# Global Commerce in the Age of Enlightenment

Combining contextual, institutional, and global perspectives, this book evaluates the impact of international trade on eighteenth-century economic thought. It meticulously delineates how economic ideas and institutions flowed between North and South Europe and across the Indian and Atlantic Oceans during the Age of Enlightenment.

*Global Commerce in the Age of Enlightenment* carefully explores contemporary debates about economic institutions, which were a crucial element in the race for controlling international trade. Eighteenth-century thinkers devoted much attention to the relative merits of existing institutions, such as free ports, grasped the dangers of economic dependence, and appraised emerging conceptions of property rights. The author draws on an impressive range of sources, including pamphlets and travel accounts, and work from lesser-known figures such as Pierre Poivre and Ange Goudar.

This volume will be valuable reading for advanced students and researchers of the history of economic thought, economic history, political economy, the history of ideas, and global history.

**J. Bohorquez** is a researcher at the Instituto de Ciências Sociais, University of Lisbon, Portugal. He was a fellow at the Freiburg Institute for Advanced Studies and the Weatherhead Center for International Affairs at Harvard University.

## Routledge Studies in the History of Economics

**European and Chinese Histories of Economic Thought**
Theories and Images of Good Governance
*Edited by Iwo Amelung and Bertram Schefold*

**Adam Smith and *The Wealth of Nations* in Spain**
A History of Reception, Dissemination, Adaptation and Application, 1777–1840
*Edited by Jesús Astigarraga and Juan Zabalza*

**Immanuel Kant and Utilitarian Ethics**
*Samuel Hollander*

**Neo-Marxism and Post-Keynesian Economics**
From Kalecki to Sraffa and Joan Robinson
*Ludo Cuyvers*

**Theology, Morality and Adam Smith**
*Edited by Jordan J. Ballor and Cornelis van der Kooi*

**Classical Economics, Keynes and Money**
*Edited by John Eatwell, Pasquale Commendatore and Neri Salvadori*

**Global Commerce in the Age of Enlightenment**
Theories, Practices, and Institutions in the Eighteenth Century
*J. Bohorquez*

For more information about this series, please visit: www.routledge.com/series/SE0341

# Global Commerce in the Age of Enlightenment

## Theories, Practices, and Institutions in the Eighteenth Century

**J. Bohorquez**

Routledge
Taylor & Francis Group
LONDON AND NEW YORK

First published 2023
by Routledge
4 Park Square, Milton Park, Abingdon, Oxon OX14 4RN

and by Routledge
605 Third Avenue, New York, NY 10158

*Routledge is an imprint of the Taylor & Francis Group, an informa business*



*British Library Cataloguing-in-Publication Data*
A catalogue record for this book is available from the British Library

*Library of Congress Cataloging-in-Publication Data*
Names: Bohórquez, Jesús, author.
Title: Global commerce in the age of enlightenment : theories, practices, and institutions in the eighteenth century / Jesús Bohorquez.
Description: 1 Edition. | New York , NY: Routledge, 2023. |
Series: Routledge studies in the history of economics | Includes bibliographical references and index.
Identifiers: LCCN 2022007144 (print) | LCCN 2022007145 (ebook) |
ISBN 9780367137069 (hardback) | ISBN 9781032310732 (paperback) |
ISBN 9780429028199 (ebook)
Subjects: LCSH: Commerce—History—18th century. | International economic relations—History—18th century.
Classification: LCC HF495 .B64 2023 (print) | LCC HF495 (ebook) |
DDC 337—dc23/eng/20220321
LC record available at https://lccn.loc.gov/2022007144
LC ebook record available at https://lccn.loc.gov/2022007145

ISBN: 978-0-367-13706-9 (hbk)
ISBN: 978-1-032-31073-2 (pbk)
ISBN: 978-0-429-02819-9 (ebk)

DOI: 10.4324/9780429028199

Typeset in Bembo
by codeMantra

# Contents

*List of figures* vii
*List of table* ix

Introduction: On global commerce: topoi, utopias, and the existential production of knowledge 1

**PART I**
**"The granary of the universe": travelogues, observations, evidence, and a global history of property** 39

1 Pierre Poivre: a microglobal life 41

2 Eighteenth-century travel accounts: platforms for economic observations 49

3 Feudal laws: liberties for a few 54

4 An empirical turn: evidence and the attack on the economists 73

5 Property rights: a global history 81

**PART II**
**"A universal warehouse of workforce": reindustrialisation, delocalisation, deurbanisation, and the propagation of economic maxims** 97

6 Ange Goudar: does the republic of economists need transgressive authors? 99

7 The will to know: the praxis of economic maxims 106

8 The will to write: North and South Europe in transnational perspective 120

9 Industry's geometry and geography 136

10 Materialising ideas: a chamber of agriculture 145

**PART III**
**"A universal intercourse of traffic as is desired": free ports, fairs, and institutional evolution in a global perspective** 149

11 Free ports: the idol of all economists 151

12 Lasting and unlasting markets: from Medieval fairs to free ports 159

13 Institutional diversity: free ports, the navigation act, and the drawback system 167

14 A Mediterranean silk road: Venice, Genoa, and Piedmont 183

15 Tyre and Carthage: failed projects and new glocal fairs 188

"Maximus totius orbis emporium" 202

*Bibliography* 205
*Index* 223

# Figures


| | | |
|---|---|---|
| 0.1 and 0.2 | English printed books (percentage and average), 1701–90 | 12 |
| 0.3 | French printed books on political economy (1660–1789) | 13 |
| 0.4, 0.5, and 0.6 | Geographical scope of printed travel accounts (1700–1800) | 24 |
| 0.1 | De l'esclavage des negres. Éphémérides du Citoyen | 26 |
| 3.1 | Geographical distribution of *Voyages d'un philosophe* (percentage) | 55 |
| 3.1 | Siam and its neighbouring countries | 58 |
| 3.2 | Elephant chasing in Siam (eighteenth century) | 59 |
| 3.3 | N-gram Google. Féodal | 65 |
| 5.1 | Cover of the Book Lettres d'une péruvienne | 86 |
| 11.1 | N-gram Google. Free port | 154 |
| 11.1 | Number of free ports established in the early modern age | 154 |

# Table

3.1 Features of despotic and feudal forms of government found in Southeast Asia 61

# Introduction

## On global commerce: topoi, utopias, and the existential production of knowledge

> Everybody here is so taken up with form, that matter is not thought of
> Ange Goudar
> The Chinese Spy (1765)

Every age has its own spectres. In the nineteenth century, there was the spectre of communism; in the twenty-first century, there was the spectre of a digital global market community. Every age fantasises its own way. We all now go virtual: we pretend we can fulfil any necessity (from essentials to sexual desires) via click-through. Enclosed, unlinked yet everlastingly connected customers and providers exchange anything for money unbrokenly. On the market platform, "all the humane" might be done or given for money. Montesquieu's dreadful nightmare seems to have eventually been realised before our eyes. The market and the marketplace – two different things[1] – have reportedly grown to be a despatialised platform in which any commodity, no matter its remotest origin or its nature, might be bought and sold all day long. A spectre was haunting Europe in the eighteenth century as well. Precisely, such anxiety is the underlying theme of this book. A dream existed that "a universal intercourse of traffic as is desired" might finally come of age. The utopia chased many enlightened minds who devoted endlessly to conjecture the successful path for its concretisation.

This book will revolve around this utopia of "universal commerce" as it was called at that time.[2] Specifically, it will shed light on how eighteenth-century "economists" dealt with the topos of universal (global) commerce at the very moment in which economics was being given the shape of science.[3] It will approach the world of economic life from a particular perspective that I call a global history of knowledge on the ground.

In the realm of ideas, discussions on the foundations of a "universal intercourse of traffic" took a particular figure: the timeless yet attainable image of a "universal magazine." Scholars imagined the rise of a global marketplace where any sort of globally produced commodities could be stored and sold. They dreamed of a mart full of global goods always ready to be shipped to purchasers worldwide. Indeed, this was at all a novelty. In classical opus,

DOI: 10.4324/9780429028199-1

this peculiar marketplace was celebrated as the *maximus totius orbis emporium*. This ageless representation of a global marketplace dated back to the primacy of Carthage and Alexandria (allegedly the first universal magazines to have ever existed, both downed by the weapons of Roman universal conquering power) and was reported to be subsequently effected in Antwerp, Livorno, and Amsterdam in the sixteenth and seventeenth centuries, respectively. The deep history told throughout this book reminds us that each age has its own Amazons. Novelties are sometimes but old refashioned ideas.

This book challenges long-ago established, prescriptive, and self-referential accounts of international trade. By placing the focus on the entanglements involving topoi and utopia along with their respective backward and forward retrospections and projections, this book takes distance from preponderant genealogical or teleological accounts. In framing the debates on global commerce from a much "mundane" outlook, the book moves away from accounts that overemphasise three main authoritative topics: theoretical justifications for free trade, the expected moralising benefits of *doux commerce*, and the intellectual origins of jealousy of trade.

My main goal here is to unveil, through a threefold concern for knowledge building, the praxis and situatedness of logical reasoning, and the anxieties for institutional innovation, how eighteenth-century reflections on global commerce were much broader than otherwise supposed. In particular, I attempt to depart from the much dominant interpretations that overstress either *doux commerce* or jealousy of trade. Instead of that, at the kernel of my sketch on international trade lies the perineal and utopical image of a "universal magazine." Over time, the image came to convey three main features: a garden (and granary) for all the plants of the world, a world factory, and a marketplace for globally produced commodities. Each part of the book will precisely cover one of those issues.

This global history of knowledge on the ground dialogues with different scholarly traditions.[4] It advances a threefold approach that seeks to reconcile three existential concerns[5]: theoretical, experiential, and institutional. Moreover, its scope is essentially global and interdisciplinary. In particular, the book aims at breaking down the walls that overspecialisation has built, bridging knowledge produced in different fields. With this goal at hand, contributions from a multivariate panoply of disciplines will be put into dialogue. The history of economic thinking will be approached from an interdisciplinary perspective that seeks to integrate the contributions of the history of science and knowledge,[6] economic theory, sociology, anthropology, and economic history.

This is not (or not merely) a book on ideas or cultural practices. Research on economic thinking has witnessed marked transformations in the last decades. Theoretically speaking, two ends seem to remain irreconcilable, though.

On the one hand, the Cambridge School of intellectual history, a perspective that overemphasises acts of speech and pragmatic approaches to languages in order to unveil plays of discourse into which inherited ideas were updated once and again over time. In the field of political ideas but related to political economy, no doubt, Hont's landmark oeuvre remains an inspiring and rigorous intellectual exercise.[7] One of the main criticisms of which Cambridge School practitioners are blamed for is the narrow number of first-rank thinkers usually integrated into the analysis. In this line, a handful of English-speaking authors are recurrently brought to the front.

On the other hand, less influential but not for that less groundbreaking stands the tradition set by Jean-Claude Perrot in the 1980s.[8] Maybe because all of his papers remain untranslated, his inputs for intellectual economic history have received far less yet unfair attention. The intellectual history of political economy, as Perrot practised it, drew on the contributions of socio-cultural history and the French tradition of the history of science in order to advance a "concrete history of ideas."[9] Attempts have recently been carried to reconcile both approaches.[10] Scholars affiliated with this concrete history of ideas have enriched our accounts not only with regard to the number of authors but also with regard to the diversity of texts that are now subjects of examination.[11] In this vein of research, theoretical oeuvres find their place beside literature books, utopian traditions, journals, etc.

In either tradition, in its concrete or pragmatic form, ideas remain rather detached from the institutional frames into which they emerged and which they created. Institutions are somehow downplayed. The intellectual history of global commerce proposed throughout this book links ideas with the practices in which they sprouted, and further, accounts for the institutions that arose from those same theories and practices Representations of global commerce are not just seen from an ideational spectre. Institutions in which those ideas materialised are a fundamental part of the account. This history of economic thinking approaches reality such as it appears: an intersection between inherited institutions, desires for transformations, and theoretical and practical groundings in which those transformations are given shape.

This introduction will explore the conceptual, theoretical, and methodological approaches into which this book is framed. To begin with, I will introduce an alternative account of global commerce that relies on the idea of marketplaces not as local but as truly global settings. Taking distance from both jealousy of trade and *doux commerce* narratives, I will account for the centuries-long recurrence of the figure of a universal magazine. In addition, I will display debates currently held in economic history in regards to the realm of ideas and institutions. I claim that a dialogue is much needed and that prospective explanations should simultaneously account for both the intellectual foundations of institutions and the institutional foundations of ideas. Along with this issue, I will elaborate on what I call innovation in persistence. A specific institution will be at the core of the analysis. In consonance, the third part will be devoted to the global history of free ports. The book will grasp the particular environments in which knowledge is produced. By putting abstract ideas into its concrete settings, I will introduce three factors that were essential in the process of knowledge building: situatedness, motion, and platforms. In doing so, I will introduce one of the first protagonists of this book: Pierre Poivre. His global life will assist us in remarking how non-theoretical formats, in this case travel accounts, contributed to the building and circulation of economic knowledge. Finally, I will attempt to reconcile theory and practice through the question of existence and its relation with knowledge production. The third protagonist of this book will be introduced: Ange Goudar. A tireless European traveller and highly renowned author, Goudar is totally unknown in today's republic of economists in spite of the fact that his books were widely read in the eighteenth century.

## Beyond *doux commerce* and jealousy of trade

*Doux commerce* and jealousy of trade have proved to be enduring and commanding topics in our understanding of global commerce. Both topics reportedly had a great influence in eighteenth-century accounts on international trade, having had a worldwide reverberation and a lasting persistence in academic records ever since.

Each topic has been tied together with a first-rank thinker. On the one hand, the notion of *doux commerce* has recurrently been linked with Montesquieu's *Spirits of the Laws* first published in 1748.[12] Even though the notion was only superficially developed by the author, the positive and moralising effects of commerce were unveiled in his history of commerce. On the other hand, a paper holding the exact same title, "On the jealousy of trade," was included in Hume's *Political Essays* and first published in 1759–60. The paper came to complement Hume's ideas on trade and political economy, being accompanied by his papers on commerce, the balance of trade, money, interest, and taxes.[13]

At first glance, both terms *doux commerce* and jealousy of trade seem to develop in locally rooted and disjoint intellectual traditions: monarchical France being the cradle of the former and republican England (in the sense that Montesquieu attached to the notion) the incubator of the latter. Both topics have even been researched from specific scholarly traditions and methodologies. Jealousy of trade along with the influences of Hume's thoughts on political and economic thinking being at the kernel of the analysis of the Cambridge School of intellectual history and its "Machiavellian moment" and "commercial humanism."[14] Relatively unsung for much time and allegedly rather uncommon in eighteenth-century parlance, the notion *doux commerce* was rescued from the shadows in Hirschman's much influential twentieth-century book on the ascendancy of political arguments in favour of capitalism. Much more than to Montesquieu himself, it was to Hirschman's impact that the civilising effects of "sweet" or "gentle" commerce should be attributed its global echo.[15] *Doux commerce* and jealousy of trade bring to mind seemingly differing understandings of commerce along with its supposed integrative or disintegrative effects, however, both notions remain much closer than one could notice.

Hirschman considered that the first mention of *doux commerce* appears in Savary's dictionary. However, he himself recognised that much talk had already been held from the late seventeenth century on the "sweetness" or "gentleness" of commerce. Montaigne, for instance, employed a similar expression to mean male's intercourse with women. Drawing on an idea that can at least be dated back to the fourth century A. D. Savary stated that the providence had endowed so differently the parts of the earth as to commercial exchanges along with gentleness to spread. Hirschman further associated Montesquieu with being "the most influential exponent" of the doctrine, and quoted a frequently used quote "it is almost a general rule that wherever the ways of man are gentle (*moeurs douce*) there is commerce, and wherever there is commerce, there the ways of men are gentle." Regardless of the lack of clarity on whether the effects were felt only among those who took part in the commercial exchanges or more broadly among all those who consumed the exchanged commodities, the term seems to have known a "successful career." Indeed, the slave trade has since been pointed out as the nemesis of those gentle manners that commerce was expected to propel.

The effects of commerce were noticeably contrasting with regard to either nations and individuals, Montesquieu's argument so reads. Peace follows trade, being its natural effect. This effect results from the interdependency that commerce engenders. Negative effects, nonetheless, were felt among individuals in those nations in which only the "spirit of commerce" drove behaviour: "They make a traffic of all the humane, all the moral virtues; the most trifling things, those which humanity would demand, are there done, or there given, only for money." Hospitality being a case in point. Discussions on *doux commerce* were in particular associated with its moralising consequences. Therefore, the focus is customarily placed on the prospective civilising effects of gradually intensified international commercial exchanges.

States "look on the progress of their neighbours with a suspicious eye." With this statement, Hume attacked an inherited malaise. In opposition to a mercantilist-like mind, he contended that "the increase of riches and commerce in any one nation, instead of hurting, commonly promotes the riches and commerce of its neighbours." The philosopher highlighted the effects that neighbouring rich countries could have on domestic industry. So "open communication" mutually benefited all the participants. Improvements lately achieved in England have resulted from a continuous process of "imitation of foreigners." Imported commodities improved manufactures, and much later, created a surplus to be exported. For these products to be demanded, however, neighbours should be rich. This pattern applies indifferently to countries or to individuals: "the riches of the several members of a community contribute to increase my riches." There was only a nation that could dread its neighbours' improvements. Enjoying no land or native commodities, the Dutch could easily lose to their neighbouring nations their brokering position. By "art and industry" the danger "may be warded off for many generations, if not wholly eluded."

Hume's jealousy of trade found inspiration in Hobbes' balance of power or jealousy of state. It was the application of reason of state to international commercial competition. In this sense, the term is framed in a neo-Machiavellian fashion. It recalls a political understanding of commerce, and further, "signaled that the economy had become political."[16] Hume asserted that war and trade were opposing ends, the former resulting in a zero-sum game, the latter creating reciprocal ties. Two forms of jealousies had chased the European nations. On the one hand, the jealousy of money, and on the other hand, the jealousy of progress. Hume dismantled both. Against the bullionist envy, Hume sustained a natural mechanism of industry and flows of money. Against fears of prosperity, Hume maintained the positive impact that emulation could have. Hume echoed a much-recurrent idea that commerce and war opposed each other, and that commerce could be a means to reach universal enrichment.[17]

A decade prior that the *Spirits of the Laws* reached its continent-wide circulation, another book also hit a large public. In one of his chapters, Melon set side by side two spirits: the spirit of conquest and the spirit of commerce. His analysis also integrated what he called the spirit of preservation. "The spirit of conquest, and the spirit of commerce, mutually exclude each other," but also, "the spirit of conquest and the spirit of preservation, are as incompatible." Melon asserted that when a conquering nation ceased to be dominant, it became "subdued." Conversely, commerce and preservation were complementary. Thereafter, Melon recounts a short history of commerce and empires, contrasting, as it was much usual in the eighteenth century, Carthage and Rome, but also, integrating into his narrative the subsequent subjugations to which people in Asia had been subdued. This historical sketch on trade appears, barely noticed, in the chapter on military government. The conclusion is not that surprising "At length the spirit of peace has enlightened all Europe. So long as this spirit prevailed, a just balance will always prevent one power from growing, by conquest, to such a degree, as to be dreaded." No nation can pretend any longer to aggrandise itself but through "wisdom in its government at home."[18]

Melon's approach is particularly close to the one that Montesquieu developed in his *Reflexions sur la monarchie universelle* and *Considérations sur les Romains*. Both pieces of thinking were contemporaneous to Melon's *Essay upon commerce* even though it is difficult to define any possible influence. There was this peculiar wish that commerce could dethrone manias for war and that a universal community could come of age through the liveness that only commerce creates. Cantillon echoed the same understanding. Nations achieve power over others through two methods: by the force of arms or by foreign trade. Both paths led to opposing outcomes. Commerce "makes all we negotiate with our friends; conquest, those we conquer, our enemies."[19] Power achieved through commerce gives a lasting reputation while conquest only generates "an imaginary and impermanent fame."

Commerce cures "the most destructive prejudices." Montesquieu stated. Later, in the chapter on the genius of the Romans with respect to commerce, the French philosopher maintained that the "Romans were never distinguished by a jealousy of trade."[20] The word jealousy is commonly associated with Hume but is barely conveyed in the analysis of Montesquieu.[21] Yet, on the French side of the Manche Channel the word jealousy was also common. Two models opposed each other, Carthage as a commercial republic and Rome as a universal monarchy. Indeed, arguments were displayed in the midst of intense European war, and were intended to counterattack the desires of the French sovereign at imposing a universal monarchy. Aspirations to achieve and retain universal power, after the Roman model, are unfit for modern times in which states should be driven by commerce. Commercial links could lead towards a universal society in which no state attempted to impose its sovereignty. Conquering along with all the evils it brought stood in opposition to the peaceful world that commerce engendered.

Already in the eighteenth century, doubts were cast on Montesquieu's model. Writing in Naples a decade later, Genovesi added a footnote to his manuscript in order to display his disagreement with the French author whom he had minutiously read, having even participated in the translation of the *Spirit of the Laws*. "This maxim does not conform to the past." History demonstrates that after the discovery of America and the Cape of Good Hope "the ambition and jealousy of commerce only perpetually inflames the European nations." A hard fact to deny. Any reader who reads the history of Europe from Tiber to Charles V "can hardly find a year without a war."[22]

## From imperium to emporium: "Maximus totius orbis emporium"

The spirit of commerce, such as it appeared to some, was the spirit of conquering wealth neither peoples nor territories. This dialectical contraposition between the spirit of commerce and spirit of war has marked so powerfully our accounts on international trade. It goes without saying that the topic was intensely present throughout the times of the Enlightenment. Scholars, either in the eighteenth century or nowadays, incessantly brought to mind the opening up of the Cape route as a watershed event in the history of humankind. Smith is often quoted at this regard yet the above Genovesi's reference shows this was a much recurrent figure. This event along with the incorporation of a new continent unleashed a path for global exchanges.

Global commerce, as historians understand it, is above all about flows and connections. The emergence of a series of interlinks that in the fifteenth century profoundly changed the fare of millions of people across the four parts of the world. Gradually, over time, commodities began to flow at a rhythm and on a scale never seen before. Prices varied according to the peculiarities of transcontinental patterns of demand and supply. Essential for the consolidation of this new global economy was the incorporation of vast sources of labour force both forced and free. Silver mined in America further propelled Euro-Asian commercial exchanges. Europeans found a fountain source through which to defray their insatiable appetite for Asian luxuries. Disagreement still exists on the proper timing in which globalisation could have emerged, and how to accurately measure its coming of age. Not only commodities circulated worldwide. Languages, religions, legal systems, plants, viruses, and art patterns, all of them in a way or another contributed to the building of overdimensioned European empires. Like Rome, back in ancient times, Europeans now faced the consequences of overseas expansion and the repercussions that much-feared universal empire could bring for domestic economies and equilibria of power. Behind the idea of global commerce appears concerns for flows, interconnections, the integration of factor and commodity prices, and the circulation of commodities across continents.

The underpinning idea of global commerce advanced throughout this book is quite dissimilar. I contend that besides this global spatialisation of flows and interconnections, another account emerged that assists us in better understanding how global commerce could be yielded and how command of it could be imposed. The unveiling of this account will oblige us to consider the theoretical imprints that this set of long-lasting conceptions had among different scholars. For instance, by pushing authors to rethink the very foundations of property rights or by placing at the core of the discussions concepts such as dependence or self-sufficient.

Overemphasis on either *doux commerce* or jealousy of trade has led to the abandonment of the study of alternative paths to the consolidation of universal commerce, which were also given much thought in the eighteenth century. It could be shortly stated: from imperium to emporium. Minor nuances, indeed, mean a lot. Accounts of global trade overall emphasise on the emergence of a global interconnected market and its repercussions for humankind. The geographical distribution of markets and their divergent economic performance have been for a long part of the scholars' agenda.[23]

The focus of this book is on emporium or what was, over the centuries, conceived of as a universal magazine. Not on the path to "global market" but on the likelihood of the emergence of a "global marketplace." At first glance, markets and marketplaces seem to be irreconcilable ends. On the one hand, we have the notion of a "depersonalised" circulation of goods and services, a "despatialised" meeting of individual interests which best finds its geometrical form (nowadays) in the Cartesian two-dimensional plane. On the other hand, we have the embedded meetings that took place in a location around which commodities and people gravitate. It is assumed that the market would gradually – in a way or another – displace the marketplace along with other "primitive" forms of exchange: its gradual aggrandisement over time makes marketplaces completely lose standing theoretically and functionally. In this perspective, marketplaces are rather fashioned like bazaars or foregone forms of commercial exchange organisation.[24] They are associated with towns and periodically held meetings.

At the end of the seventeenth century, a famous English author condensed a powerful and so influential utopia much recurrent over the whole century in England and elsewhere: "what spot of the Earth's globe were fittest for a general and universal Emporium, whereby all the people thereof may best enjoy one another's Labours and commodities."[25] The emergence of this emporium was the subject of discussion in economic books but not only. In political and utopian oeuvres like the *Commonwealth of Oceana*, Harrington's magnum opus, London was depicted as an emporium and Amsterdam was told to be a city that "sucks all the world."

This very figure of a universal emporium echoed for a long time in the minds of many on the island. As late as 1801, a paper was published which claimed the need for a free port in London. Free ports, fairs, and emporia stood closely associated over the centuries, and thereby, these institutions are at the core of part III. Fiscal impositions on carrying trade were the main object of the journal article. Governments, asserted the author, "congratulated" themselves for adroitly levying taxes on foreign nations. It should, nonetheless, be recognised that these practices that targeted carrying trade prejudiced commerce. In consequence, those taxes should be avoided, or at least, partially refunded. The author further put forward the Italian and Dutch cases not without mentioning their distinctness.

Those were two contrasting but allegedly successful models. Two models were arguably implemented in order to yield the same goal. Dutch people had emerged from slavery and obscurity through the implementation of a tax system notoriously advantageous. Slight duties were levied in an attempt to overcome the narrowness of their territory. This wise tax system could be held responsible for the country's rapid rise to maritime pre-eminence. Low impositions had transformed Amsterdam into "the great deposit for all merchandise, and consequently, the greatest mart of Europe." In turn, Livorno (a former unhealthy marsh) had risen to maritime power out of nothing. The rise of the city should be attributed to the policies enacted by the Duke of Tuscany who, as is told in the article, had followed the advice of an English Jewish expatriate. The city had, therefore, been transformed into an *entrepôt* where commodities carried from all over the world could be stored free of any charge. As a direct consequence of these policies, from being merely an unknown fishing town, Livorno had grown to be a major mart in the Mediterranean.

Any reader may be astonished at knowing, continued the author, that neither of those systems had been implemented in the "more enlightened of all nations." Fears of, and spread opposition against the establishment of a free port resulted from a prejudicial attachment to the navigation-act model and the preference granted to colonial trade. Not that that share of trade should be neglected. But it should be recognised that the island had the potential to transport a much larger tonnage. London, if the needed policies were enacted, could achieve what Amsterdam had done in the previous century, becoming the deposit of all the commodities produced on the earth. The city could with no effort store half of the commodities traded globally. The author regretted the institutional framework in which trade was conducted, and further, made an assault on the drawback system. The English model, which was presented as a third way, was somehow inefficient because "mercantile capital cannot lie unemployed without heavy loss."

Over the early modern times, the plausibility of building and preserving the pre-eminence of a global marketplace turned out to be an omnipresent and highly sound utopia. A sometimes disregarded fact is that both Montesquieu's and Hume's thesis developed in the context of a larger historical and philosophical debate. In the 1710s, Pierre-Daniel Huet's histories of trade had received much praise, having known a huge repercussion on local and European intellectual debates.[26] Even though the matter has scarcely been the object of research, it could be that histories of commerce regained a high interest, in great part owing to the impact of Huet's accounts of ancient and modern commerce. Montesquieu took on Huet's interpretation of Roman history. Disagreement existed on the underlying political foundations of a commercial society, Montesquieu holding that commerce was most appropriated for republican forms of government while Huet asserting that the rise of Antwerp to world primacy was a case in point that left no doubt monarchies could also set the grounds for commerce to prosper. Huet's book on Holland knew a wide circulation, being reprinted on several occasions over the century. Precisely, Holland's rise to commercial command was the focus of his second book. Later, in the mid-century, Jacques Acarias de Serione, in his informed analysis of the country, stated that the Dutch had built at home "the European general *entrepôt* along with huge magazines for staples and commodities, all them full of commodities carried from the four parts of the world."

It would be a mistake to attribute to Holland the lead in building the first universal magazine. This idea, which Huet explored at length, had not yet been carefully considered. This was precisely one of the arguments the turn-of-the-century protestant priest advanced in his *Le grand trésor historique et politique* in which oeuvre Antwerp is depicted as a model worth emulating; the city was portrayed as the "most famous magazine of Europe perhaps of the whole universe." At that time, the Flemish city resembled what Amsterdam "is nowadays." Around the mid-sixteenth century, 2,500 vessels could be found anchored at the harbour, all of them "loaded with all sorts of merchandise."[27] The reasons behind the rise of Antwerp, Huet believed, should be looked backward and dated back at least to the tenth century. Around 960, a set of measures had been enacted which transformed the Flemish area into a duty-free trade zone. Policies were implemented in order to attract merchants and to make commodities flaw in and out. The renown of the fairs along with the slight taxes levied upon imported and exported commodities attracted for a long-time crowds of merchants who met at Flemish marketplaces customarily.

Neither Antwerp had been the first to settle the initiative. The notion of a *universal emporium* could be rolled back to ancient times. Overall, in the literature, mention is often made of the antagonistic models that both Rome and Carthage represented. Alexandria, on the contrary, is barely brought to the front. As a piece of a history of commerce published in the mid-century told, the Egyptian city could be attributed with having been the first to have enjoyed the title of the universal emporium. The city enjoyed a peculiarity worth highlighting: it had not only been the capital of Egypt but also "the *entrepôt* of the manufactures produced in the inner country, and further, the magazine for all the commodities of the earth." Wise policies had been designed to lay the foundations of burgeoning commerce and navigation not upon foreign but local industry, at a time, they were "excellent sailors and skilled manufacturers." Rulers and merchants clearly foresaw that a maritime city could not achieve any success when its trade relied on its neighbours' production. Therefore, there was no choice but to be the factor of one's own productions; this was the maxim that led Alexandria to the commercial empire. It had been the ancient geographer Strabon who first entitled the Egyptian city as *Maximum totius orbis emporium*. This was comparable, assured the author, to "Holland's current state of affairs." This centuries-lasting recurrent figure will guide us in the theoretical and experiential discussions that took place in the mid-eighteenth century.[28]

## Ideas matter: the impact of economic thinking

Both topoi and utopias on global commerce strongly impacted the manners in which policies were designed and theories built. The same figure was shaped and reshaped over centuries. We now know that translations along with a spread circulation of ideas had a huge impact on the configuration of the eighteenth-century political economy.[29] For many, either England or Holland stood as the fountain of inspiration. In the eighteenth-century philosophical and political debates, it was hard to neatly delineate and differentiate jealousy from emulation, ambiguity remaining at the very core of the discussion. Even Hume himself ambiguously used the term "jealous emulation."[30] In the emerging field of political economy, emulation went hand in hand with translations. Balances of translations being a means through which determining which countries' economic policies and institutions attracted the most attention on the international market of ideas. This is what Reinert has called "emulation through translation." As a matter of fact, in the mid-century, there was an explosion of translations of economic oeuvres, rising from 134 to 339 at its 1760s peak. This was, as the author recalls, "an age of economic translations."[31]

A thorough examination of this European balance of knowledge shows that England stood far ahead of the rest of Europe: "as English trade "took off" internationally in the 1740s and 1750s, so translations of English economic works on the continent skyrocketed."[32] There was an increase in the number of books published in England which is still more evident from the mid-century onwards (Charts 0.1 and 0.2). For the whole early modern age, England exported 615 economic oeuvres receiving merely 144 translations. In total, by the mid-eighteenth century, 37 per cent of all European translations were made from English oeuvres. Compared with France, a country that exported a similar number of oeuvres, there is a deficit in the number of imported translations which yielded 464.

A good instance of that transnational market for ideas was the circle of Gournay.[33] Brushed aside for a long time, the role that Gournay and his fellows played in the configuration of mid-century economic debates had

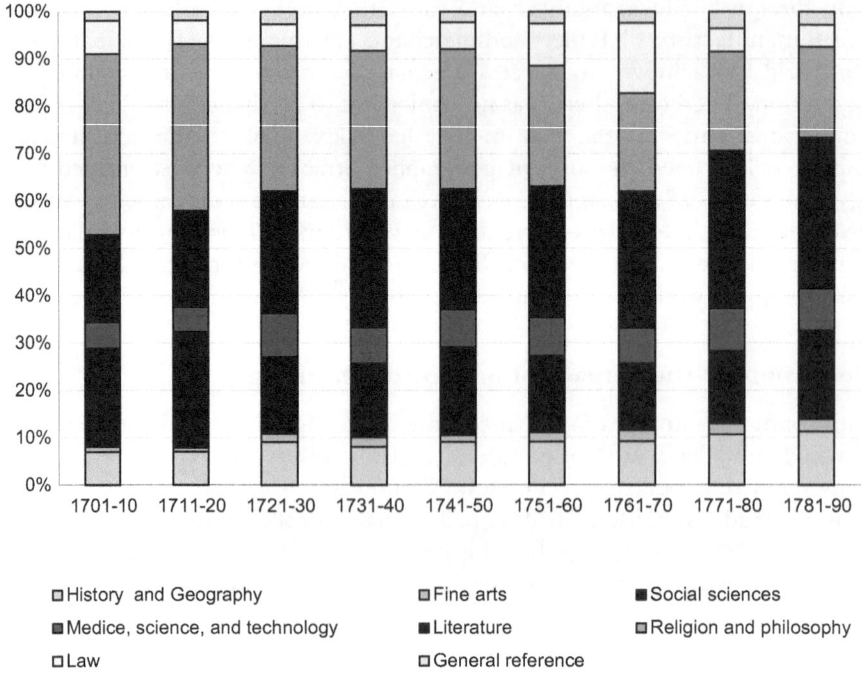


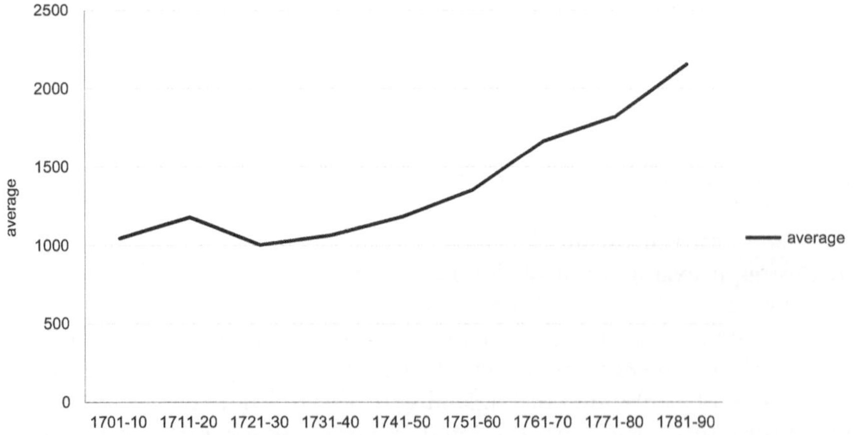


*Chart 0.1 and 0.2* English printed books (percentage and average), 1701–90
Source: Joel Mokyr, The Enlightened Economy

recently been recovered.[34] All of them had a huge influence on the transfer of knowledge from England to France. Gournay was a merchant who worked in Cadiz for some years and later became a royal official. In the 1750s, a group of fellows surrounded the Saint-Malo intendant in his ambitious official program that attempted to offer French readers a selection of the best English oeuvres on commerce. He himself translated and commented Child's *Discourse of trade*,[35] as we will see in Part III. Members of the circle not only translated books from English but also from Spanish. Forbonnais, for instance, translated Uztáriz *Theórica y práctica del comercio.*[36] Somehow ironically, even books written by French authors were advertised and sold as being translations from English. This is the case of Plumard de Dangeul's famous book *Remarques sur les avantages et désavantages de la France et la Grande Bretagne* published in 1754,[37] and thereafter, translated into English, Swedish, Danish, German, Italian, and Spanish. Perhaps, out of all the many translations the group made, there was Butel de Dumont's free translation of Cary's *Discourse on Trade* that received much interest, serving as the bases for Italian, German, and Spanish editions and in the process of internationalisation impressively increasing its length.[38]

On the French side, roughly 2,800 books were published on economic matters between 1660 and the Revolution (Chart 0.3). Crises, according to Perrot, were good moments for the market of economic books to flourish: the end of the reign of Louis XIV, the years that follow the seven-year war, and finally, the pre-revolutionary crisis. Moreover, each moment knew its economic stars: Boisguilbert and Vauban (1720s), Quesnay and his fellows (1756–63), and Isnard and Necker (1780). The 1760s, in particular, witnessed a disproportionate increase in the number of printed manuscripts, which

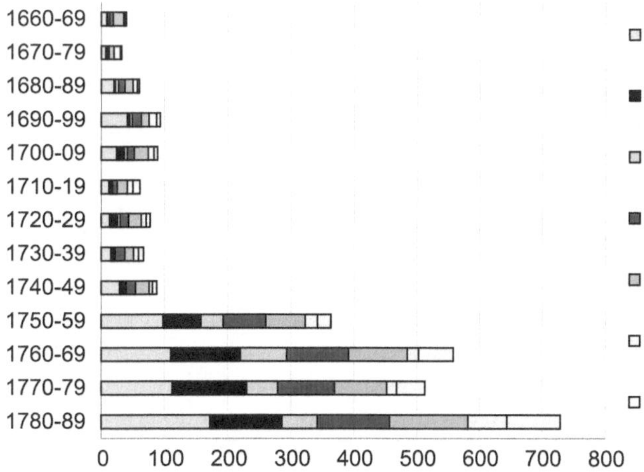


*Chart 0.3* French printed books on political economy (1660–1789)
Source: Jean-Claude Perrot, *Une Histoire Intellectuelle*

increased by threefold. The records demonstrate the specialisation of the field, a fact which is further proved by a steady increase pattern in the printing of economic treatises. After the 1750s, both agricultural and manufacturing oeuvres saw a significant increase. The same goes for the boom that books dealing with commercial topics had. Most common in the 1720s, monetary issues gradually lost interest over the century.[39]

The question remains as to whether ideas had any measurable impact on economic growth,[40] and more in specific, whether they could account for the so-called "Great enrichment," it is, the divergent economic process that set Europe apart from the rest of the world.[41] For economic growth, ideas play the same role that dark matter does for the holding of galaxies. Detecting such a matter implies, among other things, to accurately appraising how language and rhetoric "shape an economy." It also implies reconciling a mathematically-grounded economics with the human sciences and their methods. The production of economic knowledge should find support in the hermeneutics of texts, and should further, "analyze stories *and* model maxima, clarify with philosophy *and* measure with statistics, inquire into the meaning of the sacred *and* lay out the accounting of the profane."[42]

In this line of research, ideas and not institutional or material causes account for economic growth, and more in particular, long-term sustained economic growth. It is argued that a set of ideas could accurately explain why Europe got rich and the rest of the world did not. Some scholars have sought to explain England's took off while others have instead looked for the radical ideal causes that drove Europe out of the Malthusian trap. On the one hand, the expansion of useful knowledge and its cheaper access costs explain why England witnessed such an explosion of growth seen in a widespread use of the best techniques and inventions. Open science and scientific institutions further propelled access to useful knowledge. The Industrial Revolution is thus held as a by-product of an antecedent Intellectual Revolution. The Enlightenment is thus viewed as a period in the history of humankind in which reason and observation were applied in favour of human betterment. Social progress stood as one of its main claims: "Economic change in all periods depends, more than most economists think, on what people believe." On the other hand, the so-called "Bourgeois dignity." According to this interpretation, two main ideas account for Europe's rise: liberty and equality (dignity). Both beliefs found a fertile field in a corner of northern Europe where they interacted to produce a "rhetorical event."

That ideas and not capital or institutions explain sustained economic growth is a hypothesis that has generated some discomfort. The weight that beliefs had in leading to growth has not gone without criticism: they are considered to be probably necessary but unlikely sufficient enough to cause the great enrichment. As a neoinstitutionalist affiliated scholar has counter-argued: "For ideas to have an impact, a series of conditions must hold. Ideas must – somehow – be translated from the realm of abstraction to the realm of action."[43] Implementation matters. Widespread support for liberty and dignity alone cannot explain their successful implementation. Institutions and government, which are responsible for the way in which property and security are enforced in a given society, could not be taken for granted.

## Institutions matter: institutional innovation

Ideas substantialise in the form of specific institutions. In turn, institutions emerge in specific environments. Institutional design still remains an outside object for scholars of economic thinking. Books conveyed abstract reasoning and logical models yet they also transmitted knowledge on the practicability and outcomes of allegedly beneficial or harmful commercial institutions and regulations. Most authors (at least in France where a non-negligible part of them served in office) spent a lot of time deliberating about the repercussions that specific institutions could generate. Whether the importation of an institution could bring positive effects or whether its implementation could negatively impact the economy were themes that robbed the time of many. Institutions were the way through which emulation could be tested.

Economic life is built upon institutions. This is a matter of fact. Even the market, once narrowly understood as the mere spontaneous conjunction of impersonal interests, is now seen as an institutionally framed setting. In the mid-eighteenth century, the physiocrats were particularly concerned with this aspect of the market exchanges. Even though not properly from an institutional perspective, probably no other group of economists in that century considered at length and in-depth issues related to landed property. Property remained at the very core of the analysis of the economics that Quesnay and his fellows promoted, for one reason. Property rights set the foundations for market transactions not alone social bounds. Owing to this reason, taxes were held as the *vinculum sacrum* that tied the state and the individuals. "The rights of every man that even preceded any convention are the liberty to provide for one's subsistence and well-being along with the property of one's body and the things acquired with one's work."[44]

After more than a century of fading into oblivion, economists have anew brought to front property rights and their impact on economic performance.[45] North and his neoinstitutionalist fellows have devoted all their efforts to demonstrate how and why institutions matter for economic growth. In the search for an underpinning institution whose absence or inefficiency could account for economic backwardness or growth, an agreement has been reached upon that those countries in which property rights are most likely to be efficiently safeguarded follow a path to growth. The opposite occurred in those countries in which neither formal nor informal institutions achieved efficiency in the enforcement of property rights.

Property rights lay at the very core of the debate on economic performance either in the eighteenth-or in the twentieth centuries. On both occasions, the assumption has been taken for granted, and for the most part, drawn from philosophical or legal lines of thinking. As we will see in Chapter 5, either in the Enlightenment or in the last century, economists have resorted to historical proof as a way to offer evidence on the underlying principle of property rights as the underpinning foundation for social order and economic growth. These historical accounts have rather received little interest in explanations of theory building. As regards the physiocrats, for instance, debates tend to revolve around the threefold forms of property the supporters of Quesnay upheld.[46] Perhaps, in spite of the school fellows' reluctance, a global history of the property began to be drawn as a way to demonstrate the principles deduced from natural law. Notwithstanding the fact that both eighteenth- and twentieth-century economists resorted to historical evidence during both waves in which property rights became trending assumptions, the parallelism has passed almost unnoticed, and therefore, comparisons are still lacking as to how assumptions were set and thesis on property rights advanced.

In all likelihood, comparisons of this nature could allow us to get away from circular debates or avoid us falling into the case of refashioning old causations as pure novelties. Even though there is an analogy in the topics that enlightened and contemporaneous waves of economic thinking have dealt with, little efforts have yet been made at comparing their reached conclusions, hypotheses, demonstrations, etc. For instance, many in the mid-eighteenth century were particularly concerned with explaining the institutional foundations of England's rise. Many wondered whether the success of the island lay on its parliamentary form of government or on its wisely enacted commercial regulations. Both topics are of utmost interest for contemporaneous neoinstitutional economists as well. Merely anecdotally speaking, and having nothing to do with either the quality of the book or its reached conclusions, in a recent publication, Solon's shackles are carefully put forward and integrated into the narrative.[47] In the mid-eighteenth century, Sparta's case was paradigmatic in illustrating the path to decay that fared those nations which dared to violate the natural law of property.[48]

Economists have posited strong or ill-defined property rights as causes of economic growth and backwardness. Based upon this assumption, North and his co-authors have explained differences in economic performance across countries. It is believed that France's incapacity to maintain long-run economic growth and Spain's decline and stagnation, both phenomena could be attributed to the state's incapacity to efficiently safeguard property rights. Essentially owing to its absolutist form of government, in early modern Spain would have prevailed "insecurity of all property rights," a pattern evidenced by seizures, confiscations, and unilateral alteration of contractual forms.[49] Spain would have been a case in point for those countries that had failed in implementing an efficient economic organisation. Checks and balances on the executive account for why some northern European countries developed markets with clearly defined property rights. Inversely, unchecked rule unleashed a common violation of property rights, and therefore, the lack of incentives for capital investment. The rules of the game are defined in the "political market," they are the outcome of political decisions.

Many definitions exist of what exactly an institution is. Greif states that "an institution is a system of social factors that conjointly generate a regularity of behavior."[50] The system is made up of man-made, nonphysical components that not being made by any individual in specific affect individual behaviour. In other words, institutions constrain one's behaviour and help one anticipating each other's decisions. In a much recurrently quoted statement, North adventures an encompassing definition of institutions as the "rules of the game."[51] For him, "institutions are the humanly devised constraints that structure political, economic, and social interaction." They could be informal (customs, traditions, and codes) or formal (constitutions, laws, or property rights).[52] Institutions are supposed to create order and reduce uncertainty. Institutional analysis could contribute, North contends, to "explain the varied performance of economies both over time and in the current world." In this sense, the Nobel-prize-awarded economist asserted that the main task of economic history and economic development theories should be to "account for the evolution and economic institutions that created an economic environment that induces increasing productivity." A different branch of institutional economics has followed the leads settled by game theory. In mathematical parlance, institutions are conceived as "an equilibrium outcome of a game." These equilibria explain "theoretically the emergence of an institution and/or an institutional change." In this line of research, institutions can be defined as "a self-sustaining system of shared beliefs about a salient way in which the game is repeatedly played."[53]

Efforts carried at explaining institutional evolution have led many to explain the so-called Rise of the West as a path-dependent process of institutional change.[54] Greif contends that opposing institutional paths could be seen in the divergent developments of the west and the middle east. Whereas Italian mercantile institutions gradually evolved from informal to formal ones, in the Muslim world informal institutions remained as the underpinning organisational form. Relying upon formal institutions like guilds or informal ethnic or religious-based networks had a varying impact on the path to modernity. Genoese merchants were more willing to support their mercantile transactions through formal institutions in which property rights could be claimed. Maghrebi merchants, on the contrary, relied mostly on self-enforcing and coordinated mechanisms. The strong contraposition that Greif delineated between those merchant communities that resorted or not to merchant courts have been put into question. On the one hand, it is assumed that Maghrebi merchants claimed their rights before courts more commonly than previously assumed.[55] On the other hand, documentary evidence barely offers support in favour of the underlying mechanism of information circulation that served as the foundation of self-enforcement mechanisms.[56]

Regardless of the degree of impact of formal and informal institutions, courts have been taken as essential factors for economic growth. It is assumed that historically divergent legal systems were at the roots of poor-rich countries' divide.[57] In this vein, a debate exists on whether common-law legal systems were more effective at guaranteeing property rights than continental-codified ones. Even though the matter should be further analysed, underlying continental and insular differences in applied law are barely brought to debate by eighteenth-century economists. At least when compared to other sorts of institutions like the parliament or the navigation act. By the same token, scholars have examined the substitutability or complementarity of private-order institutions *vis-à-vis* public ones. On the one hand, research conducted on this frame has paid all its attention to the twentieth century therefore disregarding historical evolution. Due to this neglect, scholars have claimed that a historical test is in order.[58] On the other hand, those scholars who assess the prevalence or complementarity of self-enforcement group mechanisms over courts have basically focused on long-distance trade. Differences in the performance of legal systems have compelled economists to offer evidence as to why some countries that applied common law did not follow a path to growth.[59] The divergence is more telling in the case of British former colonies. Geographical conditions and demographic patterns are being assumed as the main cause behind those disparities.

Indeed, institutions migrate. They were far from being the outcome of a simple endogenous selection process. Not only did legal systems spread worldwide, a vast panoply of instruments, regulations, or corporations for the organisation of trade also did.[60] The underlying reasons for the emergence of an impersonal market along with the mechanisms that it required have been at the very core of the neoinstitutional research agenda. Yet, explanations are still lacking on why some institutions migrate and the spread they reached while others just vanished. One can beforehand assume that this process of selection and evolution obeyed simply to the preponderance of the most effective institutions. Even if effectiveness explains institutional migration, the question remains as to whether the endurance of lethargic institutions or as to whether some environments are less propense to institutional innovation.[61]

### *Making match to happen*

The fruitful reception of an alien institution in specific environments is no doubt a matter of match. Prevalent institutional approaches tend to disregard the intellectual horizons into which the likeliness of the transplantation could or not materialise. In this sense, the econometrics of institutions just leaves out of analysis the impacts that intellectual designs have for institutional emulation or imposition.[62] Institutions acquire a multivariate palette of forms conforming with, but not merely as a consequence of, the intellectual debates into which they materialise. Both scholars and policymakers incessantly shape and reshape institutions and are in charge of appraising whether the cultural, economic, and social conditions are or not fertile ground for the transplanted institution. On the other hand, it is very common that scholars of economic thinking barely consider institutions as an object worth studying, much of their thoughts being given to the evolution of abstract reasoning.

This book seeks to reconcile both perspectives by meticulously tracking down intellectual debates on institutional match. This is a multidirectional perspective in which institutional frames impact intellectual debates and the other way around. In particular, the book will explore this timeless and attainable idea of *maximus totis orbis emporium*. At the kernel of the survey lies what I call institutional innovation in persistence and both the theoretical and practical reverberations it generates.

The intellectual foundations of institutions remain for the most part a neglected topic. Institutions' performances and impacts on economic growth are phenomena assessed mostly from econometric and microeconomic approaches. This is not to say that a historical perspective is still lacking. All the contrary. No other branch of economic theory resorted as intensively and commonly to historical testing as those models elaborated by scholars involved in the analysis of institutional evolution. Nonetheless, a certain disconnection exists between those who research the intellectual foundations of economic theory and those who enquiry the institutional foundations of the market. By placing institutional innovation at the core of the account, this book will attempt to bridge both lines of research. In this line, I will explore the deep history of free ports, how they evolved over time and changed shape.

Changes in institutions are rather barely seen as innovations. Those modifications are modelled as institutional evolution or change. Institutional innovation impacts economic performance and sets the grounds for innovation to happen. Innovation, however, is more common the after-effect of repetition than is commonly supposed. Tarde's assumptions on innovation and repetition are worth recalling here. He calls this process "universal repetition."[63] The French sociologist wondered why "given one hundred different innovations conceived of at the same time… ten will spread abroad, while ninety will be forgotten." Four main features characterise imitation: (i) geometric progression; (ii) non-mechanical process that leads to divergence, differentiation rather than to convergence; (iii) voluntariness or involuntariness; (iv) contest between objects of imitation. Further, the spread of an innovation could result from logical causes or non-logical causes. The usefulness or appropriateness of an institution could partially explain its selection. Yet, it is also true that innovations associated with individuals, groups, communities that are taken as superior could be more likely taken as an object of imitation. Innovation is closely linked to invention. On the one hand, one finds theoretical inventions (which are related to the need to believe, affirm, or deny), an on the other one finds practical inventions (which are related to the need to desire, want, and act).

## Being an author: on situatedness, motion, and platforms

The history of economic theory has commonly been the target of strong criticism due to its overly focus on a handful of first-rank authors. Teleological and genealogical stakes still remain at the very core of much of what has been written in the field: looking for the origins, searching backward for the roots of what is going to emerge forward. The Cambridge school of intellectual history, on the other hand, set not much distance from this perspective and shared these specific features. The school's primary focus on context and "words in action" revolved around a slender number of authors, most of them within the English tradition. The intellectual history that the school advocates suffers from a narrowly political focus being extremely self-referential in text-coding. By neglecting any other context than the (written) one in which the author enacts its speech, a set of interacting concepts emerge which only have sense within the code in which they are attached. This infinite update of self-referencing meanings generates a locked-up frame that allows one to track down particular concepts. Much is interpreted as a political enactment of Renaissance political notions or the republican uses of that tradition.

Already in the 1980s, Jean-Claude Perrot stood firm in his claim that our list of economic authors should be enlarged. Departing from the idea that the analysis of economic thinking recurrently drew on a set of "successful" ideas and "renowned" authors, Perrot displayed his numbers. Between 1715 and 1775, 981 French authors published at least one text on economic matters. Between the year in which Smith published his *The Wealth of Nations* and the Revolution, 528 authors further published on economics. Thanks to the judicious and extremely careful research carried out by Théré, it is possible to unveil the sociological profiles of most of those unknown authors (87 per cent of all of them within the span period of this book). This is, in the words of Perrot, "a savant city." Most authors dwelled in Paris. Gradually, the field became more and more specialised but most authors still continued to write about different topics. The authors' social origins demonstrate that this new science was, according to Perrot (and at least for France which remains at the centre of this book) a "bourgeois science." By the revolution, almost half of the group was made up of "*roturiers*."

These numbers, in turn, resound with the ones found by Darnton, who, already decades ago, advocated the rediscovery of the "low Enlightenment."[64] The specialist of the French printing world asserted that the republic of letters should be seen from "below." The history of ideas, such as it had been inherited from the nineteenth century, placed much interest in the "big names." As Mornet put it in his 1933 influential *Les origines intellectuelles* "it is these great oeuvres that, as long as the ideas have not been realised, give them their lasting form, transmit them and transform them."[65] Darnton showed a penchant for archival research as a way out of the too-much overemphasised great philosophical treatises. Archival research came to demonstrate how narrow our list of readings was when compared to the printing material available to eighteenth-century readers. The Enlightenment was a more "down-to-earth affair than the rarified climate of opinion described by textbook writers," and added Darnton "we should question the overly highbrow, overly metaphysical view of intellectual life."

Owing to surveying and censoring concerns, we dispose of an inquiry carried out between 1748 and 1753, which was conducted by the police inspector Joseph d'Hémery. This record sheds light on the lives of at least 500 authors. These years were, as shown in Chart 0.3, particularly meaningful in regard to the number of economic publications and remain of particular interest for this book's temporal frame. Compared to the numbers that *La France littéraire* gathered, which amounted to 11,897 authors, d'Hémery's dossier only accounts for a share of all of them who the inspector himself named as *auteurs*. The focus of his political research is placed specifically on Parisian dwellers, precisely those who probably belonged to the group of authors who published on economic matters. The numbers show a relatively young group. The most active members of the republic of letters were in their thirties: Voltaire (38), Diderot (37), and d'Alembert (33). The *philosophes*, a term used with positive and negative connotations, were born in the first decades of the century. In regard to geographical origin, the large majority were born in the north and northeast, a third was born in Paris. With regard to social origins, 17 per cent of the authors were identified by the police inspector as nobles. The clergymen made up 12 per cent. The vast majority (70 per cent), belonged to the "third state." Merchants were a minority when compared to the crown functionaries or those who gained their life through intellectual activities like journalists, librarians, actors, etc.[66] Decades ago, Darnton already called attention to the fact that "the mandarins fattened themselves on pensions, most authors sank into a sort of literary proletariat."[67]

This book draws on the teachings of this socio-cultural history of the Enlightenment and seeks to enlarge our list of authors. Two-thirds of the book will be devoted to nowadays largely unknown authors: Pierre Poivre and Ange Goudar. Misplaced in the shadows of the "republic of economists," both authors enjoyed, nonetheless, a large audience in the eighteenth century. This book precisely seeks to unveil how their oeuvres were read and upon which scientific and existential conditions they were written. The choice for Poivre and Goudar is not a hazardous one. Many reasons explain in which manner the selection of those authors could contribute to our understanding of the production of economic ideas in the time of Enlightenment.

## *On situatedness, motion, and platforms*

In the realm of intellectual history, it has been a customary practice to carefully delineate the flows: from formerly and much criticised diffusionist approaches to most recent methodologies of transfers or multidirectional circulation.[68] Emerging approaches have highlighted the fact that knowledge building involves many steps in which a vast array of tasks – each one enjoying its own logics and epistemological regulations – intervenes: gathering, observation, storing and preserving, retrieving. The handling of gathered information entails, in turn, a series of undertakings that include description, quantification, classification, comparison, interpretation, verification, fact discovery, narration.[69] The production of economic theory did not escape from that pattern. Nor could it escape the spatial settings upon which knowledge is built.

Spatial patterns of knowledge production, particularly underemphasised for a long time, have begun to regain the interest of scholars of the history of science. The places in which authors conducted and developed their research remained an essential mechanism in the outcomes that can be reached. Precisely, in one of his books curiously titled *L'espion Chinois*, Ange Goudar narrates an imagined visit carried out by a Chinese spy to the library of an old European monastery. After having asked the librarian for a new release, the unwary was told that only classical oeuvres made part of the catalogue. Surprised by the reply, the spy wondered whether monks underrated the achievements of modern authors when compared to classical ones. All the contrary, the librarian replied. They would be placed first rank, if only the library disposed of the huge sums of money needed to purchase those expensive books.[70]

Whether in an old-fashioned library or in a well-endowed laboratory, physical and institutional conditions do matter. There is no doubt that the production of knowledge is situated. In this same line, scholars have also moved away from theories to practices, and one of those practices comprised the role that local knowledge had in knowledge building. Several of the routinary burdens carried by scholars are embedded in social places: laboratories, museums, universities, just to mention a few. Places and institutions that, indeed, have their own logics of productivity and rules of behaviour and scientific validation.

There goes without saying that spaces and institutions inflict their footprints on knowledge production. By the same token, they might reduce the *spectral horizon of thinking*, and therefore, consciously or unconsciously, obstruct the way for new forms of thinking to yield some success, spread or influence. Contests of different nature, in turn, exerted their dynamic and potent mark in the production of knowledge. Further, as network theory has demonstrated, structural holes, in this case, for instance, caused by an overdose of overspecialisation negatively impacted the spectral horizon of thinking.[71] Exposure, as has already been recalled a century ago, generates the conditions for the acquisition of perspective, a process of detachment that results essentially in the configuration of knowledge.[72] Briefly stated, "Ideas are produced in, and shaped by, settings. They must resonate with their environments or they could not find expression, secure agreement, or mobilize followers." That means that place is "essential to the *generation* of knowledge. It is no less significant in its *consumption*."[73]

Much efforts have recently been made at locating into their precise environments the groups, sects, and cliques that emerged in the mid-eighteenth century, tracing how the peculiarities of each of these atmospheres had an impact in the shaping of the knowledge those cliques produced. The international and vast reception of the physiocrats' models no doubt partially obeyed to the place of power in which the agrarian "speculations" (as Smith called them) sprouted.[74] Yet, spaces of power failed to wholly explain the success of a theory otherwise the *Kameralwissenchaften* could have had a larger impact. Surely, the language in which it was communicated, in contrast to the eighteenth-century *lingua franca*, could have lessened its dissemination.[75] In Germany, "political economy" rapidly found an institutional place at the university. In Milan, in contrast, the science of commerce developed in a different setting, an informal coterie called the *Accademia dei pugni* that, in turn, found its voice in the journal *Il caffè*.[76] By the same token, scholars have demonstrated how the overseas experience of some of the renowned writers in the political economy had an impact on the ideas they produced.

Knowledge was produced *in a place*, as much as it was the offspring of a life *on the move*. The fluid movement of authors created conditions upon which knowledge was gathered, analysed, and later, condensed into theories. The effect was not only felt in terms of the experiences that motion offered to potential authors, but also, in terms of the use and spread that specific kinds of platforms had in the communication of both information and knowledge. It means that the credibility of the platform itself as well as the data it conveyed were phenomena that engaged their users and provoked many discussions. Information and knowledge spread at the same rhythm with which authors did. Nothing was more common for eighteenth-century intellectuals than the practice of travelling. This was the case with the two main authors studied throughout this book. Pierre Poivre, for instance, travelled across Asia and lived in China for years. Ange Goudar lived a non-stop travel venture between north and south Europe. No doubt, those experiences had an effect on the production of their ideas and the reasons why they enjoyed some truthfulness.

In the time of the Enlightenment, travel accounts regained great success as a reliable platform. Not that this particular device was formerly unknown. All the contrary, travelogues and travel descriptions had been stored in the shelves of libraries for centuries. Marco Polo is just a famous instance. What really changed was the new dimension of their circulation, the increase in the number of travelogues written and read, and the larger geographical scope they now embraced. There is no doubt the literary genre knew a gradual enlargement over three centuries. While in the sixteenth century, roughly 456 travel accounts were published, in the age of the Enlightenment, more than 3,540 books were printed. In particular, European travels multiplied roughly tenfold, passing from 120 to 1884 (Charts 0.4–0.6).[77]

It would be no mistake in stating that travel accounts are listed among the most popular readings in the eighteenth-century republic of letters. *Voyages d'un philosophe*, the travel account that Poivre wrote, was allegedly a bestseller of the time. As we will show in the first part, his first biography was written by Pierre Samuel Du Pont de Nemours when the second edition was printed. Du Pont needs no introduction, any informed reader knows of his strong attachment to the group headed by Quesnay, being he himself who first put in inked letters the name attributed to the group. Yet, the opposite happens to Poivre.

In his biography, Du Pont tells the readers that Poivre was born in Lyon in August 1710 into a merchant family. Trained in ecclesiastical matters, he assumed missionary endeavours and relocated to Asia. Anecdotally speaking (and in an event that radically altered Poivre's life forever), Du Pont tells that

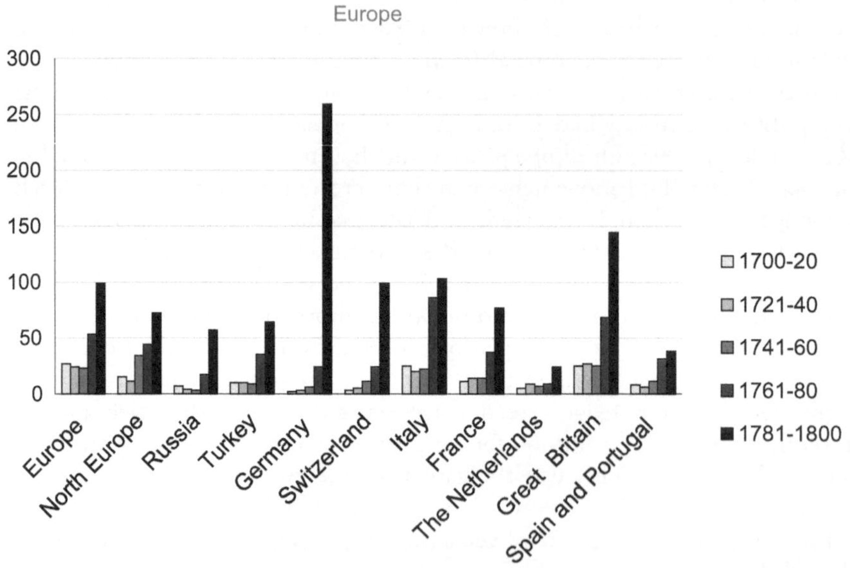


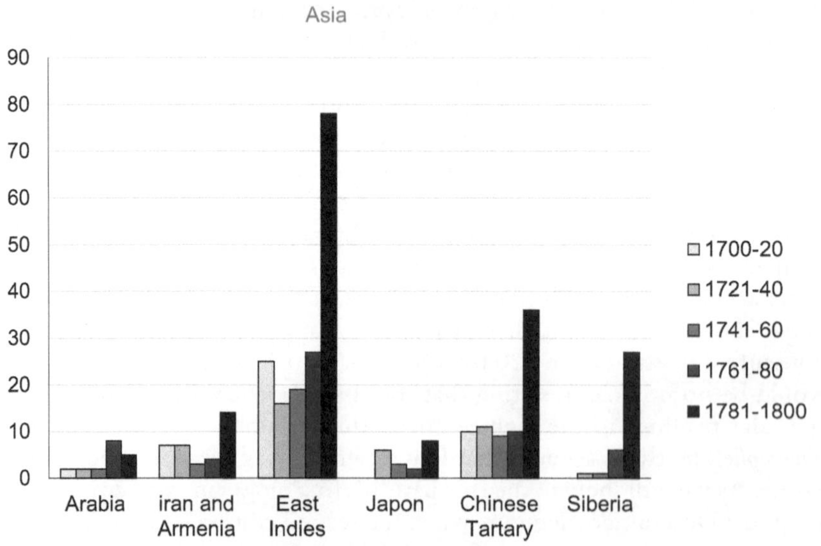


*Chart 0.4, 0.5, and 0.6* Geographical scope of printed travel accounts (1700–1800)
Source: Daniel Roche, *Humeurs Vagabondes*

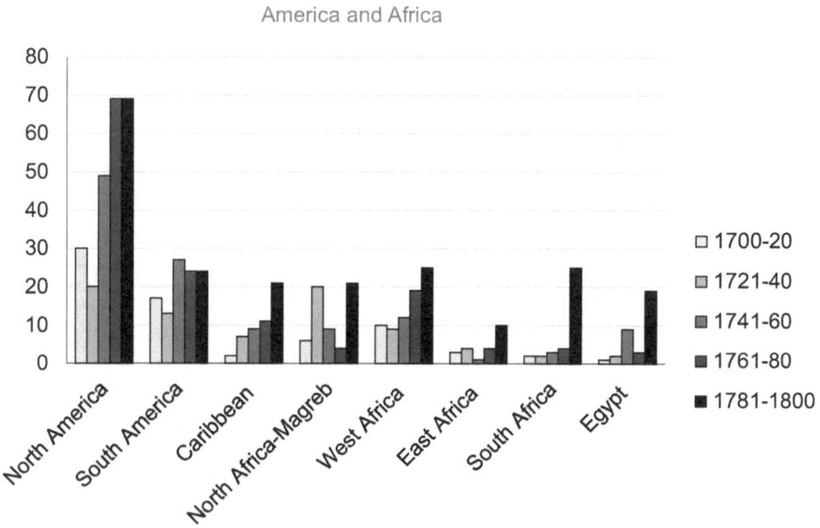


*Chart 0.4, 0.5, and 0.6* Geographical scope of printed travel accounts (1700–1800)
Source: Daniel Roche, *Humeurs Vagabondes*

after his arrival in Canton, Poivre was handed in a letter written in Chinese that was "supposed to be a recommendation letter," but, which, on the contrary, turned out to be a complaint written by a Chinese who demanded to make pay the carrier with his life the offense inflicted. While in jail, Poivre had an opportunity to learn Chinese. Later, with the support of the Canton Viceroy, he sojourned for two years inland China. In his return voyage to France, which happened to be in 1745, the vessel was rammed by an English ship and in the battle Poivre lost an arm. As Du Pont himself wrote, "life is such a singular enigme, and there is no way to know whether the events it brings are advantageous or disastrous."

Besides the lengthy biographical preface, Du Pont also added several footnotes throughout the text. Many of them were intended to offer the readers far more data on travel accounts, of which he seems to have been highly knowledgeable. Travel accounts were a recurrently employed platform for knowledge building and communication in the eighteenth century, as already said. They, indeed, have received little attention on the part of scholars working on the history of economic reflections. It goes without saying that, in the field, preference is conceded to more theoretical-grounded and abstract oeuvres.

By abstracting the ideas from their very process of production and from the spatial settings into which they sprouted, scholars ended up unconsciously overlooking the many practicalities that were involved in the building of thinking as well as the locations in which and the platforms through which thinking was given shape.

Only a couple of years after the publication of *Voyages*, Du Pont included some of his own notes in the journal Éphémérides du citoyen, the propagandistic channel of the "sect," as the physiocrats were mockingly called at that time. The review of a recently launched edition of Saint-Lambert's *Saison* transformed into an opportunity to teach the readers about the costs of slavery. The story of *Ziméo*, more in particular, offered the physiocrat fellow a chance to address some estimates on sugar growing, and with them, to voice the noxious impacts of slavery on humankind. After abridging the epic life of an African prince conducted to Jamaica, who, later, became the leader of a rebel group of slaves, Du Pont proceeded to demonstrate that free labour could improve sugar cultivation, and further, could reduce the price of the staple in the European markets. He affirmed that his estimates had been settled at least two decades ago but never shown, only occasionally to a few friends among which Franklin (Figure 0.1).

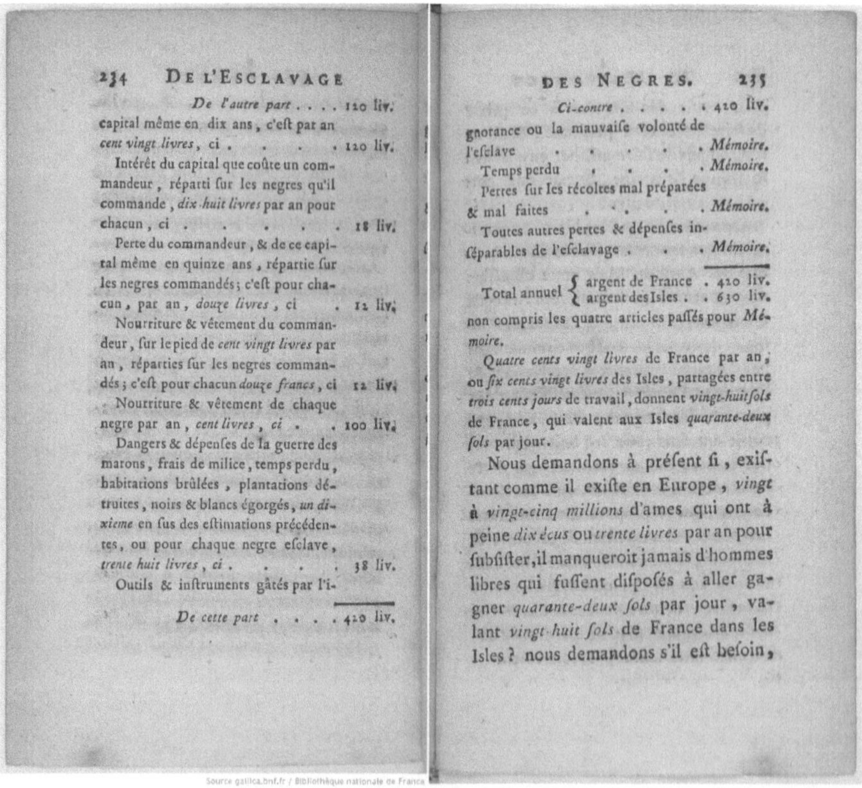

234 DE L'ESCLAVAGE

*De l'autre part* . . . . 120 liv.

capital même en dix ans, c'eſt par an *cent vingt livres*, ci . . . . 120 liv.

Intérêt du capital que coûte un commandeur, réparti ſur les negres qu'il commande, *dix-huit livres* par an pour chacun, ci . . . . . 18 liv.

Perte du commandeur, & de ce capital même en quinze ans, répartie ſur les negres commandés; c'eſt pour chacun, par an, *douze livres*, ci . 12 liv.

Nourriture & vêtement du commandeur, ſur le pied de *cent vingt livres* par an, réparties ſur les negres commandés; c'eſt pour chacun *douze francs*, ci 12 liv.

Nourriture & vêtement de chaque negre par an, *cent livres*, *ci* . . 100 liv.

Dangers & dépenſes de la guerre des marons, frais de milice, temps perdu, habitations brûlées, plantations détruites, noirs & blancs égorgés, *un dixieme* en ſus des eſtimations précédentes, ou pour chaque negre eſclave, *trente huit livres*, *ci* . . . . 38 liv.

Outils & inſtruments gâtés par l'i-

*De cette part* . . . . 420 liv.

DES NEGRES. 235

*Ci-contre* . . . . . 420 liv.

gnorance ou la mauvaiſe volonté de l'eſclave . . . . . *Mémoire.*

Temps perdu . . . . *Mémoire.*

Pertes ſur les récoltes mal préparées & mal faites . . . . *Mémoire.*

Toutes autres pertes & dépenſes inſéparables de l'eſclavage . . . *Mémoire.*

Total annuel { argent de France . 420 liv. / argent des Isles . . 630 liv.

non compris les quatre articles paſſés pour *Mémoire.*

*Quatre cents vingt livres* de France par an; ou *ſix cents vingt livres* des Isles, partagées entre *trois cents jours* de travail, donnent *vingt-huit ſols* de France, qui valent aux Isles *quarante-deux ſols* par jour.

Nous demandons à préſent ſi, exiſtant comme il exiſte en Europe, *vingt* à *vingt-cinq millions* d'ames qui ont à peine *dix écus* ou *trente livres* par an pour ſubſiſter, il manqueroit jamais d'hommes libres qui fuſſent diſpoſés à aller gagner *quarante-deux ſols* par jour, valant *vingt-huit ſols* de France dans les Isles? nous demandons s'il eſt beſoin,



*Figure 0.1* De l'esclavage des negres. Éphémérides du Citoyen
Source: Éphémérides du Citoyen

Estimates on the costs of slavery were intermingled in a review of a literature book. This practice put forward the impact that non-theoretical or non-economic oeuvres had on the emergence of economic discussions and theories, a matter that deserves further research. An instance can better illustrate this point.

Quesnay's paper on the Chinese despotic form of government has probably awaited far more interest than his short sketch on the Inca government. The latter, however, provoked a candent repercussion in the Parisian intellectual circles due to the theoretical unintended deductions it generated regarding the atemporal nature of property. If Quesnay's account were accepted, a reader recalled, it would mean that a society could function without being bound by property rights, the very foundation, and guarantor of social order. The issue will be discussed in Chapter 5, for the moment it is worth observing that scholars could be deeply concerned with the content of the paper without raising the question as to why the Incas were the fit society for elaborating this particular analysis. All things considered, the attraction that the Andean world exerted upon the leader of the physiocrats owed to some extent to the bestseller *Lettres d'une Péruvienne* and the 1730s geodesic expedition. Both the book and the scientific venture placed the Andean world at the centre of the interest of the Parisian men of letters. Peru was in vogue in the third quarter of the century in France. The years 1741–60, for instance, saw an increase in the number of travel accounts published about South America, passing from 13 to 27.

Costs incurred in keeping slavery working included the capital invested in the bartering of enslaved Africans although opportunity costs should be also considered. In particular, the interest rate that the same fund could generate when invested in overseas trade. Du Pont further calculated everyday expenses spent in feeding and clothing the enslaved workers as well as the costs of maintaining overseers. He further anticipated the low productivity of forced workers who could aspire to own but nothing, and further, foresaw that European workers could be put in charge of the plantations. Costs spent on the maintenance of enslaved workers could afford salaries for that mass of jobless Europeans who could produce all the sugar the market demanded. Moreover, Du Pont forecasted that sugar grown by free workers could be sold at a cheaper price, making unnecessary the sustainment of a regime of work that violated the very principles of natural law. He thus cited Poivre's travel account and held that in Cochin-China, where sugar was farmed and processed by free workers, that was the price on the market.

Poivre considered that Cochin-China could be seen as a colony. He compared the different sorts of cane farmed in the country and also described the refinement practices employed there. In Southeast Asia, he stated, techniques had not achieved yet the level of refinement already yielded in the Caribbean though plenty of sugar was sold, much of which was purchased by Chinese merchants. As much as the abundant quantities of commercialised sugar, cheap prices also amazed the eyes of the traveller. The most important fact to remark was, nonetheless, that "sugar cane is there cultivated by free men, and all the process of preparation and refining, the work of free hands."[78] When prices of sugar grown by slaves and free workers were compared, the resulting conclusion was that the maintenance of a regime of slavery resulted completely useless. His observations led him to think that "if our West-India colonies had been distributed without reservation amongst a free people, they would have produced double the quantity."[79] Du Pont added a footnote to the text and explained that the observations came to refute the claims of mill owners who claimed that only enslaved people could farm the sugar. Du Pont also advised the readers that the "apology" of that system could be found in another travel account entitled *Travel to the Sierra-Leone*, and further warned the public that a contradiction to this author has been elaborated in an "excellent book in English" titled *Essay on the colonization*.

Du Pont conceived of Poivre's comparison as an observation. In Chapter 4, I will discuss the difference between evidence and observation and point out how the unleashed discussion on proof served to attack the main ideas the économistes upheld. However, many readers remained rather unconvinced of the conclusions that the travelling philosopher had reached. Shortly after being published, an extensive review was included in the journal *Correspondance littéraire*. It is worth saying that the periodical was the voice of the most tenacious contradictors the physiocrats found. The reviewer fully disqualified the gathered observations, and in particular, wondered how a traveller who had never been to America could convey any idea on that continent. More in general, the reviewer casted doubts on the reliability of travel accounts. His ideas are worth bringing forward as they shed light on the discussions that the truthfulness of travel accounts provoked. In other words, the "uses and misuses" of that platform.

A sharp discontent resulted from the inflated worth of China found throughout the narrative. Much of the discomfort lies (as the reviewer blamed the traveller for) in that Poivre shared with a large number of the "best spirits" of the time a delight for the most eastern empire. Told as immutable since the dawn of time, and for the most part fantasised by misguided European authors, China was sold as the model to follow. Elsewhere in the same journal, an author who advertised the sole whole novel to have ever been translated the same journal, an author who advertised the sole whole novel to have been translated from Chinese to English, and then, from English to French, appraised the dilemma in-depth. It could be easily agreed upon that there was only little information available on that faraway country. This insurmountable society was, therefore, a lucky chance for "system makers to deploy the sources of their imagination." After having read reverend Percy's translation of *Hau Kiou Chooan*, readers could wonder whether or not Europeans should emulate China. In a short time, the country (mostly shaped by the ideas of some misleading panegyrists) had become the "asylum of virtue, wisdom, and happiness." Said to enjoy the superior and most ancient form of government, mistaken advertisers wanted the public to believe that its laws, police, arts, and industry were models that everybody should aspire to follow.[80]

To make his point clear, the anonymous reviewer judged the prospect of writing on Ancient Rome. Let's suppose, he argued, that Rome would have left no record of any kind: no history books, philosophical treatises, or monuments. Upon that condition, no smart spirit would dare to raise any opinion on the behaviour and morals of the Romans only assisted by a few traces left by Greek merchants or philosophers. The only way to get the right impression of the customs and manners of a country was to dwell there for years, learn the language, and read their authors. Nothing of those requisites were found in most of the authors that displayed such a compelling attractiveness for China. As for faraway or forgoing cultures, the tendency was for authors to find all of them more virtuous or smarter: "the farther the distance, the larger the capacity of the imagination to believe whatever it pleases." Experience shows that travel accounts contradicted each other, making them less reliable when not reliable at all.[81]

Evoking a point that had also been scrutinised by the above reviewer, a decade later Smith mused on the reliability of travel accounts. In China, roads and canals were reported to be the responsibility of the government. Smith further affirmed that provincial governors were asked to be diligently occupied with the maintenance of those roads, which were said to "exceed very much everything of the same kind which is known in Europe." In a straightforward manner, Smith asserted that "the accounts of those works, however, which have been transmitted to Europe, have generally been drawn up by weak and wondering travellers; frequently by stupid and lying missionaries." The trustworthiness of that kind of sources was then put into criticism. Those wonderful impressions could be debunked "if they had been examined by more intelligent eyes and if the accounts of them had been reported by more faithful witnesses."[82]

Smith made extensive use of travel accounts, though. Exactly the same can be said of many other first-rank economists like Quesnay. This is an issue that has seemingly deserved little research. A few instances could be mentioned. In the chapter on colonies, Smith drew comparisons between the Spanish and the English colonies with regard to population patterns. In that case, Ulloa is quoted. Numbers for Mexico are said to have been drawn from Gemelli Carreri "a pretended traveller, it is said, indeed, but who seems everywhere to have written upon extremely good information." Those numbers, even in the case they suffered from the "exaggerations of the Spanish writers," overpassed the ones of cities like Boston, New York, and Philadelphia. Agricultural techniques practiced in North America were reported to have been taken from the observations the Swedish traveller Mr. Kalm had gathered. Further, precisely with regard to agricultural matters, and placed in the chapter on the agricultural system, Smith compared the fluvial engineering works built in Ancient Egypt and those of the Ganges. After offering some insights on social organisation (which are very likely to be taken from historical narratives or travel accounts), Smith asserted that both governments were particularly attentive to the "interest of agriculture." Genovesi had already used the same instances.

Averted to the sea, both Egyptians and Indians seemed to have depended on other nations to export their agricultural surpluses, which might "have confined the market" and with them the increase of manufactures which "require a much more extensive market than the most important parts of the rude produce of the land." The comparison allowed the Scottish author to draw some conclusions on the market extension, a topic central to the first book of The *Wealth of Nations.* In the subsequent sections, Smith compares Greece's and Rome's agrarian policies. The question remains as to whether the assumption regarding the extension of the market developed in an inductive manner and was thereafter illustrated with historical cases or the other way around.

For the sake of this book, Smith's notes on Chinese agriculture and taxes are worth bringing forward, still more due to the fact that they stood at the kernel of Smith's theory. The chapter on the wages of labour put into dialogue a lot of data, though Smith barely stated from whence the information had been drawn. Let's discard for a moment the theoretical deductions and let's pay attention to the data upon which the abstraction was elaborated. After having compared wages paid both in England and North America, Smith focused on China, a country which, as was overall accepted, was "one of the most fertile, best cultivated, most industrious, and most populous countries in world." It seems, nonetheless, that since long ago a stationary trend prevailed. This pattern could be deduced from the fact that Marco Polo's description closely matched the recent observations offered by modern travellers. "The accounts of all travellers, inconsistent in many other respects, agree in the low wages of labour, and in the difficulty which a labourer finds in bringing up a family." Still of most interest is the mention that Smith made of Poivre's travel account. In a try to abstract some patterns on the rent of land, Smith compared colonial sugar production to French vineyards' production. Cochin-China appears at the centre of the comparison. In that country, sugar was commonly sold for three piasters the quintal, "as we are told by Mr. Poivre a very careful observer of the agriculture of that country." He continued on saying that the greater part of the land was employed to cultivate corn and rice, which maintain a natural price between the three staples in total contraposition to what happened in the American colonies.

Both Du Pont and Smith cited Poivre for different purposes. Even though Quesnay should have heard of or read the book, *Voyages* are not cited in the *Despotisme de la Chine.* Turgot was a great reader of Poivre whom he knew. Precisely, during his voyages inner France, the to-became minister asked Du Pont to post him a second copy of *Voyages.* Regarding Chinese taxation, he commented that he had learned through Poivre and Verthamont that the tenth imposed upon the crops was the main source for the Chinese emperor. According to the former, the share of the tax varied depending on land fertility: the most fertile lands were charged a tenth while those less productive only paid a thirtieth.

In drawing on Poivre, Smith indirectly made an underhand double use of travel accounts. For one reason. As we have seen, doubts have been cast on the conclusions that Poivre reached on the American colonies and slavery. The question, therefore, arises upon which sources the French traveller built his comparison. It is not doubt that the comparison had been possible thanks to the observations gathered by travellers journeying the French Caribbean colonies. One of those travellers was Chanvalon who published *Voyage à la Martinique* whose subtitle recalled the one Poivre placed in his book *Diverses observations sur la physique, l'histoire naturelle, l'agriculture, les moeurs, et les usages de cette isle.* Data had been gathered in 1751 and presented before the *Académie Royale des Sciences* in 1761. It coincides with the years in which Poivre read his lectures at both Lyon and Parisian societies. In his preface, Chanvalon cautioned his readers that during his voyage he had looked with the eyes of a philosopher and insisted that the travel account should be read as a series of observations.

## Theory and practice: existence

These are a few of the issues an author faced. The process of gathering data or giving shape to that information into a precise format – either a book or a paper – is commonly left out of the analysis because most of the attention is paid to abstract ideas. In his *L'espien Chinois*, Goudar unveiled the trap: "the theory of the society has in a way absorbed the practice, we read too much about men, and we do not observe them enough." The best book on the world was the world itself, Goudar underlined. The intellectual world was, according to the same author, "radically different" from the one in which people lived.

Ange Goudar, the author who wrote this piece of criticism, might sound unfamiliar to many. In spite of this fact, Goudar's name was recurrently evoked in the eighteenth century and his books were widely read. The second part of this book will revolve around his vast oeuvre. The assessment of Goudar's books (as it could be alleged) might add little to our understanding of the theoretical apparatus elaborated in the eighteenth century, however, it might contribute much to our understanding of the inextricable entanglements involving theory and practice. While Poivre produced his thoughts embedded in the practical world of botanical knowledge, Goudar, instead, elaborated his ideas in a constant motion between the rich north and backward south Europe. For him, intellectual salons were highly appealing although not less than underground worldly places seem to have been.

Goudar's life has been extensively researched, or at least, inquired as far as his faint presence in both private and public records has allowed. Interest in his oeuvre and life have come from the part of scholars who have seen him as an adventurer of the Enlightenment or a *libertin.* Born into a merchant family on the outskirts of Montpellier, Goudar proved to be a tireless traveller. In 1733 and with an inherited sum of money at hand, Goudar moved to Paris where he spent much of the heritage in hazard games. This was the first of his sojourns in the French capital. Previously, he had spent at least two years in Istanbul. Through a petition allegedly written for Goudar himself in 1777, we learn that in those years he worked in Turkey overseeing the quality of French clothes of which at that moment many complaints were heard of. Son of an inspector of manufactures, he had practical knowledge on the arts of weaving wool. He would later profit from this knowledge and it is reported that he moved first to Lisbon and much later to Naples where he was supposed to sell this know-how through either the settling of a fabric or the transfer of knowledge for improving textile qualities.

Goudar's life is one of someone who uninterruptedly travelled between North and South Europe. As it is widely known, in the mid-century, many scholars showed a particular interest in explaining why England had risen to maritime control. Most of the answers overstated the peculiarity of the political institutions that existed on the island. Commercial regulations and political institutions were alternatively said to explain why English merchants had overcome Dutch contestants and had set domination upon North Atlantic markets. Even though the topic remained far less studied, scholars were likely to be less concerned in identifying the reasons why southern countries remained in backward conditions. Spain, indeed, was a commonly mentioned instance. Yet, one should be aware of the fact that it was not only Spain, Portugal, or other southern countries which caused curiosity due to their apparent lethargy. For many mid-eighteenth-century authors, France was also depicted in a backward condition when compared to other countries.

Goudar addressed the underlying causes that explained the rise of England and the backwardness of Portugal. He was among the few authors who conceived of the South of Europe as a unity and who advanced a series of explanations for the preponderant backward conditions in Portugal and Naples. Indeed, those issues were studied mostly from local perspectives for local cliques, and with local stakes at hand. Conversely, the kernel of the debate sought to shed light on the path followed by, and the conditions prevailing in rich countries. This was the usual manner in which the debate reached some degree of internationalisation. Goudar approached the issue from a different perspective. He offered his readers a series of explanations with mainly a local character. Besides, he wrote for the large public (it means for layman in economic matters) a series of oeuvres in which he explained the basics of the theoretical debates.

Unlike most widely known authors, Goudar was not seemingly well connected to any of the contemporaneous powerful cliques. Neither was him arguably and at first glance influential in the community of economists. Yet, he sold very well. He gained his life from what he wrote. For instance, according to Darnton, books ordered to the *Société Typographique de Neuchâtel* in the 1760s and 1770s placed Goudar among the most sold authors. In a list made up of 23 authors headed by Voltaire and D'Holbach, he is, along with Mirabeau, among the few economists to appear. Ordered books authored by Mirabeau reached 312 copies while Goudar followed close with 214 ones. Both authors could not be more different.

Goudar could be seen as an outsider or an alien both in the local Parisian circles or elsewhere. Somehow because of this feature, however, he enjoyed certain freedom to express his thoughts without constraints. In one of his books, he criticised the massive number of economics books published recently, alleging that most of them only generated confusion. But at the same time, he mocked the quixotic attempt to organise all existing knowledge in alphabetical order in an attack against Diderot, d'Alembert, and their group.

## Notes

1 Karl Polanyi, Conrad M. Arensberg, and Harry W. Pearson, eds., *Trade and Market in the Early Empires: Economies in History and Theory* (Glencoe: Falcon's Wing Press, 1957); Karl Polanyi, *The Great Transformation: The Political and Economic Origins of Our Time* (Boston, MA: Beacon Press, 2001); Fernand Braudel, *Civilisation Matérielle, Économie et Capitalisme (XVe–XVIIIe Siècle)* (Paris: Armand Colin, 1979); Clifford Geertz, 'The Bazaar Economy: Information and Search in Peasant Marketing', *American Economic Review* 68, no. 2 (1978): 28–32.

2 Karl Mannheim, *Ideology and Utopia* (New York: Routledge, 1998); George H. Taylor, ed., *Lectures on Ideology and Utopia. Paul Ricoeur* (New York: Columbia University Press, 1986); Franco Venturi, *Utopia e Riforma Nell'illuminismo* (Turin, 1970).

3 For overviews of international or global commerce from economic or intellectual history perspectives see, Fernand Braudel, *Civilisation Matérielle*; Ronald Findlay and Kevin H. O'Rourke, *Power and Plenty: Trade, War, and the World Economy in the Second Millennium* (Princeton, NJ: Princeton University Press, 2007); Andre Gunder Frank, *ReOrient: Global Economy in the Asian Age* (Los Angeles: University of California Press, 1998); Dennis O. Flynn and Arturo Giraldez, 'Born with a "Silver Spoon": The Origin of World Trade', *Journal of World History* 6, no. 2 (1995): 201–22; Emma Rothschild, 'Global Commerce and the Question of Sovereignty in the Eighteenth-Century Provinces', *Modern Intellectual History* 1, no. 1 (2004): 3–25.

4 Michel Foucault, *Sécurité, Territoire et Population. Cours Au Collège de France (1977–78)* (Paris: Gallimard/Seuil (Collection Hautes Études), 2004); Michel Foucault, *L'herméneutique Du Sujet. Cours Au Collège de France (1981–1982)* (Paris: Seuil/ Gallimard, 2001); Michel Foucault, *L'archéologie Du Savoir* (Paris: Gallimard, 1969); Pierre Bourdieu, *Esquisse d'une Théorie de La Pratique (Précédé de Trois Études d'ethnologie Kabyle* (Paris: Seuil, 2000); Pierre Bourdieu, *Le Sens Pratique* (Paris: Les éditions de minuit, 1980); Pierre Bourdieu, *L'ontologie Politique de Martin Heidegger* (Paris: Les éditions de minuit, 1988); Michel de Certeau, *The Practice of Everyday Life* (Berkeley: University of California Press, 2011).

5 Martin Heidegger, *Being and Time* (New York: State University of New York Press, 2010); Hannah Arendt, *The Human Condition* (Chicago, IL: Chicago University Press, 2018); Jeff Kochan, *Science as Social Existence. Heidegger and the Sociology of Scientific Knowledge* (Cambridge: Open book publishers, 2017); Jeff Malpas, *Heidegger's Topology: Being, Place, and World* (Cambridge: MIT, 2006).

6 Peter Burke, *What Is the History of Knowledge?* (Cambridge: Polity Press, 2016); Peter Burke, *A Social History of Knowledge: From Gutenberg to Diderot* (Cambridge: Polity Press, 2000); Martin Mulsow, *Prekäres Wissen. Eine Andere Ideengeschichte Der Frühen Neuzeit* (Berlin: Suhrkamp, 2012); David N. Livingstone, *Putting Science in Its Place: Geographies of Scientific Knowledge* (Chicago, IL: Chicago University Press, 2003); James A. Secord, 'Knowledge in Transit', *Isis* 95, no. 4 (2004): 654–72; Kapil Raj, *Relocating Modern Science. Circulation and the Construction of Knowledge in South Asia and Europe, 1650–1900* (New York: Palgrave Macmillan, 2007).

7 Istvan Hont, *Jealousy of Trade: International Competition and the Nation-State in Historical Perspective* (Cambridge, MA: Harvard University Press, 2010); J. G. A. Pocock, *Virtue, Commerce, and History: Essais on Political Thought and History. Chiefly in the Eighteenth Century* (Cambridge: Cambridge University Press, 1985).

8 Jean-Claude Perrot, *Une Histoire Intellectuelle de l'économie Politique* (Paris: EHESS, 1992).

9 Roger Chartier, *Inscrire et Effacer. Culture Écrite et Littérature. XIe-XVIIIe* (Paris: Seuil/Gallimard, 2006); Roger Chartier, *Culture Écrite et Société: L'ordre Des Livres XIVe–XVIIIe* (Paris: Albin Michel, 1996).

10 Paul Cheney, *Revolutionary Commerce: Globalization and the French Monarchy* (Cambridge, MA: Harvard University Press, 2010).

11 Simone Meyssonnier, *La Balance et l'horloge. La Genèse de La Pensée Libérale En France Au XVIIIe Siècle* (Paris: Éditions de la passion, 1989); Loïc Charles, Frédéric Lefebvre, and Christine Théré, *Le Cercle de Vincent de Gournay: Savoirs Économiques et Pratiques Administratives En France Au Milieu Du XVIII* (Paris: Institut National d'Études Démographiques, 2011); Arnaud Orain, *La Politique Du Merveilleux. Une Autre Histoire Du Système de Law (1695–1795)* (Paris: Fayard, 2018).

12 Montesquieu, *The Spirit of the Laws* (Cambridge: Cambridge University Press, 1989).

13 David Hume, *Political Essays* (Cambridge: Cambridge University Press, 1994).

14 Istvan Hont, *Jealousy of Trade*; J. G. A. Pocock, *Virtue, Commerce, and History.*

15 Albert O. Hirschman, *The Passions and the Interests: Political Arguments for Capitalism before Its Triumph* (Princeton, NJ: Princeton University Press, 2013); Laurence Dickey, 'Doux-Commerce and Humanitarian Values. Free Trade, Sociability and Universal Benevolence in Eighteenth-Century Thinking', *Grotiana (New Series)* 22/23, no. 2 (2001): 271–318; Catherine Larrère, 'Montesquieu et Le "Doux Commerce": Un Paradigme Du Libéralisme', *Cahiers d'histoire. Revue d'histoire Critique* 123 (2014): 21–38; Anoush Fraser Terjanian, *Commerce and Its Discontents in Eighteenth-Century French Political Thought* (Cambridge: Cambridge University Press, 2016), 9–13; Marco Platania, 'Montesquieu Und Der "Doux Commerce": Wie Der Handel Gesellschaft Und Politik Verwandelt', in *Der Moderne Staat Und 'Le Doux Commerce': Politik, Ökonomie Und Internationale Beziehungen Im Politischen Denken Der Aufklärung*, ed. Olaf Asbach (Baden-Baden: Nomos, 2014), 69–90.

16 Istvan Hont, *Jealousy of Trade*; Sophus Reinert, *Translating Empire: Emulation and the Origins of Political Economy* (Cambridge, MA: Harvard University Press, 2011); Sophus Reinert, 'The Sultan's Republic: Jealousy of Trade and Oriental Despotism in Paolo Mattia Doria', in *Enlightenment Reform in Southern Europe and Its Atlantic Colonies, c. 1750–1830*, ed. Gabriel Paquette (Farnham: Ashgate, 2009), 253–70.

17 Benoît Walraevens, 'Jealousy of Trade in Hume and Smith', *History of Economic Ideas* 25, no. 2 (2017): 11–36.

18 Jean-François Melon, *A Political Essay upon Commerce.* Written in French by Monsieur M. Translated, with Some Annotations, and Remarks by David Bindon (Dublin: Printed for Philip Crampton, 1738), 135–44.

19 Philip Cantillon, *The Analysis of Trade, Commerce, Coin, Bullion, Banks, and Foreign Exchanges Wherein the True Principles of This Useful Knowledge Are Fully but Briefly Laid down and Explained, to Give a Clear Idea of Their Happy Consequences to Society When Well Regulated Taken Chiefly from a Manuscript of a Very Ingenious Gentleman Deceased and Adapted to the Present Situation of Our Trade and Commerce* (London: Printed for the author, 1759), v.

20 Céline Spector, 'Commerce', in *A Montesquieu Dictionary*, n.d., http://dictionnaire-montesquieu.ens-lyon.fr/en/home/.

21 Benoît Walraevens, 'Jealousy of Trade in Hume and Smith'.

22 Antonio Genovesi, *Lezioni Di Commercio o Sia d'economia Civile* (Bassano: Spese Remondini, 1769), Vol. I, 297.
23 Kenneth Pomeranz, *The Great Divergence. China, Europe, and the Making of the Modern World* (Princeton, NJ: Princeton University Press, 2009); Jean-Laurent Rosenthal and Bing Wong, *Before and Beyond Divergence: The Politics of Economic Change in China and Europe* (Cambridge, MA: Harvard University Press, 2009).
24 Karl Polanyi, *The Great Transformation.*
25 William Petty, *An Essay Concerning the Multiplication of Mankind: Together with Another Essay in Political Arithmetick, Concerning the Growth of the City of London: With the Measures, Periods, Causes, and Consequences Thereof, 1682* (London: Robert Clavel and Henry Mortlok, 1698).
26 Pierre Daniel Huet, *Le Grand Trésor Historique et Politique Du Florissant Commerce Des Hollandais, Dans Tous Les États et Empires Du Monde. Quelle Est Leur Manière de Le Faire, Son Origine, Leur Grand Progrés, Leur Possessions & Gouvernements Dans Les Indes. Comment Ils Se Sont Rendus Maîtres de Tout Le Commerce de l'Europe* (Haye: Henry Frik, 1713).
27 Pierre Daniel Huet, 15–16.
28 M. Auffray, 'Considérations sur les Manufactures dans les Villes Maritimes et Commerçantes', *Journal de l'agriculture, du commerce, et des finances* Juillet (1768): 130–81.
29 Sophus Reinert, 'The Empire of Emulation: A Quantitative Analysis of Economic Translations in the European World, 1500–1849', in *The Political Economy of Empire in the Early Modern World*, eds. Sophus Reinert and Pernille Roge (New York: Palgrave Macmillan, 2013), 105–30.
30 Sophus Reinert, *Translating Empire*, 32.
31 Sophus Reinert, 46.
32 Sophus Reinert, 52.
33 Loïc Charles, Frédéric Lefebvre, and Christine Théré, *Le Cercle de Vincent de Gournay.*
34 Simone Meyssonnier, *La Balance et l'horloge*, 161–209.
35 Josiah Child, *A New Discourse of Trade* (London: T. Sowle, 1698).
36 Gerónimo de Uztáriz, *Theórica y Práctica de Comercio y de Marina: En Diferentes Discursos y Calificados Exemplares Que, Con Específicas Providencias, Se Procuran Adaptar a La Monarquía Española, Para Su Pronta Restauración, Beneficio Universal y Mayor Fortaleza Contra Los Émulos de La Real Corona, Mediante La Soberana Protección Del Rey Nuestro Señor Don Phelipe V* (Madrid: Imprenta Antonio Sanz, 1757).
37 Plumard de Dangeul, *Remarques Sur Les Avantages et Les Désavantages de La France et de La Gr. Bretagne, Par Rapport Au Commerce, et Aux Autres Sources de La Puissance Des État. Traduction de l'anglais Du Chevalier John Nickolls* (Leiden: s.n., 1754).
38 Sophus Reinert, *Translating Empire.*
39 Jean-Claude Perrot, *Une Histoire Intellectuelle*, 75–77.
40 David Landes, *The Wealth and Poverty of Nations Why Some Are So Rich and Some So Poor* (New York: W.W. Norton Company, 1999); Joel Mokyr, *The Gifts of Athena: Historical Origins of the Knowledge Economy* (Princeton, NJ: Princeton University Press, 2004); Joel Mokyr, *The Enlightened Economy: An Economic History of Britain 1700–1850* (Princeton, NJ: Princeton University Press, 2012); Deirdre McCloskey, *Bourgeois Dignity: Why Economics Can't Explain the Modern World* (Chicago, IL: Chicago University Press, 2010).
41 Kenneth Pomeranz, *The Great Divergence*; Jean-Laurent Rosenthal and Bing Wong, *Before and Beyond Divergence.*
42 Deirdre McCloskey, *Bourgeois Dignity: Why Economics Can't Explain the Modern World* (Chicago, IL: Chicago University Press, 2010), 372.

43 Barry R. Weingast, 'Exposing the Neoclassical Fallacy: Mccloskey on Ideas and the Great Enrichment', *Scandinavian Economic History Review* 64, no. 3 (2016): 190.

44 Pierre du Pont de Nemours, *De l'origine et Des Progrès d'une Science Nouvelle* (Londres: Chez Desaint, libraire, rue du Foin, 1778), 18; Rafe Blaufarb, *The Great Demarcation: The French Revolution and the Invention of Modern Property* (Oxford: Oxford University Press, 2016), 15–47.

45 Pierre-Joseph Proudhon, *What Is Property? Or an Inquiry into the Principle of Right and of Government* (Cambridge: Cambridge University Press, 1994); Harold Demsetz, 'Toward a Theory of Property Rights', *American Economic Review* 57, no. 2 (1967): 347-59; Geoffrey M. Hodgson, 'Much of the "Economics of Property Rights" Devalues Property and Legal Rights', *Journal of Institutional Economics* 11, no. 4 (2015): 683–709; Daron Acemoglu and Simon Johnson, 'Unbundling Institutions', *Journal of Political Economy* 113, no. 5 (2005): 949–95; Joshua Getzler, 'Theories of Property and Economic Development', *Journal of Interdisciplinary History* 26, no. 4 (1996): 639–69; Gary D. Libecap, 'Property Rights in Economic History: Implications for Research', *Explorations in Economic History* 23 (1986): 227–52; Rosa Congost, 'Property Rights and Historical Analysis: What Rights ? What History?', *Past and Present* 181 (2003): 73-106.

46 Arnault Skornicki, 'Liberté, Propriété, Sûreté. Retour Sur Une Devise Physiocratique', *Corpus, Revue de Philosophie* 66 (2004): 17–36.

47 Daron Acemoglu and James Robinson, *The Narrow Corridor: States, Societies, and the Fate of Liberty* (New York: Penguin Press, 2019).

48 Françoise Ruzé, 'L'Utopie Spartiate', *Kentron. Revue Pluridisciplinaire Du Monde Antique* 26 (2010): 17-48.

49 Douglass North, *The Rise of the West World: A New Economic History* (London: Cambridge University Press, 1973), 137.

50 Avner Greif, *Institutions and the Path to the Modern Economy: Lessons from the Medieval Trade* (Cambridge: Cambridge University Press, 2006), 30.

51 Douglass North, *Institutions, Institutional Change and Economic Performance* (Cambridge: Cambridge University Press, 1991); Douglass North, *Understanding the Process of Economic Change* (Princeton, NJ: Princeton University Press, 2010).

52 Douglass North, 'Institutions', *Journal of Economic Perspectives* 5, no. 1 (1991): 97–112.

53 Masahiko Aoki, *Toward a Comparative Institutional Analysis* (Boston: MIT, 2001), 10.

54 Avner Greif, *Institutions and the Path to the Modern Economy*; Jarced Rubin, *Rulers, Religion, and Riches: Why the West Got Rich and the Middle East Did Not* (Cambridge: Cambridge University Press, 2017).

55 Jeremy Edwards and Sheilagh Ogilvie, 'Contract Enforcement, Institutions, and Social Capital: The Maghribi Traders Reappraised', *Economic History Review* 65, no. 2 (n.d.): 421–44.

56 Jessica Goldberg, 'Choosing and Enforcing Business Relationships in the Eleventh-Century Mediterranean: Reassessing the Magrhibi Traders', *Past and Present* 216, no. 3 (n.d.): 3–40.

57 Rafael La Porta et al., 'Law and Finance', *Journal of Political Economy* 106, no. 6 (1998): 1113–55.

58 Aldo Musacchio and John D. Turner, 'Does the Law and Finance Hypothesis Pass the Test of History?', *Business History* 55, no. 4 (2013): 524–42.

59 Daron Acemoglu, Simon Johnson, and James Robinson, 'The Colonial Origins of Comparative Development: An Empirical Investigation', *American Economic Review* 9, no. 5 (2001): 1369–401.

60 Ron Harris, *Going the Distance: Eurasian Trade and the Rise of the Business Corporation, 1400–1700* (Princeton, NJ: Princeton University Press, 2020).

61 Daron Acemoglu, Georgy Egorov, and Konstantin Sonin, 'Institutional Change and Institutional Persistence', *Becker Friedman Institute-Political Economics Initiative Working Papers* 127 (2020).

62 Daron Acemoglu and Simon Johnson, 'Unbundling Institutions'; Daron Acemoglu et al., 'The Consequences of Radical Reform: The French Revolution', *American Economic Review* 101, no. 7 (2011): 3286–307; Michael Kopsidis and Daniel W. Bromley, 'The French Revolution and German Industrialization: Dubious Models and Doubtful Causality', *Journal of Institutional Economics* 12, no. 1 (2016): 161–90.
63 Gabriel Tarde, *The Laws of Imitation* (New York: Henry Holt and Company, 1903).
64 Robert Darnton, 'The High Enlightenment and the Low-Life of Literature in Pre-Revolutionary France', *Past and Present* 51 (1971): 81–115.
65 Daniel Mornet, *Les Origines Intellectuelles de La Révolution Française, 1715–1787* (Paris: éditions Tallandier, 2010), 1.
66 Robert Darnton, *The Great Cat Massacre: And Other Episodes in French Cultural History* (New York: Basic Books, 1984), 145–90.
67 Robert Darnton, 'The High Enlightenment', 94.
68 Michel Werner and Bénédicte Zimmermann, 'Penser l'histoire Croisée: Entre Empirie et Réflexivité', *Annales. Histoire, Sciences Sociales* 58, no. 1 (2003): 7–36.
69 Peter Burke, *A Social History of Knowledge.*
70 Ange Goudar, *L'espien Chinois, Ou l'envoyé Secret de La Cour de Pekin, Pour Examiner l'état Présent de l'Europe. Traduit Du Chinois* (Cologne: 1765, n.d.), Vol. III, 174.
71 Ronald S. Burt, *Neighbor Networks: Competitive Advantage Local and Personal* (New York: Oxford University Press, 2010); Mario Cedrini and Magda Fontana, 'Just Another Niche in the Wall? How Specialization Is Changing the Face of Mainstream Economics', *Cambridge Journal of Economics* 42, no. 2 (2018): 427–51.
72 Karl Mannheim, *Ideology and Utopia.*
73 David N. Livingstone, *Putting Science in Its Place*, 7, 11.
74 Christine Théré and Loïc Charles, 'The Writing Workshop of François Quesnay and the Making of Physiocracy', *History of Political Economy* 40, no. 1 (2008): 1–42; Arnault Skornicki, *L'économiste, La Cour et La Patrie. L'économie Politique Dans La France Des Lumières* (Paris: CNRS Éditions, 2011).
75 Guillaume Garnier, État, Économie, Territoire En Allemagne. L'espace Dans Le Caméralisme et l'économie Politique, 1740–1820 (Paris: EHESS, 2006); Keith Tribe, *Governing Economy: The Reformation of German Economic Discourse, 1750–1840* (Cambridge: Cambridge University Press, 1988); Marten Sepppel and Keith Tribe, eds., *Cameralism in Practice: State Administration and Economy in Early Modern Europe* (Cambridge: Boydell & Brewer, 2018); Albion W. Small, *The Cameralists: The Pioneers of German Social Polity* (Chicago, IL: University of Chicago Press, 1909).
76 Sophus Reinert, *The Academy of Fisticuffs: Political Economy and Commercial Society in Enlightenment Italy* (Cambridge, MA: Harvard University Press, 2019).
77 Daniel Roche, *Humeurs Vagabondes. De La Circulation Des Hommes et de l'utilité Des Voyages* (Paris: Fayard, 2003).
78 Pierre Poivre, *Travels of a Philosopher, or Observations on the Manners and Arts of Various Nations in Africa and Asia* (Augusta: Kennebec, 1797), 113.
79 Pierre Poivre, 114.
80 *Correspondance Littéraire, Philosophique et Critique de Grimm et Diderot, Depuis 1753 Jusqu'en 1790. Nouvelle Édition, Revue et Mise Dans Un Meilleur Ordre, Avec Des Notes et Des Éclaircissements, et Ou Se Trouvent Rétablies Pour La Première Fois Les Phrases Supprimées Par La Censure Impériale* (Paris: Chez Furne, librairie quai des augustins, n. 37 et Landrage, même quai, 19, 1829), Vol. V, 151.
81 *Correspondance Littéraire*, Vol. V, 450–59.
82 Adam Smith, *An Inquiry into the Nature and Causes of the Wealth of Nations* (Edited and with an Introduction, Notes, Marginal Summary, and Index by Edwin Cannan. With a New Preface by George J. Stigler (Chicago, IL: University of Chicago Press, 1977), 973.

# Part I

# "The granary of the universe"

## Travelogues, observations, evidence, and a global history of property

# 1 Pierre Poivre

## A microglobal life

Pierre Poivre was a highly renowned eighteenth-century French botanical explorer and royal functionary who travelled across Asia in the 1740s and served as an intendant in the Isle de France (nowadays Mauritius) in the 1760s. In the island, he settled the roots of a centuries-long botanical garden (currently named Sir Seewoosagur Ramgoolam Botanical Garden) where he experimented with the acclimatisation of tropical plants, especially spices that he himself smuggled from the other corner of the Indian Ocean. At once, missionary, merchant, and traveller; Poivre's life was by all its features perplexingly global and vividly local. His experiences bridged different disconnected spaces across a few continents as well as multiple branches of knowledge.

After his death in 1786, Pierre Samuel Du Pont de Nemours (one of the most tenacious and active members of the Physiocratic circle and Quesnay's relentless advocate) prefaced at length the second edition of Poivre's unique but exceedingly popular 1768 book titled *Voyages d'un philosophe.*[1] Du Pont also drafted a first detailed biography, and furthermore, added several explanatory and bibliographical footnotes. Poivre's account no doubt generated much interest in the mid-eighteenth-century republic of letters, and more in particular, among his fellow *économistes.* Turgot read the travel account judiciously, as his correspondence indicates. Jefferson, in turn, quoted him. Smith used Poivre's observations to estimate differences in salaries as we already have seen. Just to mention a few of those commonly quoted economists who read and cited the French traveller.

The account chronicles Poivre's 1750s journey across the Indian Ocean, Southeast Asia, and China. *Voyages* was first launched in 1768, and before the century was gone, at least ten French editions had already been released. The number of editions clearly demonstrates the high esteem in which readers held the book. Furthermore, the book swiftly found potential readers abroad.[2] Translations were promptly made into English,[3] and later, into German.[4] Just one year after its release, the English audience disposed of an edition translated by the renowned eighteenth-century English agriculturalist Arthur Young, who, in turn, published his own travel accounts of journeys conducted in the 1760s–80s. Alongside, chunks of the book were

DOI: 10.4324/9780429028199-3

published in Portugal. Just to mention some instances that demonstrate the rapid international reception that the book regained.

In the academic milieu, Poivre has commonly been credited with the credentials of a botanist.[5] It is uncommon for him to be ascribed any role in the configuration of mid-eighteenth-century socioeconomic ideas. His observations, however, knew a large impact in manifold ways far beyond botany. His contributions in the agrarian field, and particularly, in the domestication of tropical plants and seeds are beyond doubt. [6] On the contrary, his inputs in the field of economic theory and the advancement of empirical evidence concerning the intricate interrelations involving government, agriculture, and economic growth have found a rather narrow repercussion.

This first part will unveil Poivre's contributions, the context in which the oeuvre was read, as well as the intellectual debates in which the book took form and circulated. It will be divided into five chapters. In Chapter 1, I will introduce the life and adventures of Pierre Poivre, paying particular attention to the different scales in which *Voyages* would take shape. Poivre travelled across Asia, but his existence was also marked by his intense participation in local scholar societies like the *Académie de Lyon*. Chapter 2 will bring into focus the repercussions that a particular platform, travelogues, had in the configuration of eighteenth-century economic thinking. This kind of platform was much in vogue in the eighteenth century and was believed to conduct accurate observations on far-flung lands and societies. Before taking into consideration the unfolding of what I call an "empirical turn in economics" (a move that took shape at the very same moment that political economy came of age in the mid-century), I will consider a sizzling debate that engaged most authors in different moments in the eighteenth century: the idea of a feudal age versus the existence of a feudal system. Contemporary debates on Feudalism, which will be analysed in Chapter 3, have largely been disregarded. Finally, I will demonstrate that the empirical turn included the writing of a global history of the property. In Chapter 5, I will show that history became trending in the mid-century and that a large palette of societies (Incas, Sparta, China) were called into attention through which cases many scholars expected to offer evidence on the deduced laws physiocrats upheld but many intellectuals refused to agree with.

## Outer geographies

Three junctures silhouette Poivre's private life neatly: the missionary, the merchant-explorer, and the royal functionary. He was born in Lyon in August 1719 into a family of merchants. Before leaving France and heading over for his first journey to China and Cochin China, he pursued some academic training. His membership in the Catholic church offered him the opportunity to conduct intercontinental ventures. One of the endeavours of his missionary mission was to learn Asian languages. Unexpectedly, in China, disputes happened and Poivre was compelled to abandon his religious community. In 1747, he was back in Europe from whence he returned to Asia now working as a servant for the French East-India Company (Feic).[7]

Poivre had already demonstrated his high interest in economic matters well before his first return home. In the 1740s, he drafted a paper on Asian painting techniques hoping it would be useful in the improvement of French manufactures. Therein, he considered the skills of, but also the natural resources that Asian weavers employed in the fabrication of inks. By that time, cotton textiles were in high demand in Europe.[8] Poivre was of the mind that differences in qualities obeyed not to a competitive disadvantage in the mastering of threats but that they were mainly a result of the natural composition of dyes that Asian weavers used. Already in this very first paper, he combined his two long-life interests: botanical know-how and reflections on economic life.

Back in France, Poivre made a proposal to the Feic regarding trade in Southeast Asia and agricultural improvements in the Isle de France. Basically, he committed to carry on two tasks. His proposal fit in with the company's interests, which was keen in settling enduring commercial relations with Cochin-China (a region with which Poivre was already acquainted) and in acclimatising Asian plants in the Isle de France. Poivre was asked the hard task of smuggling nutmeg and clove seeds and introducing them into the island. As a matter of fact, France had obtained the island from the Ducht a few years ago, and now pretended to improve the economic potential of the recently acquired colony. The Isle de France had been under Dutch control until 1721. That year, the island passed over to the Feic's management. In 1764, a government reform happened, and the crown started administering the overseas colony itself. Poivre's life was tightly linked to Mauritius' fate: in the first moment working for the company as a servant, and much later, serving as an intendant. This is precisely the period of his life that has most called the attention. For Poivre, as for others, the crossroad between the Atlantic and Indian Oceans could be transformed into a laboratory where spices and tropical plants introduced from all over the world could be acclimatised at the benefit of global consumers. Glove, nutmeg, but also rice and fruits, all of these plants awoke his intellectual interests.

In 1748, Poivre's second decade-lasting journey began. This experience offered him the time to gather the data later employed in his *Voyage*. The trip led Poivre from Mauritius across the Indian Ocean to Southeast Asia and China. A journey account posted back to the company directors in Paris informs us in full detail about his itinerary and observations. The account spans nine years from 1748 to 1757. Therein, Poivre reported the difficulties to settle lasting trading relations with Cochin-China and narrated the adventures incurred in his desperate search for spices.

His first endeavour consisted in the settling of lasting commercial relations with Cochin-China. On 16 April 1749, Poivre left Mauritius and headed off to Pondicherry where he arrived after two months of the crossing. By the end of August, he was already in Faifu, one of the leading trading ports in the Peninsula, not far away from the court and home for many Chinese merchants. He unfortunately happened to arrive in the wrong term when merchants used to move inland for four months. Therefore, he headed over to the court, where, according to his own account, the King granted him the required permissions to trade. He reported to Paris about the ways in which trade was conducted in the Kingdom and devoted particular attention to currency matters. One year after his departure, Poivre arrived at Mauritius with a cargo made up of sugar, an assortment of goods and currencies. More importantly, as he himself highlighted, more than 300 different plants had been carried from Cochin-China, namely fruits and a type of rice.

On the other hand, the envisaged acclimatisation of different spices compelled Poivre to journey to the Philippines and the Moluccas. Two months after having left Mauritius, Poivre was in Canton on 14 August 1750. In the Chinese port, he underwrote a contract intended for the manufacturing of silks to trade in the Philippines. After an eight-month stay, he finally arrived in Manila on 15 May 1751. Poivre described the hard efforts undertaken in the procurement of spices. He purchased 300 nutmeg seeds from a Chinese merchant. Obtaining glove seeds was a nightmare due to regulations that forbade any extractions out of the Moluccas. Poivre reported that he had spent a long time in the Philippines gathering information on the Moluccas and on the cultivation of spices. Further, he profited the time and learned Malay, an asset that could spare him the need for translators and made the task safer. He also had conducted research in the Manila archives, finding particularly useful the Spanish *Relaciones*. After a fourteenth-month sojourn and unable to procure the seeds, he left Manila for Pondicherry. He brought with him a cargo of nutmeg, many of which plants could not survive the crossing.

Poivre returned to Mauritius in November 1753. Some of the carried nutmeg plants survived the oceanic crossing and were transplanted in some plots scattered across the island. Next May, he embarked once again to the Philippines, this time with hopes to bring back the very dear glove seeds. The business, however, proved hard to accomplish. Poivre navigated to Celebes and Timor. In the latter, he arranged with a Portuguese governor the purchase of clove plants in exchange for a sum of money. Finally, he departed from Lifao, and in June 1755, he was back in Mauritius. Ultimately, Poivre embarked for France, where he arrived on 22 April 1757. He would return to the island as intendent in the 1760s. The second edition of his book included the discourse he read when he took office.

## Inner spaces

*Voyages* was first published in 1768. It means that a decade had elapsed before Poivre's thoughts, impressions, and experiences were pressed into inked letters. Indeed, this was a very long time even for eighteenth-century standards. The mid-century was a blistering and convoluted intellectual epoch that witnessed the coming of age of new science at which not everyone looked fully convinced.

On 1 January 1770, one of the Parisian journals informed its readers, in a mocking, disapproving, and dismissing tone, that the city had incubated a new-born sect, one that was "at first as humble as the dust from which it sprang, as poor as its doctrine, as obscure as its style," but soon to become "imperious and arrogant." The sect's members had self-identified as *philosophes économistes*: the physiocrats.[9] The journal that published this bizarre warning was the channel of one of the cliques that reluctantly raised its voice against a peculiar and seemingly incomprehensible manner of rethinking human behaviour. Grimm, who was the journal's co-editor, remained close to, and sided with the network of *encyclopédistes* whose leading figures were Diderot and d'Alembert. The journal vindicated classical and literature studies along with the humanist tradition.[10] Their sympathisers were further attached to a particular type of empiricism and refused evidence (a word that recalls a Cartesian parlance) as the foundation of science.[11] Patrons were commonly updated with bibliographical references and book reviews, among which a demolishing one on Poivre's *Voyages*. The journal thus became the main trench from whence opposers to the économistes propelled their attacks on the emerging "credo." A prominent fellow of this network was Ferdinando Galiani, far more knowledgeable on economic theory than others yet an outsider. The rebellious and unbearable young Neapolitan (who had published his first book on money when he was only 21 years old) left the city not without publishing a comical, Socratic-style, and daring manuscript with the help of Grimm himself and Mme. d'Epinay. The book sought to exacerbate the *économistes* and voiced criticism against their stubborn enforcement of the liberalisation of grains.

*Voyages* was warmly welcomed and entered the public sphere of an already sizzling intellectual atmosphere. Economic issues were not only discussed in print; salons transmuted into spots in which many intellectual cliques furiously discussed, perhaps as never before, economic matters. Many of these meetings were organised and entertained by noble women like Mme. d'Houdetot, Mlle. de Lespinasse, Mme. Necker, or Mme. Saurin.[12] Taxation, inflation, money, and particularly corn, all these matters captured the interest of many in Paris and elsewhere. Suddenly, everyone was concerned about corn. It was the only topic of conversation. Voltaire's phrase regained fame. Others, like Ange Goudar, believed that it was manufactures that robbed everybody's attention.

It is safe to assert that those years witnessed a boom in the number of publications, in particular, those concerning economic government, commerce, and agriculture, which increased by at least fourfold compared to the preceding decade.[13] The emerging political economy had suddenly become a coveted object of discussion. Debates were held among different "circles, sects or groups" that advanced antithetical explanations on the natural economic order or the true sources of wealth.[14]

Poivre's sojourn in Asia coincided with the release of the first edition of Montesquieu's *The spirit of the law*.[15] Twenty years had already passed and Montesquieu's reflections on government and virtues began to be challenged. Quesnay stood among those scholars who hankered to voice alternative explanations about the underlying and structural conditions upon which humans created durable and spontaneous social links. In fact, in 1757, ten years after the release of *L'esprit de lois* and ten years prior to *Voyages*, Quesnay – to whom his disciples granted the title of the European Confucius – rendered a bewildering framework that accounted for the natural laws of wealth's circulation and reproduction: *Le tableau économique*. At that point, only a handful of followers were able to capture and comprehend the full message of Quesnay's model.[16]

All the above intellectual debates should be carefully considered in order to single out the reasons why *Voyages* was published. By 1768, nonetheless, the *économistes* had already yielded their apogee and their intellectual standing began to crumble under uncompromising criticism. Both the knowledge they produced and the methodologies they endorsed became targets of furious intellectual disapproval. Soon later, Turgot's disgrace proved that the policies this group expected to enact were simply unachievable, having rather brought chaos and famine.

This effervescent intellectual mid-century atmosphere coincided with uncertain and harsh socio-economic conditions. Intellectual debates accelerated in line with the increasing quantity of publications on political economy. This was also a time in which economic policies, mainly the ones concerning the commoditisation of corn, were drastically and suddenly remodelled. Networks in power, like Turgot's or Gournay's, could all of a sudden fall on disgrace: those who were at the top of the economic debate and who pretended to have penetrated the natural rules of market government could unexpectedly find themselves on disfavour.

The release of *Voyages* was marked by two main political and economic events. On the one hand, the highest grains' prices known for eighteenth-century France, which, no doubt, negatively impacted the quinquennium.[17] On the other hand, a royal policy of clearing which apparently showed itself highly effective in a very short run.[18] It is important to bear in mind that scholars have essentially devoted their attention to the images and ideas on Asia that Poivre's book brings to light yet far less devotion has been paid to the local, cultural, and intellectual conditions upon which the book was written. Lives are at some points locally rooted. Indeed, books adhered to this same logic. It seems that, from its very formulation, *Voyages* was not thought of as a book. Most probably, it was thought of merely as a series of lectures to be read before the *Académie de Lyon* of which Poivre had been appointed fellow at his return in 1759.[19]

Before his fellows, Poivre read two lectures, one on Asian trade and another one that summarised his Asian travelling experiences. *Voyages* thus underwent a process of divulgation which was rather common for eighteenth-century standards. Two years later, he read the papers again, this time before the *Société Royale d'agriculture* in Paris. Reviews of the lectures or chunks were rapidly published in two journals. This fact plainly demonstrates that his impressions on Asian agriculture and government regimes were already on the market of ideas prior to the publication of the full manuscript in 1768.

In July 1766, the *Journal d'agriculture, commerce et finance* published a review of the lecture. Only a year later, in August, the official channel of physiocratic advertising, the Éphémérides du citoyen, offered a piece of the manuscript, more specifically, the part on the Kingdom of Ponthyamas which was described as the granary of South Asia and a paradise of natural rights. One can thus deduce that, to some extent, the first draft was thought of as a conference intended for a very precise public: the fellows of the *Académie*.

## Notes

1 Pierre Poivre, *Oeuvres Complètes de P. Poivre, Intendant Des Isles de France et Bourbon, Correspondant de l'académie Des Sciences, Etc. Précédées de Sa Vie et Accompagnées Des Notes* (Paris: Chez Fuchs, libraire, rue de Mathurins, 1797).

2 On European translations and the international building of eighteenth-century economic knowledge see, Sophus Reinert, *Translating Empire: Emulation and the Origins of Political Economy* (Cambridge, MA: Harvard University Press, 2011); Sophus Reinert, 'The Empire of Emulation: A Quantitative Analysis of Economic Translations in the European World, 1500–1849', in *The Political Economy of Empire in the Early Modern World*, eds. Sophus Reinert and Pernille Roge (New York: Palgrave Macmillan, 2013), 105–30.

3 Pierre Poivre, *Travels of a Philosopher, or Observations on the Manners and Arts of Various Nations in Africa and Asia* (Augusta: Kennebec, 1797).

4 Pierre Poivre, *Reisen Eines Philosophen: Mit Betrachtungen Über Die Gebräuche, Sitten,Künste, Ackerbau Und Den Handel Verschiedner Völker in Asien Und Afrika: Aus Dem Englischen Übersetzt* (Daniel Ludwig Wedel, 1773).

5 Richard Hug Grove, *Green Imperialism: Colonial Expansion, Tropical Island Edens and the Origins of Environmentalism, 1600–1860* (Cambridge: Cambridge University Press, 1995); Dorit Maria Nicola Brixius, *French Empire on the Ground: Plants, Peoples, and Knowledge in the Services of Eighteenth-Century Isle of France* (Florence: European University Institute, 2017).

6 Richard Drayton, *Nature's Government: Science, Imperial Britain and the Improvement of the World* (New Haven, CT: Yale University Press, 2000); E. C. Spary, *Utopia's Garden: French Natural History from Old Regime to Revolution* (Chicago, IL: Chicago University Press, 2000); Sarah Easterby-Smith, *Cultivating Commerce: Culture of Botany in Britain and France, 1760–1815* (Cambridge: Cambridge University Press, 2018); Daniela Bleichmar, *Visible Empire: Botanical Expeditions and Visual Culture in the Hispanic Enlightenment* (Chicago, IL: Chicago University Press, 2012).

7 Massimiliano Vaghi, *La France et L'Inde. Commerce et Politique Impériale Au XVIIIe Siècle* (Fano: Éditions Mimésis, 2016).

8 Felicia Gottmann, *Global Trade, Smuggling, and the Making of Economic Liberalism: Asian Textiles in France 1680–1760* (London and New York: Palgrave Macmillan, 2016); Giorgio Riello and Roy Tirthankar, eds., *How India Clothed the World: The World of South Asian Textiles, 1500–1850* (Leiden: Brill, 2009); Giorgio Riello and Prasannan Parthasarathi, eds., *The Spinning World: A Global History of Cotton Textiles, 1200–1850* (Oxford: Oxford University Press, 2011).

9 Georges Weulersse, *Le Mouvement Physiocratique En France (1756–1770)*, 2 vols (Paris: Félix Alcan éditeur, 1910); Catherine Larrère, *L'invention de l'économie Au XVIIIe Siècle. Du Droit à La Physiocratie* (Paris: Presses Universitaire de France, 1992); Arnault Skornicki, *L'économiste, La Cour et La Patrie. L'économie Politique Dans La France Des Lumières* (Paris: CNRS Éditions, 2011); Liana Vardi, *The Physiocrats and the World of the Enlightenment* (Cambridge: Cambridge University

Press, 2012); Steven L. Kaplan, *Raisonner Sur Les Blés. Essais Sur Les Lumières Économiques* (Paris: Fayard, 2017); Jean-Claude Perrot, 'La Comptabilité Des Entreprises Agricoles Dans l'économie Physiocratique', *Annales. Économies, Sociétés, Civilisations* 33, no. 3 (1978): 559–79; Christine Théré and Loïc Charles, 'The Writing Workshop of François Quesnay and the Making of Physiocracy', *History of Political Economy* 40, no. 1 (2008): 1–42; Loïc Charles and Christine Théré, 'Jeux de Mots, Narrative and Economic Writing: The Rhetoric of Anti-Physiocracy in French Economic Periodicals (1764–1769)', *European Journal History of Economic Thought* 22, no. 3 (2015): 359–82; Alain Clément, 'Nicolas Baudeau, an Anti-Physiocrat? Éphémérides Du Citoyen Prior to "Conversion" (1765–1766)', *European Journal of the History of Economic Thought* 22, no. 3 (2015): 534–63; Pierre Henri Goutte and Gérard Klotz, 'Turgot: A Critic of Physiocracy? An Analysis of the Debates in Éphémérides Du Citoyen and in Correspondence with Dupont', *European Journal History of Economic Thought* 22, no. 3 (2015): 500–33; Théophile Pénigaud, 'The Political Opposition of Rousseau to Physiocracy: Government, Interest, Citizenship', *European Journal History of Economic Thought* 22, no. 3 (2015): 473–99; Arnaud Orain, 'Figures of Mockery. The Cultural Disqualification of Physiocracy (1760–1790)', *European Journal History of Economic Thought* 22, no. 3 (2015): 383–419.

10 Yves Citton, *Portrait de l'économiste En Physiocrate: Critique Littéraire de l'économie Politique* (Paris: Harmattan, 2000).

11 Jessica Riskin, *Science in the Age of Sensibility: The Sentimental Empiricists of the French Enlightenment* (Chicago, IL: Chicago University Press, 2002).

12 Antoine Lilti, *Le Monde Des Salons: Sociabilité et Mondanité à Paris Au XVIIIe Siècle* (Paris: Fayard, 2013).

13 Jean-Claude Perrot, *Une Histoire Intellectuelle de l'économie Politique* (Paris: EHESS, 1992).

14 Simone Meyssonnier, *La Balance et l'horloge. La Genèse de La Pensée Libérale En France Au XVIIIe Siècle* (Paris: Éditions de la passion, 1989); Catherine Larrère, *L'invention de l'économie Au XVIIIe Siècle. Du Droit à La Physiocratie*; Loïc Charles, Frédéric Lefebvre, and Christine Théré, *Le Cercle de Vincent de Gournay: Savoirs Économiques et Pratiques Administratives En France Au Milieu Du XVIII* (Paris: Institut National d'Études Démographiques, 2011); Arnault Skornicki, *L'économiste, La Cour et La Patrie.*

15 Catherine Larrère, *Actualité de Montesquieu* (Paris: Sciences Po, 1999).

16 Loïc Charles, 'The Visual History of the Tableau Économique', *European Journal of the History of Economics* 10, no. 4 (2010): 527–50.

17 Camille-Ernest Labrousse, *Esquisse Du Mouvement Des Prix et Des Revenus En France Au XVIIIe Siècle* (Paris: Librairie Dalloz, 1933); James C. Riley, *The Seven Years War and the Old Regime in France: The Economic and Financial Toll* (Princeton, NJ: Princeton University Press, 1986); Olwen Hufton, 'Social Conflict and the Grain Supply in Eighteenth-Century France', *Journal of Interdisciplinary History* 14, no. 2 (1983): 303–31.

18 Anonymous, *Mémoire Sur Les Défrichements* (Paris: Chez la veuve D'houry Imp. Lib. de Magr. le duc d'Orléans, rue de la vieille Bouclerie, 1760); Jean Rives, 'Dîme et Défrichement En Gascogne et Query Au XVIIIe Siècle', *Annales Du Midi: Revue Archéologique, Historique et Philologique de La France Méridionale* 92, no. 146 (1980): 57–66; Louis Mazoyer, 'Exploitation Forestière et Conflits Sociaux En France- Comté, à La Fin de l'Ancien Régime', *Annales d'histoire Économique et Sociale* 16 (1932): 339–58.

19 Roger Chartier, 'La Académie de Lyon Au XVIIIe Siècle: Étude de Sociologie Culturelle', in *Nouvelles Études Lyonnaises*, eds. Roger Chartier, L. Desgraves, and J.-M Dureau-Lapeyssonie (Paris: Librairie Droz, 1969), 133–250.

# 2 Eighteenth-century travel accounts

## Platforms for economic observations

Scholars who study the production and circulation of economic thinking barely consider travelogues as a means through which economic ideas emerged and spread. Travelling was beyond doubt a very dear undertaking for enlightened economists. Many of them embarked on transnational journeys, which, for some, like for Poivre, lasted for years.

Indeed, only the travels of a few are commonly mentioned yet most "writers or authors" (as they were called in the mid-century) travelled across Europe and outside the continent. The list of travelling economists is as vast as their journeys and accounts. Gournay travelled in Spain, Germany, Holland, and England; Cantillon travelled to Spain; Hume and Smith sojourned for a while in France; Beccaria and Galiani visited France, the latter also lived in England; Du Pont de Nemours lived in Germany, Poland, and the United States; Forbonnais, Morellet, and Condillac travelled to Italy (the first also to Spain), von Justi visited Austria and Denmark. Much less known authors also travelled. Ange Goudar, lived in England, Portugal, Austria, and Italy, as we will see in the second part. The same goes for Montesquieu who, like Poivre, wrote a famous travel account.

Keeping a diary or writing a travel account was part of this experience as much as was the habit of exchanging letters. Diaries and letters have by far been less mined for, in regard to economic thinking, preference is usually given to standard academic, scientifically-shaped, theoretically-grounded, and first-rank corpora. While letters have received recent attention, travel accounts remained outside sight no matter the huge impact they had on the diffusion of data and the circulation of ideas. Quesnay, Smith, Malthus (just to mention a few), all of them cited and used data gathered in travelogues. Thanks to the notes that Du Pont de Nemours added to the second edition, we can have an idea of some of the travel accounts that called the economists' attention in the mid-century. He referred six times to Thumberg's *Voyages au Japon* and to Saint-Pierre's *Voyage au Cap et a l'isle de France*. Further, Crawdford's sketch on the history of the Hindostan is also cited among many others.

DOI: 10.4324/9780429028199-4

## Travelogues

By the eighteenth century, travelogues were no doubt an aged device. Since antiquity, travellers had nourished their congeners with particulars on faraway lands. In the western tradition, two classic journeys along with their specific narrative techniques set the standards for the ages to come: Homer's *Iliad* and Herodotus's *History*. Dated as they both were, these texts featured hallmarks on how travelogues have since been analysed and refashioned. Homer narrated an imaginary venture across the Mediterranean coastline. Herodotus, in turn, claimed to have told what he had actually observed or inquired: his was a *research* (the meaning of the word history in Ancient Greek).[1] Observing and observations (witnessing), as we will see later, were a clear feature in Poivre's account. Another famous Medieval traveller, Marco Polo, like Herodotus, alleged to have told what he had seen in the farmost eastern regions of the planet: he, like the Ancient Greek historian, self-defined as a witness. The observations he narrated could be taken as a reliable description of the Asian lands he had visited during his long journey. Bringing the sight to front served to prove the truthiness of the narrative: the traveller's eyes filtered to the reader's eyes a reality distant in space and drawn on sheets of paper. Travelogues were thus apprehended as a device through which reliable information could be transmitted.

Travelogues, on the other hand, were also perceived as a channel through which "marvellous things" could be diffused. Consequently, the question arises as to where exactly the division between reality and imagination actually lies. Indeed, it was a very tenuous line. That issue is particularly hot concerning the information on Asia that European travel descriptions echoed, a matter which is at the very core of this part.

Currently, at least two frameworks prevailed in debates about travel accounts. Drawing on Foucault's ideas, scholars within the field of cultural studies and postcolonial perspectives describe travel accounts as "technologies of power": Europeans would have written accounts on the outside world longing for domination and control. In this vein, orientalism should be understood as a strategy deployed for imperial expansion and cultural dominion: knowledge gathered or produced that intended to depict extra-European societies under specific labels or that sought to collect precise data on wealth. Most influential for a long time, this approach has shown extremely oversimplifying in regard to the variety of travels, travellers, and travel descriptions.[2] Scholars have started to gradually move away from such a perspective although many remain still loyal no matter the approach's drawbacks. Even within the field of cultural studies, scholars have expressed their objections to the above perspective. For the sake of this chapter, three arguments are worth highlighting.

To begin with, voyage journals were framed within "the colloquy of their community." It means that writers compared notes, raised questions, and supplemented each other's information. Voyage journals were not only committed with discursiveness and language plays but also with the "real world." Travellers were far to see the peoples they met through their journeys as mere colonial subjects. Most of the time, they interacted with brokers from whom data and information were regained. When it comes to the East India Company servants, for instance, shareholders in London asked for the most possible reliable and accurate information on routes and markets. Servants should carefully account for funds, goods, and transactions. All those tasks generated a specific protocol on data gathering, and particularly, on how information should be collected, organised, preserved, and communicated. This is why a "rhetoric of wonder" opened up room for narrative techniques in which itemisation, reporting, and details acquired utmost interest. At least at the beginning of his career, Poivre should have performed within this "colloquy of community."[3]

In addition, European travellers relied on oriental literate traditions. The availability of non-European sources along with a large variety of genres (historical and geographical) lead to think that travel descriptions were far from being only "imaginary constructs."[4] For instance, sixteenth-century travel accounts, which indeed remained closer to Medieval marvellous descriptions, were far from simply offering readers a coherent set of stereotypes on Asia. By the same token, non-European sources provided European travellers with worthless data and also counterpoints against which travel accounts could be critically engaged with.

Let's take an eighteenth-century Indo-Persian travel account as a counterpoint. Poivre described some areas of Southeast Asia as a "forest paradise." According to his narrative, cities were surrounded by dense forests. Yet, Indo-Persian travellers, munshis, scholars, and artists provided Asian readers with a highly similar version. The South Asian kingdoms are characterised in Mughal literature "as a sublime forest world stewarded by an ideal universal sovereign." A case in point of this literature being Abd al-Latif Khan Shushtari from Iran who journeyed across India and South Asia at the turn of the eighteenth century. His account depicted the Burmese Empire as a "land of dense jungles, herds of wild elephants, and mines rich in precious stones."[5] This view perfectly coincides with the version Poivre told his European readers. Indeed, this does not mean both travellers told what they actually saw, it merely implies that we are able to critically engage with the traveller's impressions.

Finally, travels suited diverse goals. Botanical expeditions were a highly prized kind of travel in the Age of Enlightenment. They were above all a field in which accurate knowledge and unmistaken observations were indispensable. Scientific global expeditions were financed and put together with the intent to identify and classify plants and seeds. New techniques were displayed although classical authors like Polibios and his *Natural history* regained fame again after centuries. A commitment with accurate botanical knowledge became the aspiration of a generation of scholars who travelled across the world and who resorted to precise techniques to acclimatise plants, to conserve seeds, to design flora, to transmit information in memoires. Herbariums gathered across the world were shipped to Paris, London, Amsterdam, and Madrid. Medicinal concerns were at the core of all those scientific undertakings. These were cross-disciplinary explorations that encompassed simultaneously botanical taxonomy, economic botany, and collecting.[6]

As a matter of fact, economical plants were of the utmost interest.[7] Classifying the whole natural world (Linnaeus' life dream) required an army of travellers, a vast network through which reliable information flowed. Books should errorlessly reproduce the most recent observations so travellers could be in the position to further identify and classify new flora. Botanophiles were trained in reading, describing, and distinguishing among plants, and generally left their countries accompanied with catalogues and lists. In turn, botanists in Paris, London, and Leyden, who were unable to travel, depended on accurate knowledge reported from far-flung and remote zones. Travellers were in charge of collecting new plants, forwarding information, and correcting inconsistencies.[8] They were connected to institutions like the royal gardens, which, like Adam and Eva's paradise, intended to gather all the riches of the world in a spot.[9] The aspiration was to cultivate the precious Asian spices in a garden closer to European consumers.

Poivre actively participated in all these scientific undertakings. He corresponded with Buffon who in turn mentioned him in his *Histoire Naturelle*.[10] The concept of liberty, which Poivre called frequently to mind throughout his book, was widely employed in natural history as well. After publishing his book and coming back to Mauritius as an intendant, he himself devoted many efforts to establish a botanical garden. This, of course, was a chance for him to put into practice the acquired know-how.

All the above points make clear that travelogues were an aged device, which, nonetheless, regained great success in the Enlightenment. The genre acquired great success and became a precious item in enlightened libraries: travel accounts were written and printed as never before. Managing such a high number of incessant publications became a troublesome task and publishers decided to print compilations, which, like the *Encyclopédie*, could help readers to handle information in an easy and friendly way.

## Notes

1 François Hartog, *Le Miroir d'Hérodote: Essai Sur La Représentation de l'autre* (Paris: Gallimard, 1980).

2 Daniel Roche, *Humeurs Vagabondes. De La Circulation Des Hommes et de l'utilité Des Voyages* (Paris: Fayard, 2003); Jürgen Osterhammel, *Unfabling the East: The Enlightenment's Encounter with Asia* (Princeton, NJ: Princeton University Press, 2018); Mary Louise Pratt, *Imperial Eyes: Travel Writing and Transculturation* (London and New York: Routledge, 1992); Joan-Pau Rubiés, *Travel and Ethnology in the Renaissance: South India through European Eyes, 1250–1625* (Cambridge: Cambridge University Press, 2004); Richmond Barbour, *The Third Voyage Journals: Writing and Performance in the London East India Company, 1607–10* (New York: Palgrave Macmillan, 2009); Sanjay Subrahmanyam, *Three Ways to Be Alien: Travails and Encounters in the Early Modern World* (Waltham, MA: Brandeis University Press, 2011).

3 Richmond Barbour, *The Third Voyage Journals: Writing and Performance in the London East India Company, 1607–10*, 3, 19–20.
4 Joan-Pau Rubiés, *Travel and Ethnology in the Renaissance: South India through European Eyes, 1250–1625*, 11, 25, 28.
5 Arash Khazeni, 'Indo-Persian Travel Writing at the Ends of the Mughal World', *Past and Present* 243, no. 1 (May, 2019): 141–74.
6 Daniela Bleichmar, *Visible Empire: Botanical Expeditions and Visual Culture in the Hispanic Enlightenment.*
7 Staffan Müller-Wille, 'Nature as a Marketplace: The Political Economy of Linnaean Botany', *History of Political Economy* 35, no. Annual Supplement (2003): 154–72; Lisbet Rausing, 'Underwriting the Oeconomy: Linnaeus on Nature and Mind', *History of Political Economy* 35, no. Annual Supplement (2003): 173–203.
8 E. C. Spary, *Utopia's Garden: French Natural History from Old Regime to Revolution*, 68, 83.
9 Richard Drayton, *Nature's Government*, 17, 41.
10 E. C. Spary, *Utopia's Garden*, 123.

# 3 Feudal laws

## Liberties for a few

In his book, Poivre unveiled the underlying conditions upon which agriculture could prosper or stagnate. In so doing, he advanced a comparative global perspective. Fitting in with his observations gathered in the eastern hemisphere was the idea that agriculture flourished in those countries in which three conditions prevailed: liberty, property, and security. At first glance, the claim appears to be rather wonted. This was a set of broadly echoed ideas in the mid-eighteenth-century French intellectual circles, and particularly among the physiocrats. Poivre's claims leave no room for doubt that he was closely associated with, and admirer of the *philosophes économistes*. The claim was further enriched with assertions on the negative incentives that despotic and feudal forms of government inflicted upon economic growth.

The traveller began his journey in West Africa and guided the reader east across the Indian Ocean to a final destination in China. Finally, the book recapitulated all the arguments and, from a comparative global perspective, delivered an explanation for the developments of agriculture in Africa, Europe, Asia, and America.

"What an extensive object has an attentive traveller, to remark the state of agriculture amongst the different nations of the world."[1] The current flourishing state of land cultivation that could be observed in Europe resulted from the latest enactment of the rights of liberty and property. Compliance with those rights had diverted Europe from a long-lasting barbaric age during which the continent begged for its subsistence. Africa had followed a divergent path. The continent that had formerly been famous for enjoying the "granaries of the universe" now presented a desolate landscape, which was "miserably cultivated by slaves." Slavery had refrained agriculture in South America from flourishing, especially in the northern regions of the continent. Enslaved humans "removed from the laws of nature" "make efforts in vain to procure that happiness" that agriculture provided with. Asia, in contrast, offered a canvas hard to be interpreted. In some countries, feudal lords and despots harnessed the development of agriculture, in others, like China where natural laws were rigorously endorsed, agriculture prospered.

As already mentioned, prior to its release in a whole edition, chunks of the *Voyages* had already been delivered in two Parisian journals. The 1768 edition

DOI: 10.4324/9780429028199-5

was shaped in a narrative manner that offered the reader the impression of an eastward journey. Poivre combined their observations on political economy and agriculture with botanist know-how. Particular attention is paid to profitable plants that could be acclimatised outside Asia. Rice and sugar remained at the core of his analyses on Southeast Asia.

The number of pages could give us an impression on the areas that reclaimed the most interest from the traveller. Chart 3.1 displays the information. Cochin-China and China demanded the largest room. In turn, Malaysia and the Kingdom of Siam occupied a non-negligible space. All those regions, however, were brought into the narrative in order to fit different purposes. It is worth noting that the Cape of Good Hope received a big deal of attention. This turns out to be comprehensible if one takes into account how dependent the French African colonies were on the Dutch ones.

The section on the Cape of Good Hope circulated separately in manuscript form.[2] Poivre's interest in the Dutch colonies was twofold. He looked at them as a model worth emulating: regardless of its hard climatic conditions, geographical situation, and soil sterility, in those colonies agriculture had flourished. This was not only a model worth emulating but also one which had been implemented by French settlers who had fled their country following the revocation of the Nantes edict. French and Dutch colonies had followed opposing directions no matter how their soils and climate resembled The Cape of Good Hope served to demonstrate that backwardness in cultivation was far from being the offspring of a sterile soil. Plenty of all sorts of corn, vegetables, and fruits farmed in the Dutch colony was an explicit proof

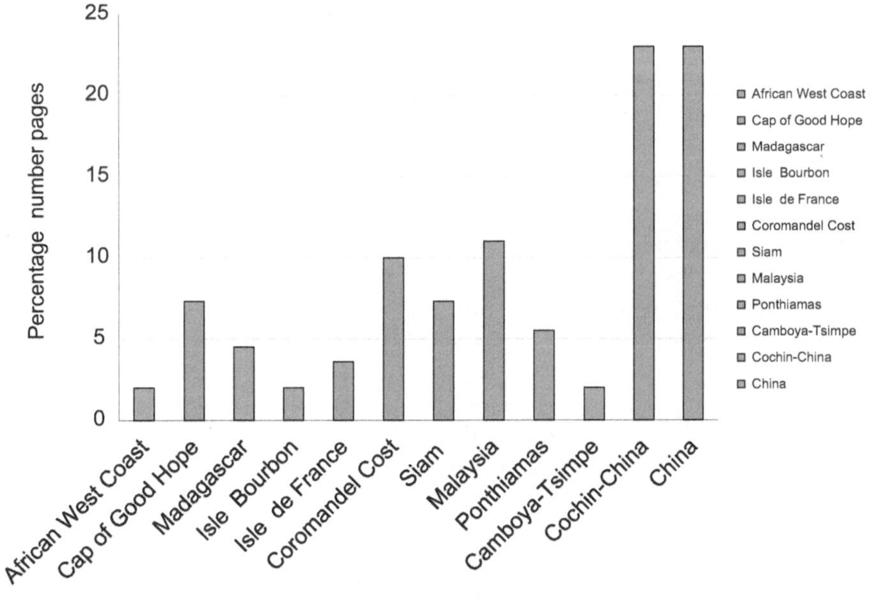


*Chart 3.1* Geographical distribution of *Voyages d'un philosophe* (percentage)

that no progress could be yielded without a good government or the right institutions. As he himself put it "earth denies her favours only to the tyrant and the slave."[3] The first French settlers had sowed the "drivers" that agriculture needed to flourish: security, property, and liberty. These were "the only principles of abundance." Thanks to those drivers the Cape had escaped from a destiny of infertility and fatalism. Those drivers had converted the colony into the richest granary found on the interoceanic journey.

Despite the sharp contrast drawn among regions under European and African control, Poivre advanced no clear explanation on the negative impacts that African governments had on cultivation. He confined himself to condemn slavery and the trade in enslaved humans so one can safely assume that slavery was held as the main cause of the prevailing underdeveloped agriculture. It is true that he merely spent a couple of pages on the Cape and that his focus lay on the achievements that Dutch settlers had yielded. However, French settlers and their ineffective cultivation practices received as much criticism as did the obstinate support for slavery that African societies showed.[4] Poivre's narrative went deeper and richer when he advanced an explanation on the underlying reasons why backward agriculture prevailed in Southeast Asia. To him, the dreadful situation in Siam was rooted in an impairing tyranny, a pervasive form of government that prevented any agricultural improvements in a richly endowed "terrestrial paradise."

## Tableau de comparaison: Siam, Malacca, and Ponthiamas

Comparing was at the very core of Poivre's practice: A *tableau de comparison* or a "comparative representation" as the English translator translated the expression. In this vein, observations and observing, and more in particular, the sense of sight gains the attention. The main purpose of the *tableau* was to "let see." "How do economists observe the world" "What are economic observations?" The question was asked then and now.[5] In current economics, observations regain much more attention than the act of observing itself. Manipulable data concern much more their practitioners than the act through which observations are gathered (practices like sampling, describing, typifying, and mapping). In current economics, observing is barely seen as both a practice and a process. Observing, indeed, involves at the same time doings and outcomes.

In the emerging economics, the most famous visible representation of economic circuits was without doubt the *Tableau* printed by Quesnay himself in 1757. Quesnay's *tableau* has recently been reinterpreted as encompassing a two-dimensional perspective: it is at a time a scientific device and a visual artefact. In other words, a "visual machine." Drawing on the *Encyclopédie* (*table* and *tableau*), Charles asserted that, in mid-eighteenth-century France, the word *table* meant a set of arranged data whereas *tableau* implied a synthesis of elements united in a single piece without regard for its format: written, spoken or visual. In this sense, *Tableau* had three connotations. It meant a painting, a blackboard, and a literary metaphor. On the contrary, *table* stood much closer to mathematics, meaning only "a method for presenting numerical data."[6]

Eighteenth-century books' titles incorporated the word *tableau* with frequency. Poivre also mentioned the word observation in his subtitle: *Observations on the customs, manners, arts.* The action of observing was recalled to mind alike by both the physiocrats and its enemies, Forbonnais with his *Principes et Observations oeconomiques* being a case in point.[7] As Du Pont de Nemours put it himself "as truth exists by itself – and it is in nature – to demonstrate only means to make see, and the art of judging is nothing else than the talent to open the eyes."[8] In his preface to *Principes et observations*, Forbonnais forewarned the reader that in times of ignorance (his own age), the search for causes was sacrificed at the expense of a certain penchant for mistaken observations that led to wrong teachings. In those times in which a false philosophy dominated, "the observation of facts was disdained" and "brilliant paradoxes" commanded. Forbonnais further asserted that the determination of facts has ceded its place to an obsession for good arguments based on general truths. He, on the contrary, was convinced that "To observe the facts accurately, abstract principles are the compass that must guide: but to make a safe route in practice, it is necessary to know the variations of the needle and the value of the currents."[9]

The different kingdoms of Southeast Asia, to which Poivre allocated half of the total room of his book, are placed side by side. Four contrasting kingdoms that offered an acute observer a field in which identifying causality relationships between natural rights (liberty and property) and agriculture. These four countries (already known to many of Poivre's readers) were Siam, Malacca, Cambodia, and Ponthiamas. Cartographically speaking, the region had been represented as a unit. As a matter of fact, Poivre was far from being the first to observe and depict this Asian trading crossroad. Missionaries had since the seventeenth century preceded him as well as many other writers. Further, writing representations had been complemented with draws (Figure 3.1).[10]

Elephants, in particular, fascinated the imagination of travellers and readers alike. In line with an intense debate on population, Poivre stated that the king of Siam valued more his elephants than his own subjects, "he conceives an idea of his greatness, more from the number of his elephants, than from the number of subjects." Many of them were preferred to the "first dignities in the kingdom" and the only service they accomplished was to destroy the crops of those who refused to pay tributes (Figure 3.2).[11]

Some historical details are mentioned throughout the narrative although the main goal of the book was to unveil the underpinning differences in agriculture performance across countries. The excerpt on the Kingdom of Ponthiamas (a land that, in full contrast to its neighbours, enjoyed high levels of agricultural output), had already been delivered separately. Poivre backed

*Figure 3.1* Siam and its neighbouring countries
Source: BNF, Placide de Saint-Hélène, Carte du Royaume de Siam et des pays circonvoisins

the idea that compliance with natural rights led the country to become a rich agricultural nation. Given the channel in which this piece circulated, one can suppose that it was of utmost interest for some physiocrats. For them, this

*Figure 3.2* Elephant chasing in Siam (eighteenth century)
Source: BNF, Usages de Siam, 1655–1700

very small nation cornered by despotic governments represented a case in point of a country that, like China, obeyed the rules of natural order.

The comparative operation lets the reader transpire that it was the kind of government and not the climate what explained the state of agriculture in any given country. Both Siam and Malacca were described as richly endowed countries in which the vastness of their forests overwhelmed travellers. In spite of their similar climatic conditions and regardless of their identical endowments, agriculture remained in a stagnant condition in Malacca and Siam in full contrast with Ponthiamas, which could be considered the richest granary of the peninsula: "if the other nations of the globe, who have the misfortune to be governed by the feudal system, inhabited a climate as happy, and land as fertile as those of the Malais, their agriculture would be as much neglected."[12] Poivre distanced himself from Montesquieu. Agricultural development pended on natural rights, neither in the form of government nor in the climatic conditions. Montesquieu stated that agriculture was the "principal labour of man." Laws and religion should push inhabitants to plough in those adverse climates where an inclination for laziness and honour prevailed. In chapter XIV of his *The Spirit of the Laws*, Montesquieu tells that in India, for instance, laws "which give the land to the prince, and destroy the spirit of property among the subjects, increase the bad effects of the climate."

This is the debate on the existence or non-existence of property rights in India.[13] Poivre coincided with Montesquieu on the negative effects of a lack of property rights. In India, agriculture had flourished for centuries, the decadence of this country being unleashed only by the Mughal conquest "When the conquerors took possession of the country, they appropriated to themselves at the same time all the lands." Lands were then allocated in "moveable fiefs" to the grandees "these farmed them out to their vassals, and those again to others." Consequently, "only the servants and day-labourers of the sub-farmers cultivate the fields."[14] In a country so penchant for revolutions neither the possessor nor the tenant could have certainty of their rights, and in consequence, agricultural improvements were not a matter of concern. Only a natural inclination for agriculture and the power of religion compelled people to plough the land; "the Malabar contemning and pitying the master whom he obeys, cultivates as ardently as if he was proprietor, the fief of his ancestors."[15] No matter the soil's qualities (dry, light, and sandy), two crops were produced every year thanks to the "industry and work" of the peasants.

The opposite conditions could be observed in Siam. This was a "very fruitful" kingdom, a land blessed by nature whose soil produced a great assortment of fruits with no much work required. Besides, mines were scattered all over the country. Notwithstanding, people living in "such great riches, are, perhaps, the most miserable of the mortals."[16] Siam's government was a despotic one in which uniquely the king enjoyed the "liberty which is natural to all mankind." Under such conditions "there is no law that can afford protection to individuals against violence, or in the smallest degree secure them in their property." A similar situation could be observed in Malacca, where, no matter the nature and its privileged geographical position, the inhabitants were so unhappy. Here, instead, the traveller found feudal laws. I follow Poivre's way of arguing and demonstrate that feudal laws were characterised by despotism yet one of a very peculiar nature.

Despotic government and Feudal laws could be observed in Siam and Malacca respectively. The former was featured by a common violation of property rights, workers' overtaxation, and recurrent excesses impelled both from the King and the "grandees." In that sense, Siamese people were no more than mere "slaves." Poivre avoided the term serf, even though one can assume he had in mind serfs' duties. Those slaves were annually taxed at six-month personal service without receiving wages or food. The remaining time was left free for them to procure their livelihood. This despotic government ruled in such a manner that no property rights were secured and rights could commonly be violated. Only religion could protect against the evils that that tyranny inflicted. The prince's excesses were boundless and his unbridled power was backed by the avarices of the grandees who themselves were no more than "chief slaves." The king was adored like a divinity "though subject to the most dangerous caprices."[17] This vicious form of government explained why agriculture had declined in this kingdom. Poivre went even further and held that agriculture was nonexistent: the largest tracts of land remained uncultivated. This despotic form of government discouraged inhabitants who devoted little effort to cultivate an extremely fertile land that, in spite of a lack of industriousness, provided people with rich rice harvests (Table 3.1).

The Malais, instead, were ruled by feudal laws. It is of the utmost interest for the sake of this chapter to clearly determine the underlying differences between despotic and feudal forms of government. Both forms of government had a different nature yet they are commonly encompassed under the same label: despotism. In despotic states, Montesquieu says, "the nature of government requires the most passive obedience, and when once the prince's will is made known, it ought infallibly to produce its effects. Here they have no limitations or restrictions, no mediums, terms, equivalents, or remonstrances" In

*Table 3.1* Features of despotic and feudal forms of government found in Southeast Asia

| *Despotic form of government Siam* | *Feudal form of government Malacca* |
|---|---|
| 1. Personal service<br>2. No protection to individuals against violence<br>3. No property rights<br>4. Excesses of power by the Prince<br>5. Avarices of the grandees<br>6. King adored like a divinity<br>7. Only religion protected against tyranny | 1. Laws, manners, customs, and prejudices of ancient north Europeans<br>2. Liberty of a few against the tyranny of one<br>3. Honour, bravery, and ferocity<br>4. The strong oppressed and destroyed the weak<br>5. Armed people |

chapter III, he says that upon this government "man is a creature that blindly submits to the absolute will of the sovereign."

Malacca was ruled by the laws, manners, customs and prejudices of the ancient northern European peoples. As we will see, Poivre shared exactly the same set of assumptions advanced in a huge body of literature published in the 1770s. While despotism meant a form of government that found its foundations on the excesses of one overbearing person, feudal laws instead meant the "defense of the liberty of a few against the tyranny of one." Yet, in either form of government the multitude remained subjected to slavery and oppression. Under despotism, the king inflicted outrageous and immoderate behaviour. Instead, under the command of feudal laws, a handful of lords enjoyed unchecked power. A specific set of values characterised such an order: Malacca was a society in which honour, bravery and ferocity prevailed. Afraid of falling prey to frequent violations, everyone was always armed "the industry of this nation even surpasses itself, in the fabric of this destructive weapon."[18] Briefly said, the Feudal form of government was a system intended for a few to oppress and destroy at a time the weaker and the state.

Neither despotism nor feudal laws ruled in the small kingdom of Ponthiamas. This was a relatively young and very small polity established by a Chinese merchant only fifty years prior to Poivre's travel. He had hired Chinese peasants and peasants from neighbouring countries to cultivate the land. He distributed lands "without the less reservation of any of those duties or taxes known by the names of service or fines of alienation, duties which by allowing no real property, become the most fatal scourge to agriculture."[19] In building this labouring and trading nation, he only ruled through the laws with which nature had provided humankind. Even he himself obeyed those natural laws: he fashioned simplicity, industry, frugality, humanity, and good faith "he formed, then, no system of laws – he did more – he established morals." He could have emulated his neighbours and could have implemented feudal laws and arbitrary taxation. Further, he could have exhibited luxury in a splendid court dwelled by "multitudes of fawning slaves," treating "his associates as slaves." But this was not the case. He, on the contrary, was persuaded that "he should be always rich, if his labourers were so."[20]

## The government of "feudal legislators"

Indeed, despotism is a term that had been in use long before Montesquieu made it trending. Previous to and after *The Spirits of the Laws*, the term came to be a means through which to demur against the absolutist monarchy.[21] In the enlightened discussions, despotism was recurrently associated with orientalism.[22] Some fellows of the physiocratic circle published extensively on the topic: one famous instance being Quesnay's *Despotisme de la Chine.* In this case, it was the despotism of the natural order itself, though. As happened with Poivre, mid-eighteenth-century French philosophers availed of "eastern despotism" as a means through which to raise their voices against their own forms of government.

Yet, no pure form of despotism was likely to have ever existed. Any kind of power faced its own limitations. The actual distinctiveness between despotism and much more balanced forms of government lay elsewhere. The former had external limits (religion, *moeurs*, climate) whereas the latter had internal ones (political). Hot climates, for instance, favoured despotism by impacting women's fertility, making work annoying or exacerbating sexual desires. Indeed, China's despotism aroused enthusiasm among many French thinkers. Not for Montesquieu, for whom this was a much more benign form of despotism, despotism though. This very peculiar political system was characterised by the interrelations between available natural resources and a high population: the ever-growing Chinese population made the country vulnerable to frequent famines compelling the despot not to enforce his will, and rather, to ensure his vassals' well-being. Under these particular conditions, China's arguably good government was far from being an outcome of minded governmental policies; on the contrary, the despot's self-control derived from external conditions.[23]

Almost identical forms of government yet diverse in nature could be found in both Siam and Malacca. The slight variation, nonetheless, recalls an essential, long-lasting, and multivariate debate. As it is evident, the traveller availed himself of Asia as a means through which to channel his thoughts on Europe, and more in particular, on France. As Du Pont de Nemours himself pointed out in a footnote added to the second edition, even though Poivre had not mentioned that, the author was convinced that France was ruled by the same pattern under which the Malais found their misfortune.

Essentially, the Feudal order was understood as a system characterised by a despotic form of government. Issues related to land tenancy and land distribution were at the very core of the discussion: property rights were one of the main concerns. Poivre agreed with Montesquieu in that it was liberty and not the soil's fertility the reason why agriculture developed in some countries while it stagnated in others. "Countries are not cultivated in proportion to their fertility, but to their liberty," as Montesquieu stated in chapter XVIII. Poivre, nevertheless, went still far and claimed the need for land distribution. Ponthiamas' case demonstrated that respect for natural rights was necessary for agriculture to flourish.

The 1770s, in particular and for reasons which are beyond the goals of this book, witnessed a tenacious debate on the impacts, origins, history, and features of the so-called Feudal order. Feudalism and the Feudal system have received a great deal of attention on the part of the economic historians.[24] Nonetheless, as Kaplan has recently called to mind, the topic has barely been approached from intellectual history or economic thinking perspectives.[25] Little is actually known about how eighteenth-century thinkers approached and dealt with the topic. Osterhammel has unveiled the features that European eighteenth-century travellers attributed to those nations that they considered under the Feudal system. Poivre enlisted Malaysia as a feudal country yet other travellers found similar features of "feudal-chivalry fashion" among the Afghan, Ceylonese, Sikhs, Marathas, Kurds, Circassians, Crimean Tatars, and Tahiti.[26] The system prevailed not only across Asia, it also had survived in most parts of Europe. The debate essentially sought to identify the system's nature and principles.

Two branches of the debate bifurcated. On the one hand, those with Voltaire who praised England and its (republican) parliamentary form of government.[27] This group of intellectuals was basically concerned with the executive's unrestricted will. On the other hand, those with Mirabeau who displayed apprehensiveness for the havoc of the Feudal order and the dangers of an extremely weak and ironed shackled state (or king), which could easily turn prey to a small group of grandees.[28] They were mainly concerned with the grandees' overpower.

The whig narrative has recently been refashioned in explaining convergent and divergent patterns of economic growth globally. In the last decades, economists working from a neo-institutional perspective have attributed differences in national economic performance to political institutions. For instance, England's eighteenth-century rise is ascribed to its parliamentary form of government.[29] This idea, indeed, is closely linked to Montesquieu's tripartite division of power. This dominant perspective (basically a depiction of the state within a Leviathan, rent-seeking depredator frame)[30] falls short at demonstrating the impacts of a weak state incapable of refraining the wills of intermediate powers. Named as Hayek's mistake,[31] economists have recently started revisiting this widely echoed assumption (the state is now even conceived of as an agent which promotes innovation).[32] Consequently, a call has been made for a more balanced approach in which strong states and well-organised societies counterbalance each other.[33]

The debate is framed within a republican conception in which civil society and representative institutions could constrain the executive. Yet, liberal explanations seem to downplay the potential distorting effects of intermediate powers dictated by strongly powerful and extremely well-off individuals. The polemic on the misfortunes of the Feudal system, to which the *économistes* seem to have particularly been attached, brought to the front the issue of the "feudal legislators" (to borrow D'Holbach's words).

If google n-gram unveils accurate tendencies, it seems plausible to state that the word feudal was common prior to the revolution but somehow lost track after August 1791. The term was seemingly again in vogue in the years that preceded the 1848 wave of revolution after which time it tends to be less constant over the second half of the nineteenth century and the whole twentieth century, with the exception of the 1960s. If google n-gram reflects correct trends for eighteenth-century French books, thus, the adjective feudal seems to have been popular in the 1730s, and again, in the 1770s. By the time Poivre published his book, the mention of the word had gradually lost track yet it would be trending once again in the years that followed the launching of *Voyages*. It is hard to ascertain whether or not this has something to do with the success that *Voyages* yielded (Figure 3.3).

*Figure 3.3* N-gram Google. Féodal

In the mid-century, the main strand of the debate opposed Montesquieu to Voltaire. The discussion apparently had taken wing in 1727 after the publication of Boulainvilliers' book.[34] In the introduction to his masterpiece *The Feudal Society*, Bloch tracked down the origin of the word and revealed that Boulainvilliers seemed to have been the first to introduce it with an enduring impact in eighteenth-century intellectual debates.[35] Montesquieu updated Boulainvilliers' hyperinflated positive image of the Feudal order,[36] and further, refashioned his ideas into a new concept. Substituting the substantive form (Feudalism) and introducing the expression Feudal laws, a concept that would become trending afterwards. Already in the preface of his *The Spirit of the Laws*, Montesquieu recognised that his "ideas are new, and therefore I have been obliged to find new words, or to give new acceptations to old terms, in order to convey my meaning." This was the concept most commonly used over the eighteenth century, and more in particular, the one employed when the debate apparently reached its zenith in the 1770s.

Feudalism as either order or event. This was the underlying contradiction that framed the discussion. The chapter 30 of the second book of *The Spirit of the Laws* dealt with the theory of the Feudal laws. Montesquieu advised his readers that the subsequent pages narrated the history of how those laws had emerged among the Franks and how they had contributed to the establishment of the monarchy. The historical process could be seen as the emergence of a system of laws that had no connection with former prevailing institutions; a system of laws "which suddenly appeared all over Europe." The chapters should be held more like a general survey than a properly designed treatise on those laws. However, offering this sketch was preferable to pass in silence "an event which never again, perhaps, will happen." Here, precisely, lies the core of disagreement.

Voltaire countered Montesquieu and offered an antagonistic version in which Feudalism was not seen as an event, an unrepeatable event that had happened at the dawn of European history to never reappear. For him, on the contrary, Feudalism should be conceived of as an ancient system of government that still ruled in immense parts of the hemisphere no matter the form it might take. In this sense, the Great Mogul and the German Emperor clearly resembled. Voltaire envisages Feudalism as an order in which the "petit tyrants" rule, people being no more than their "slaves." In his widely read *Le siècle de Louis XIV*,[37] he raised his voice against the Comte de Boulainvilliers whom he blamed for having asserted that the Feudal order should be considered as the "masterpiece of the human spirit." In Voltaire's mind, in contrast, this social order prevented industries, commerce, and property to burgeon. An order fit for a hundred lords to impose their will with no restrictions: at the same time oppressors of the land and enemies of the king.

One could, therefore, deduce that this was the framework within which Poivre produced his ideas on feudal laws and arranged his observations. The years following the intellectual pre-eminence and governmental apogee of the physiocratic school witnessed an explosion of curiosity on the harmful impacts that Feudalism had brought about. Many authors from many perspectives approached the subject in many books. At least three elements were at the core of the discussion. To begin with, Feudalism mingled with despotism. In addition, Feudalism's main characteristic, it is, the overpowering of a few grandees and the slavery condition of the majority. Finally, the global extension of the system, it is, whether it had ever emerged outside Europe.

The dispute on free trade offered some a precious opportunity for approaching the topic from a political-economic perspective.[38] The debate that opposed Galiani to Morellet is interesting in this regard.[39] Morellet himself had travelled across the Italian Peninsula and had corresponded with members of Italian intellectual circles like *Il Caffè*,[40] being himself the translator into French of Beccaria's famous *Dei Delitti e delle Pene* only a year and a half after its being printed by Guiseppe Au-bert at Livorno.[41] In an intensely contentious book, which was written in a total derisive tone, titled *Dialogues sur les grains*, the irreverent but highly charismatic Neapolitan economist used the words despotism and feudal to mean a form of despotic government: "that anarchy that you can call Feudal government or Despotism."[42] For him, despots like Tibere only feared famines. Wherever one puts the eyes, wherever a despot rules like in Constantinople, Cairo, Maroc, "the caution to maintain abundance and low prices in the cities is the first and almost the only care of the government." For those despots, supplying the market came at any cost and deserved the enactment of any law, no matter whether commerce perished, navigation languished, or agriculture faded. The feudal government was a military one in which the grandees were all commensals and the free men were soldats who lived at their expenses "all the rest were slaves."[43]

Many were curious about the seemingly existence of feudal laws outside Europe. In this vein, the observations gathered by travellers across the globe could be a very precious source of information. Attributing feudal features to Asian polities dated back to the sixteenth century when the first European travellers met Asian nations and got aware of their history. For instance, Portuguese reported the social organisation of the kingdom of Vijayanagar through the lenses of a Feudal society.[44] In an eighteenth-century English translation of the *Lusíadas*, the word feudal was brought up several times. As already said, Poivre was not the only traveller to have ascribed European feudal features to Asian societies.[45] In his *Fragment sur l'Inde*, Voltaire claimed that the Mogol government was, since Genghis Khan and probably long before, a feudal government that resembled the German contemporaneous system, which, in turn, operated in the same manner in which it had operated among the Lombards, the Spaniards, the English, and French people: "it was the ancient form of administration of the Scythes and Tartares."[46] This was an ancient system yet one that still ruled over vast areas of Europe.

The situation in Asia was not that different. This branch of the debate was nourished by travellers' accounts. By drawing on those sources, many maintained the global spread of that noxious economic system. Poivre held that feudal laws ruled in Malacca. One contemporary traveller found the same situation in the Pacific, more specifically on the O-Taheitee island: "Their government seems greatly to resemble the early state of every nation in Europe under the feudal system." There was a three-class social order, land tenure patterns, and labour interacted like in some areas of Europe. There were two kings each ruling one of the peninsulas of the island. Lords ruled over one or more districts. Another class (the *mahounonis*) superintendent land cultivation, which was carried by the lowest class (*Towtows*) which "seem to be nearly under the same circumstances as the villein in feudal governments: they do all the laborious work, they cultivate the land under the *mahounonis*, who are only nominal cultivators for the lord."[47]

Observations were gathered in Europe as well. A highly renowned travel account written by two Swedish travellers attributed the backward conditions that had made the Kingdom of Naples fell behind other northern European countries to an old-centuries, customarily, and unmutated feudal legal system.[48] Fixed feudal laws, which dated back to the Normand conquest, ruled over the country. Centuries and centuries under such a harmful legal system had offered the nobles of the northern Italian republics (places in which much more egalitarian social systems had been settled) a very precious opportunity for them to acquire vast fiefs upon no restriction. Further, succesorial laws had allowed landholders to inherit land with no restriction. So, many fiefs across the Kingdom of the Two Sicilies belonged to the Venetians, Genoese, and other northern Italian inhabitants. A conclusion could be thus drawn: certain forms of land tenure negatively impacted economic growth.

Indeed, the southern Italian kingdom was not the only country in which travellers could observe feudal Laws. Poland and Russia, in particular, called the attention of the writers and travellers alike. Poland's and Denmark's conditions could be no more different. The former was far from enjoying the good legislation that had put the latter on the road of economic progress. Regardless of its factor endowments, Poland had remained poor: "The feudal government upon which the people languish put insurmountable obstacles." In such a government "the lords are everything, the people are nothing" ("les seigneurs sont tout, le peuple n'y est rien"). The king himself was no more than an instrument of a "multitude of tyrants." For this reason, a "vicious constitution" had annihilated nature's gifts. A very likely situation prevailed both in Russia and Germany. In the former, peasants groaned under feudal servitude, and in the latter, a large number of *Nabats* had submitted the whole country to the same conditions the Moguls had imposed elsewhere. A plethora of scattered small feudal governments had converted the country into a prey of foreign enemies and had prevented the strengthening of the state. For many, this was a constitution worthy of admiration, though. Laws snatched all power from the "chief of confederates" while gave no power to the people. The chief could be satisfied because all his wishes were fulfilled: "he crushed the peasants to provide for the futile maintenance of his equipment, theatre, and luxuries."[49]

Some authors displayed a special concern for the negative incentives that the Feudal system brought for the society as a whole. They sought to unveil the political causes and effects of the Feudal order. In 1773, D'Holbach published *La Politique naturelle,* and two years later, Mirabeau sent to print his *Essais sur le despotisme.*[50] Both authors employed the word despotism, a word very much in vogue in eighteenth-century books. Even though both Despotism and Feudalism were closely related yet they referred to distinct forms of government. While Montesquieu clamoured for checks and balances on the executive as the only condition upon which liberty could be unleashed, mid-eighteenth century French *économistes* weighted up the overbearing and tyrannical power imposed and maintained by a few grandees.

Both D'Holbach's and Mirabeau's books explored at length the features of the Feudal system. Many of their ideas resembled the observations read in travel accounts. D'Holbach even devoted an entire chapter to what he called the Feudal government. For several authors, the Feudal order or system was a centuries-lasting, European-wide order that unfortunately still ruled in at least two-thirds of the continent. When one compares D'Holbach's and Mirabeau's lines of reasoning two features stand out: (i) The executive's strengths had been shrunk at the bottom level: this was actually a despotism inflicted not by the monarch but rather by a handful of "feudal legislators;" (ii) This was a system in which the idea of property rights was non-existent.

Robbery, disorder, and war had been the ground upon which the system had flourished. According to D'Holbach's account, the conquerors had imposed an independent and disastrous power that had ultimately led to an extremely weak monarchical power. People had been crushed by a multitude of tyrant devotees of "anarchic life" for whom liberty was no more than their capacity to oppress people unrestrictedly and upon no impunity. These tyrants had tied the monarch's hands so tightly that nobody could refrain them from committing profligacy. In the same vein, Mirabeau stated that feudal legislators held to a system in which love for pillage and military honour led to the suppression of property rights. Conquerors coming from the northernmost regions had implanted chaos. The enemies of royal sovereignty had established a particular form of dominion in which no check and balance could refrain their will.

Only one year after the launching of Mirabeau's *Essais sur le despotisme*, the *Wealth of Nations* was printed in England. Therefore, both books are contemporaneous. The "engrossing of uncultivated lands," this is how Smith introduced the topic from a historical perspective. Chapter II of book III explains the causes behind the discouragement of agriculture in the ancient state of Europe, a question which no doubt remembers the one Poivre evoked in his travel account. The fall of the Roman Empire ended up in a chaotic situation that had led to the concentration of lands in the hands of a few great landholders although the actual occupiers were all tenants. Smith like Poivre and most mid-century authors resorted to the term slaves: all of them or almost all were actually slaves. Slaves of a different kind to the ones found in Ancient Greek, Rome, or the West Indies, though: "they were supposed to belong more directly to the land than to their masters. They could, therefore, be sold with it, but not separately."

One more feature of this wide and enduring slavery was the slaves' incapability to acquire property "whatever they acquired they did for the master" "Such slaves could acquired nothing but their daily maintenance." To Smith, as for the authors above, this "species of slavery" subsisted in large parts of Europe: Russia, Poland, Hungary, Bohemia, and Moravia. Smith went on with the impact that slavery brought for economic growth. In the same chapter, he stated that it was a universal rule (or rather one deduced from the experiences of all ages and nations) that work done by slaves, no matter how cheap this work could be, negatively impacted the economy. Ancient classic texts clearly demonstrated that point. For instance, both Plinio and Columella proved "how much the cultivation of corn degenerated, how unprofitable it became to the master when it fell under the management of slaves." It seemed accurate to hold that

> The pride of man makes him love to domineer, and nothing mortifies him so much as to be obliged to condescend to persuade his inferiors. Wherever the law allows it, and the nature of the work can afford it, therefore, he will generally prefer the service of slaves to that of freeman.

Smith's interpretation of Feudal laws is slightly different from the account offered by the above French physiocratic-affiliated authors. For him, the consolidation across Europe of that system could be seen as an attempt to moderate "the authority of the great allodial lords." Feudal laws were intended to establish regular duties "from the king down to the smallest proprietor." Even though the implementation sought to strengthen the king's authority and to weaken the power of the great proprietors "it could not do either sufficiently for establishing order and good government among the inhabitants of the country; because it could not alter sufficiently that state of property and manners from which the disorders arise." The result was a weak authority in the head and strong in the inferior members, therefore, causing a certain disequilibrium "the open country still continued to be a scene of violence, rapine, and disorder."

## Notes

1 Pierre Poivre, *Travels of a Philosopher*, 167.
2 Chambre de Commerce de Marseille, *Fonds Monteil*, L XIII, n. 4.
3 Pierre Poivre, *Travels of a Philosopher*, 9.
4 It is worth highlighting that a lack of information on South African indigenous people was not an issue. In 1719, a book had been published in Nuremberg whose European-wide impact would last long well into the end of the century: Peter Kolb's travel account. The diary was first published in three volumes, and then, it was translated into English and French, and additionally, published in an abridged version. Kolb's travel account offered the reader plenty of information on the geography, nations, and customs. On Kolb's book see: Ann Good, 'The Construction of an Authoritative Text: Peter Kolb's Description of the Khoikhoi at the Cape of Good Hope in the Eighteenth Century', *Journal of Early Modern History* 10, no. 1–2 (2006): 61–94.
5 Harro Maas and Mary S. Morgan, 'Observation and Observing in Economics', *History of Political Economy* 44, no. Annual supplement (2012): 1–24; M. Norton Wise, 'Making Visible', *Isis* 97, no. 1 (2006): 75–82.
6 Loïc Charles, 'The Visual History of the Tableau Économique'.
7 François Véron de Forbonnais, *Principes et Observations Oeconomiques*, 2 vols (Amsterdam: Chez Marc Michel Rey, 1767).
8 Georges Weulersse, *Le Mouvement Physiocratique*, T. II, 121.
9 François Véron de Forbonnais, *Principes et Observations Oeconomiques*, T. I, III–V.
10 Bibliothèque National de France, Manuscrits, Usages du Royaume de Siam: Cartes, vues et plans: sujets historiques.
11 Pierre Poivre, *Travels of a Philosopher*, 60.
12 Pierre Poivre, 84.
13 Dharma Kumar, 'Private Property in Asia? The Case of Medieval South India', *Comparative Studies in Society and History* 27, no. 2 (1985): 340–66.
14 Pierre Poivre, *Travels of a Philosopher*, 36.
15 Pierre Poivre, 37.
16 Pierre Poivre, 51.
17 Pierre Poivre, 58.
18 Pierre Poivre, 73.
19 Pierre Poivre, 97.
20 Pierre Poivre, 91.
21 Catherine Larrère, *Actualité de Montesquieu*, 83.
22 Jürgen Osterhammel, *Unfabling the East: The Enlightenment's Encounter with Asia*; Sophus Reinert, Farnham 'The Sultan's Republic: Jealousy of Trade and Oriental Despotism in Paolo Mattia Doria', in *Enlightenment Reform in Southern Europe and Its Atlantic Colonies, c. 1750–1830*, ed. Gabriel Paquette (Farnham: Ashgate, 2009), 253–70; Jarced Rubin, *Rulers, Religion, and Riches: Why the West Got Rich and the Middle East Did Not* (Cambridge: Cambridge University Press, 2017).
23 Catherine Larrère, *Actualité de Montesquieu*, 91–92.
24 Marc Bloch, *La Société Féodale* (Paris: Albin Michel, 1968); Witold Kula, *Théorie Économique Du Système Féodal* (Paris: Mouton, 1970); T. H. Aston and C. H. E. Philpin, eds., *The Brenner Debate: Agrarian Class Structure and Economic Development in Pre-Industrial Europe* (Cambridge: Cambridge University Press, 1985).
25 Steven L. Kaplan, *Raisonner Sur Les Blés*, 130.

26 Jürgen Osterhammel, *Unfabling the East*, 425.
27 Voltaire, *Letters Concerning the English Nation*. The Second Edition, with Large Additions (London: Printed for C. Davis in Pater-noster-Row, 1761).
28 Honoré-Gabriel Riqueti Mirabeau, *Essais Sur Le Despotisme. Seconde Édition Augmentée et Corrigée Par l'éditeur de Cet Ouvrage* (Londres, 1776).
29 Douglas North and Robert Weingast, 'Constitutions and Commitment: The Evolution of Institutional Governing Public Choice in Seventeenth-Century England', *Journal of Economic History* 49, no. 4 (1989): 803–32; Douglass North, *The Rise of the West World: A New Economic History* (London: Cambridge University Press, 1973); Daron Acemoglu and James Robinson, *Why Nations Fail? The Origins of Power, Prosperity and Poverty* (New York: Crown Publishers, 2012); Daron Acemoglu and James Robinson, *The Narrow Corridor: States, Societies, and the Fate of Liberty* (New York: Penguin Press, 2019); Jean-Laurent Rosenthal, 'The Political Economy of Absolutism Reconsidered', in *Analytic Narratives*, ed. Robert H. Bates (Princeton, NJ: Princeton University Press, 1998), 63–108; Jean-Laurent Rosenthal and Bing Wong, *Before and Beyond Divergence: The Politics of Economic Change in China and Europe* (Cambridge, MA: Harvard University Press, 2009); Hilton Root, *The Fountain of Privilege. Political Foundations of Markets in Old Regime France and England* (Berkeley: University of California Press, 1994).
30 Regina Grafe and Oscar Gelderblom, 'The Rise and Fall of the Merchant Guilds: Re-Thinking the Comparative Study of Commercial Institutions in Pre-Modern Europe', *Journal of Interdisciplinary History* 40, no. 4 (2010): 477–511.
31 F. A. Hayek, *Law, Legislation and Liberty* (New York: Routledge, 1982).
32 Mariana Mazzucato, *The Entrepreneurial State: Debunking Public vs. Private Sector Myths* (London: Penguin Press, 2018).
33 Daron Acemoglu and James Robinson, *The Narrow Corridor.*
34 M. de Boulainvilliers, *Etat de La France, Contenant XIV. Lettres Sur Les Anciens Parlements de France Avec l'histoire de Ce Royaume Despuis Le Comencement de La Monarchie Jusqu'a Charles VIII. On y a Joint Des Mémoires Présentés à M. Le Duc d'Orléans* (Londres: Chez W. Roberts; & se vend chez J. Brindley in New Bond-street, où on trouve les deux premiers volumes, 1728).
35 Marc Bloch, *La Société Féodale.*
36 For a similar situation in the first decades of the twentieth century see, Otto Brunner, *Land Und Herrschaft: Grundfragen Der Territorialen Verfassungsgeschichte* (Darmstadt: Wissenschaftliche Buchgesellschaft, 1984).
37 Voltaire, *Le Siècle de Louis XIV. Nouvelle Édition Augmentée d'un Très Grande Nombre de Remarques Par Mr. de La B* (Francfort: Chez la veuve Knoch et J. G. Eslinger, 1753).
38 Abbé de Mably, *Doutes Proposés Aux Philosophes Économistes Sur l'ordre Naturel et Essentiel Des Sociétés Politiques* (Haye: Chez Nyon quai des augustins, Veuve Durand, rue S. Jacques, 1768); Anonymous, *Lettres à Un Ami Sur Les Avantages de La Liberté Du Commerce Des Grains et Le Danger Des Prohibitions* (Amsterdam: Chez Desaint, libraire, rue du Foin, 1768); Anonymous, *Résultats de La Liberté et de l'immunité Du Commerce Des Grains, de La Farine et Du Pain* (Amsterdam: Chez Desaint, libraire, rue du S. Jacques, 1768); Anonymous, *Observations Sur La Liberté Du Commerce Des Grains* (Amsterdam: Chez Michel Lambert libraire-imprimeur rue de la Comédie, 1759); Steven L. Kaplan, Raisonner Sur Les Blés, and Judith A. Miller, *Mastering the Market: The State and the Grain Trade in Northern France, 1700–1860* (Cambridge: Cambridge University Press, 1998).
39 *Correspondance Littéraire, Philosophique et Critique de Grimm et Diderot, Depuis 1753 Jusqu'en 1790. Nouvelle Édition, Revue et Mise Dans Un Meilleur Ordre, Avec Des Notes et Des Éclaircissements, et Ou Se Trouvent Rétablies Pour La Première Fois Les Phrases Supprimées Par La Censure Impériale* (Paris: Chez Furne, librairie quai des augustins, n. 37 et Landrage, même quai, 19, 1829), V. 6, 56, 134, 321, 332, 330,

338, 370, 418; Paolo Amodio, *Il Disincanto Della Ragione e l'assolutezza Del Bonheur. Studio Sull'Abate Galiani* (Naples: Alfredo Guida, 1997); Augusto Bazzoni, ed., *Lettere Ferdinando Galiani al Marchese Bernardo Tanucci* (Florence: Gio. Pietro Vieusseux, 1880); Epistolario Bernardo Tanucci, vol. 20 (Naples: Società Napoletana de Storia Patria, 2000), Vol. XV: 147; XVI: 167; XVII: 248, 391, 402, 407, 409, 415; XX: 28.

40 Franco Venturi, *Settecento Riformatore. De Muratori a Beccaria* (Torino: Giulio Einaudi, 1969); Sophus Reinert, *The Academy of Fisticuffs: Political Economy and Commercial Society in Enlightenment Italy* (Cambridge, MA: Harvard University Press, 2019).

41 Jean Pandolfi, 'Beccaria Traduit Par Morellet', *Dix-Huitième Siècle* 9 (1977): 291–316.

42 Ferdinando Galiani, *Dialogues Sur Le Commerce Des Bleds* (Londres: s.n., 1770), 114.

43 Ferdinando Galiani, 247.

44 Joan-Pau Rubiés, *Travel and Ethnology*, 30–31.

45 Jürgen Osterhammel, *Unfabling the East*, 424–26.

46 Voltaire, *Fragments Sur l'Inde, Sur Le Général Lalli et Sur Le Comte de Morangiés* (s.n.: s.n., 1773).

47 *New Discoveries Concerning the World, and Its Inhabitants. In Two Parts. Part I Containing a Circunstancial Account of All the Islands in the South-Sea, That Have Been Lately Discovered or Explored; the Situation, Climate, and the Soil of Each; Their Natural Productions, Including Many Species of Animals and Vegetables Hitherto Unknown; the Persons, Dresses, Extraordinary Manners and Customs, Manufactures, Buildings, Government, and Religion of the Various Inhabitants, Their Domestic Utensils, and Weapons of War, Their Ingenuity, Mental Endowments, Skill in Navigation, and Other Arts and Sciences. Comprehending All the Discoveries Made in the Several Voyages of Commodore (Now Admiral) Byron, Captains Wallis, Carteret, and Cook, Related by Dr. Hawresworth, Sidney Parkinson, Mr. Forster, and Captain Cook. Together with Those of M. de Bougainville. The Whole Compared with the Narratives of Former Celebrated Navigators, Viz. Mendoza, Quiros, Tasman, Le Maire, Schouten. Dampier, Roggewein, Anson, and Others. Part II Containing a Summary Account of Captain Cook's Attempts to Discover a Southern Continent in 1773, 1774, and 1775. Also Voyage of the Honourable Constantine John Phipps (Now Lord Mulgrave) towards the North-Pole, in 1773.* WIth Maps and Prints (London: Printed for J. Johnson, St. Paul's Church-Yard, 1778), 104–7.

48 *Observations Sur l'Italie et Sur Les Italiens, Données En 1764, Sous Le Nom de Deux Gentilshommes Suédois. Par l'auteur Du Livre Intitulé Londres* (Amsterdam: Chez Costard, Fils & Compagnie, rue S. Jean de Beauvais, 1774), Vol. III, 272–74.

49 J. P. Brissot, *Testament Politique de l'Angleterre* (Philadelphie: s.n., 1780), 64–66.

50 Paul Henri Dietrich D'Holbach, *La Politique Naturelle ou Discours Sur Les Vrai Principes Du Gouvernement* (Londres, 1773); Honoré-Gabriel Riqueti Mirabeau, *Essais Sur Le Despotisme. Seconde Édition Augmentée et Corrigée Par l'éditeur de Cet Ouvrage.*

# 4 An empirical turn

## Evidence and the attack on the economists

In a letter written on 10 September 1776, Poivre told the Parisian banker Jean-Marie Galles his feelings on the lately implemented economic policies, and further, recounted his deep regret for the sad situation his dear friends had gone through.[1] As he noticed, news had spread with the word being that "the *économistes* had been mistreated and exiled." He felt terrorised at realising that the *économistes* have been ill-treated because of their desire to behave wisely and reasonably. In his eyes, the *économistes* were intellectuals attached to the principles of reason and natural justice. And he continued: "all the Chinese savants are *économistes* and the great science of the Chinese Empire is the same that our *économistes* had started publishing since recently." There was a difference between Europe and China, though: the Chinese government had been enforcing this knowledge for more than 400 years. Expelling the *économistes* from office meant, on the one hand, falling into barbarity, and on the other hand, refusing to obey nature and its universal laws.

More in particular, Poivre expressed his full regret for Turgot having been expelled from office due to the debacle that the 1760s grain crisis unchained. In an attempt that sought a final solution to the continuous famines, the devotees of the sect rushed into action and sought to demonstrate the validity of the universal laws they endorsed with headstrong impulsiveness. Total freedom to trade was supposed to be the final solution: this was the way in which an extremely thin group of fellows at that point made up of no more than eight adherents understood the issue. The enactment of such policies would lead to the settling of a natural price, benefiting equally producers and consumers both nationals and foreigners. Their unbending efforts carried at passing universal principles ultimately led to a catastrophe.

Turgot was very well acquainted, as all the *philosophes économistes* seemed to have been, with the work of Poivre.[2] Prior to his tenure in the office of French Finances, Turgot had travelled across inner France. He himself, like Poivre had carefully observed a poor, peasant, socio-economic world. Yet, contrary to Poivre, who had witnessed how well fed Chinese peasants were, Turgot's French congeners suffered unstoppably the pains caused by

DOI: 10.4324/9780429028199-6

famines and mounting prices. From Limoge, he wrote a letter to Du Pont de Nemours asking for a second copy of the book Poivre had published.

China was held in high regard in the eighteenth-century European intellectual milieu.[3] The eastern foremost empire drew the *économistes*' attention particularly in the 1760s. Around those years, the *Ephémérides du citoyen* published Quesnay's thoughts on what appeared to European eyes as a perplexing, immemorial, and almost atemporal government. Le *despotisme de la Chine* preceded only for a couple of years the publication of *Voyages* although Poivre had previously read his papers in Paris. Quesnay himself conveyed his uses of travel accounts. Alongside Duhalde, he quotes Mac Paul, Emmanuel Pinto, Navarette (a Spanish and Dominican missionary), Dutch travellers, Giovanni Franceso Gemelli Careri, the Russian special envoy Laurant Lange, Eberhard Isbran, and admiral Anson.[4] One can assume that Poivre's observations might well have nurtured Quesnay's understanding of his legal despotism. Poivre had allegedly observed an economic system in which nature's principles ruled. The idea itself of a natural order or system was at the very core of the debates.

The market, as Newton's universe, fit within a universal order of things and laws that were beyond human control. A sect of self-willed *économistes* had sought to enact innovative grain policies that at the beginning showed little effect. The unforeseen repercussions and the seriousness of the subsequent events transformed the dilemma into a deeply studied topic. The *économistes'* fall into disgrace not only demonstrated the inapplicability of their recently uncovered market gravitational laws, but also confirmed the mistaken way in which they pretended to idealise both social order and human behaviour.

Compare to the debate on grains, which indeed was essential at that time, much less attention has been paid to another different phenomena that partially explained why *Voyages* reached such a welcoming audience among the *philosophes économistes*. In the following remaining chapters of this first part, I will demonstrate that an empirical turn happened in the 1760s. Despite firmly upholding a science supported by geometric evidence and laws deduced from the natural law theory, the *économistes* were compelled to offer empirical proof to their held assumptions. Opposers believed that without empirical proof their ideas should be considered as mere aprioristically endorsed universal principles. The challenge came not from within the sect itself but from rival intellectual Parisian groups. Poivre's book precisely appeared in time to refrain the critics and counter the disbelievers. His travel account could assist with observations that came to prove the solid ground and validity of the new trinity faith: Liberty, property, and security. All those principles had first been deduced from natural law, being framed into a physicist's approach to the social world. Those axioms had become fashionable in 1767 backed by an oeuvre that is reported to have reached a high impact. That year Lemercier de la Rivière arranged the credo and submitted a solid philosophical ground for a natural approach to social order in his *L'ordre naturel et essentiel*.[5]

One of the branches of this empirical turn took the form of a sizzling discussion on the uses and misuses of the past both in a broad sense (the past as a laboratory) and in a narrower one (the lessons scholars could draw from classical erudition). While some fellows of the Parisian intellectual milieu (particularly the ones entrenched in the journal *Correspondance littéraire* and the *Encyclopédie*) attacked the *économistes* in reason of his disdain for Classical studies and their contempt for erudition and ancient history, the *économistes* blamed their adversaries for their contemptuousness to incorporate nations outside Europe to the analysis. The former looked backward; the latter looked eastward. The *économistes* believed that the clue to many economic theoretical issues could be found if a look were given to the Asian socio-economic systems.

## Celestial evidence or earthbound observations?

Evidence was a recurrent term in the 1760s. The concept was as much dear to the *économistes* as the concept system would later be to Adam Smith who encompassed previous explanatory or practical frameworks as mercantile and agricultural systems. Indeed, this is not to say that evidence and system meant the same. According to Melon, a system is a set of linked propositions "whose consequences tend to establish a truth or an opinion". The term came from the idea of the Tolomean or Copernican system and had been "generalised and applied to all.[6]" Before the word system became trending, the word evidence was in fashion. In the 1760s, the term was reiteratively employed in economic journals, and more in particular, in the one that served the economists' propagandistic purposes. On the other hand, the word observation was, as already said, a term frequently used in book titles throughout the century. Even though both words implied the same kind of action (the act of bringing forward a proof), they, nonetheless, implied a verification of a distinct and completely opposite nature.

The gulf that separated evidence from observation reported on a tenacious intellectual battle fought in the mid-century. Observations should offer support to evidence. This was the absolute condition upon which the *économistes'* assumptions could be endorsed and shared. This empirical turn sheds light on why and how seemingly universal, incontestable, and self-evident truths started to crumble before unconvinced eyes. Criticism arose which expressed suspicion about the validity of logically-deduced laws that the *économistes* reckoned as evidence. Steadily, suspicion transformed into scepticism on the shaky wall that separated evidence from opinion (or rather ideology[7]).

This turn informs us in particular on how the fellows of the sect reacted. An empirical turn was deployed with the intent to fight back the attacks on the credo. This was far to be a process of endogenous disciplinary and scientific evolution, being rather the outcome of pressure coming from exogenous forces that sought to compel the *économistes* to prove their beloved truths. There were at times forces mobilised in the battleground of the public opinion and counterarguments placed in theoretical corpora written by highly radicalised fellow members that belonged to contenders' intellectual cliques. In particular, fellows of the Encyclopaedic circle showed themselves as the most punctilious and stubbornly enemies of the *économistes'* evidence. In the journal *Correspondance littéraire*, Diderot and Grimm propagated continuous assaults against the supposed validity of the *économistes'* way of reasoning and proving.[8] For shielding and bolstering their truths, the *économistes* were gradually compelled to make a move from evidence to observation. They were gradually pushed to revisit the realism of their unrealistic evidence. Poivre's observations played an indisputable role in this battle.

According to the *Encyclopédie*, Evidence and Observation made part of different philosophical branches. While the former belonged to metaphysics the latter did to physics. It means that one truth found proof in the inner mind while the other did in the outside world. Such a dichotomy transpired a transcendental debate that drove the minds of mid-century French intellectuals, which sharply opposed Newton's and Descartes' notions on nature. As Riskin notices, the vision was the "supreme sense" in the Enlightenment.[9] Newton had published *Optica,* in which book he expressed his ideas on the nature of light and its interaction with the senses and the configuration of human ideas. Blindness called, in particular, the attention of many philosophers: people wondered whether or not a blinded person who unexpectedly recovered the vision could associate figures with things.

Empiricists like Diderot warned against mechanical models that came to be denounced as "spirit of systems." The mathematical-mechanist approach to nature went through attack in the 1740s when the sympathisers of Cartesian philosophy of nature were discredited for their tendency to "capture and internalize the natural world by reducing it to a mechanical model that could be fully contained within a single mind."[10] Further, evidence and observation alluded to two ways of living the philosophy: philosophical modesty versus rationalist vanity. Vanity for assuming that one can capture in one's mind the natural world after having reduced it into a system of mechanical causes and effects. The evidence that the *économistes* preached was closely linked to this rationalist vanity. This partially explained the rage coming from empiricist intellectuals. In full contrast to the natural-law foundations of political economy, Cartesian philosophy remains less explored. Weulersse had long ago already called attention to the impact that Cartesianism had had among the physiocratic fellows but his insights had barely been taken further.[11]

For Quesnay's allies, the 1760s were essentially lived as a propagandistic time.[12] The group of economists agreed on the need to reach a much broader public outside the court palace and noble salons in Paris. Time has come to spread a new credo that blindly believed in market autoregulation and the defence of *fermiers*. Shovlin, who focuses essentially on the spirit of patriotic ideas, assumes instead that the decade was featured by the attacks that patriotic intellectuals propelled against the economists.[13] Perrot and Larrière depict the span as one in which a dispute on concrete observations flourished.

Their focus basically lies on arithmetical discussions that set the basis for the *Tableau économique*.[14]

In the 1760s, the *économistes* tasked themselves with the task to disseminate their doctrine.[15] The idea emerged that pedagogical efforts should be carried in the hope that this new social order be enacted consciously. This view is plainly developed in Lemercier de La Rivière's book. According to Weulersse, the propagandistic rupture went through two very specific stages. In the first phase, Quesnay's followers basically focused on economic matters: agriculture, finance, and commerce. Afterwards, juridical and political issues were at the head of the debate. This shift is particularly noticeable in some papers published in the *Éphémérides du citoyen*. There is no doubt that this propagandistic phase is somehow a reaction against the attacks infringed by contender circles. Shovlin demonstrated that the *économistes* were accused of defending the interests of speculative grain merchants and rich farmers.[16] Criticism notably arose because of the distance that the sect had taken from civic and patriotic principles, a style that caused rage among authors who upheld the learnings of the Humanistic and Classical world. In line with Pococks' Machiavellian moment, this patriotic rhetoric has recently been emphasised in regard to the assault infringed on the Physiocrats.[17]

As much critical as patriotic ideals were issues concerning mathematical proof, especially the data Quesnay needed to draw the *Tableau économique*. Historians have shown how data was gathered and analysed at both the local and national levels. Many efforts were carried not only to make the observations, but also, to adequately organise the figures later incorporated into the *tableau*. Curiously, the *tableau* represents the circulation process as an abstract model by hiding its underlying empirical data. This "arithmetical economy," as it was developed by the sect, allowed their fellows to virtually validate economic axioms on mathematical deductions presented as empirically supported calculations. Mathematical evidence came to give a boost to the irrefutability of the advanced arguments. One instance of this debate being the large versus small ownership. Physiocrats raised their intellectual weapons against those who defended small farming. In one of the very first papers published on the dogma, in which Quesnay advocated the interests of the *Fermiers*, several estimates were made in order to calculate capital advances, land resources, and productivity. Data along with the deductions these observations made possible were assumed as "concrete observations."[18]

This obsession with mathematics and mathematical evidence led the *économistes* to what Larrière calls "dogmatic rationalism." This dogmatism further escalated unsympathetic voices that were fully averse to the sect's overgeneralisations and arbitrarian and rather ideologically-rooted models. Many believed that overgeneralisations underestimated the peculiarities of contexts and cases, for instance, on land's uses and yields.

Patriotic ideals have been overrated without considering the scientific context in which they were expressed, used, and misused. They are mostly read within the frames of a "Republican tradition." Here I advance the idea according to which the 1760s witnessed an empirical turn in economics. I explored more in detail the overlooked role of history, and more specifically, what I call the collective writing of a global history of the property. I hold that this was a move that resulted less from an internalist evolution driven by the devotees of the sect themselves, and more from an externalist path set by the pressure coming from outside circles. This global history of property contributes twofold. On the one hand, it shows that "patriotic ideals" should not be decontextualised. They received different uses, some of which obeyed the logics of scientific agendas. On the other hand, I advance some arguments on the nature of history and the past as a field in which proof could be unearthed.

## "Walking in the night preceded by a torch"

The *économistes'* claim on the pretended irrefutability of mathematical evidence caused much intellectual discomfort and discontent among most members of the Parisian republic of letters. Yet, it seems likely that the true Achilles' heel of the sect was found not in the irrefutable mathematical dimension of the new science. Detractors threw the arrow towards what they considered to be the most fragile of all the targets: opponents devoted their attempts to disclose the philosophical foundations of a rather naive emerging celestial and pretended-to-be universal science. Up to now, a big deal of attention has been paid to the disgruntlement that the implementation of free trade policies originated. Scholars have also revealed the criticisms that the *économistes'* obstinacy with market natural laws caused. Their self-identification as *philosophes* has, on the contrary, received much less attention. What exactly did *philosophes* stand for in this name?

In spite of its ferrous endorsing of mathematical and geometrical evidence, the new science's foundations rested essentially upon philosophical grounds. It was precisely on this battlefield that a scientific fight broke out. Antagonists of the sect came to the conclusion that its practitioners were obliged to prove the seemingly self-evident principles they blindly embraced. In other words, an agreement seemed to have been reached that not everyone saw what they claimed to clearly see. The *économistes* took the challenge over and ultimately attempted to put deduced evidence upon a rationalist and empirical test. Eventually, the *économistes* got a dose of their own medicine. The debate ended up unveiling the extremely thin line that separated evidence from opinion.

Precisely, one of Quesnay's fellows, Lemercier de la Rivière, had pointed towards this polarisation. For him, evidence was the antithesis of opinion.[19] In consonance with the credo, the recently emerging science should stick to evidence and avoid any opinions. "A body of exact science, indubitable, demonstrative, based on evidence,"[20] evidence which was "the palladium of societies, & of the whole humanity."[21] According to the *Encyclopédie*,

"The term evidence means a certainty so clear and so manifest by itself, that the mind cannot refuse it." Indeed, this is a Cartesian way of seeing. Evidence resulted from the observation of one's own sensations. A certainty that was impossible to refuse because it appears as much clear as an actual sensation.

This implied the upholding of universality and atemporality. The natural order was, in Lemercier de la Rivière's own words, "a perfect set, made up of different parts, all of which are equally necessary to each other." Evidence lies essentially in the perfect harmony among the parts. According to Weulersse, the *économistes* "had absolute confidence in their principles, and, by a sort of inversion of judgment, they were inclined to believe that the rigor of the consequences they drew from them conferred on them an equal certainty."[22] Therefore, any knowledge on the social order should comply with a basic axiom: it should be at once "explicit and evident." It should reveal immutable rules (this was precisely the feature that physiocrats liked so much on China's model, one country ruled by an immutable order set up since the dawn of time).

Opinion, on the contrary, was pure arbitrariness. Two main features could be ascribed to evidence. Firstly, it could pass any test, therefore, total freedom of speech and print should be guaranteed for evidence to be contradicted. Secondly, evidence should be submitted to sufficient examination: it should appear sensible, manifest. A new trinity thus consolidated as evidence, it means, as a truth which was so explicit that everyone was compelled to agree with. The harmonic perfect set was made up of three universal principles: property, liberty, and security.

## Notes

1 Bibliothèque Municipale d'Angers, Manuscript 613. Available on Pierre-Poivre.fr.
2 Gustave Schelle, ed., *Oeuvres de Turgot. Et Documents Le Concernant* (Paris: Institut Coppet, 2018), Vol. I, 467, II, 18, 350.
3 Jürgen Osterhammel, *Unfabling the East*; Ashley Eva Millar, *A Singular Case: Debating China's Political Economy in the European Enlightenment* (Montreal: McGill Queen's University, 2017).
4 *Éphémérides Du Citoyen, Ou Bibliothèque Raisonnée Des Sciences Morales* et Politiques (Paris, 1767), Vol. III, 14.
5 M. de la Rivière, *L'ordre Naturel et Essentiel Des Sociétés Politiques*, 2 vols (London: Chez Jean Nourse, libraire and Chez Desaint, Libraire, 1768).
6 Jean-François Melon, *A Political Essay upon Commerce.* Written in French by Monsieur M. Translated, with Some Annotations, and Remarks by David Bindon (Dublin: Printed for Philip Crampton, 1738), 358.
7 For a discussion on ideology see, Thomas Piketty, *Capital et Idéologie* (Paris: Seuil, 2019).
8 Yves Citton, *Portrait de l'économiste En Physiocrate: Critique Littéraire de l'économie Politique*; John Shovlin, *The Political Economy of Virtue.*
9 Jessica Riskin, *Science in the Age of Sensibility*, 10.
10 Jessica Riskin, 69–70.
11 On evidence see Liana Vardi, *The Physiocrats and the World*, 76.
12 Georges Weulersse, *Le Mouvement Physiocratique*, Vol. I, 131.
13 John Shovlin, *The Political Economy of Virtue.*

14 Jean-Claude Perrot, 'La Comptabilité Des Entreprises Agricoles Dans l'économie Physiocratique'; Catherine Larrère, 'L'arithmétique Des Physiocrates: La Mesure de l'évidence', *Histoire et Mesure* 7, no. 1–2 (1992): 5–24; Loïc Charles, 'The Visual History of the Tableau Économique'.
15 *Éphémérides Du Citoyen, Ou Bibliothèque Raisonnée Des Sciences Morales et Politiques*, Vol. II, 55.
16 John Shovlin, *The Political Economy of Virtue*, 113.
17 "Much of the political economy elaborated and embraced by ordinary elites was animated and shaped by a patriotic impulse…Patriots sought to create a political community in which citizens subordinated their private interests to the welfare of the public, a polity stirred by the same spirit of the civic virtue that had characterized the republics of the ancient world" John Shovlin, 5. In the same line see, Arnault Skornicki, *L'économiste, La Cour et La Patrie.*
18 Catherine Larrère, 'L'arithmétique Des Physiocrates'.
19 M. de la Rivière, *L'ordre Naturel et Essentiel Des Sociétés Politiques.*
20 *Éphémérides Du Citoyen, Ou Bibliothèque Raisonnée Des Sciences Morales et Politiques*, Vol. I, 22.
21 *Éphémérides Du Citoyen, Ou Bibliothèque Raisonnée Des Sciences Morales et Politiques*, Vol. II, 54.
22 Georges Weulersse, *Le Mouvement Physiocratique*, Vol. II, 125.

# 5 Property rights

## A global history

When economics emerged as a science, the *économistes* self-identified as *philosophes*. This is a rather bizarre feature that would surprise many of its current practitioners. This word involves multiple meanings proper to the eighteenth century. In the words of Chesneau who wrote the entry for the *Encyclopédie*: "nothing is easier to acquire today than the name philosopher, an obscure and retired life, a few outward signs of wisdom, with a bit of reading, are enough." According to him, a philosopher endeavours to "bring causes to light." The philosopher "forms his principles on the basis of an infinite number of discrete observations." A very feature set apart philosophers from other people. The latter "adopt a principle without thinking about the observations that produced it: they believed that the maxim exists, so to speak, in itself." Instead, the philosopher "follows the maxim to its source; he examines its origin; he knows its true value, and only makes the use of it that is appropriate."

Ownership was one of those principles that should be chased to their very first origins. The search for ownership's roots and origins (abstract and empirical) paved the way for an algid debate. Contrary to the prevailing tendency in much of the nineteenth century and the first decades of the twentieth century when the property was somehow taken for granted by economists,[1] in the mid-eighteenth century it lay at the very core of the main economic theoretical debates. Its foundations lie in natural law theory and philosophy. Indeed, explanations on the origins and evolution of property rights were closely linked to the contradictions between common well-being and private interests.[2] In a paper published in the physiocratic journal, the author advocated that "Provided that personal interest is not unjust, vexatious and tyrannical, it never tends to anything but the general good. Everybody can and must try to make his fate the best, without harming anyone else."[3]

The devotees of the sect contended that clearly defined property rights were a precondition for farmers to willingly increase productivity. Otherwise, nobody would be interested in investing their capital and labour, and in consequence, agriculture would not prosper. This seems somehow self-evident. Yet, offering an unbeatable philosophical foundation for the sacrality of the

DOI: 10.4324/9780429028199-7

property was easier said than done, especially when what was at stake was the need to convince a highly sceptical intellectual milieu.

The debate on the landed property was closely linked to the above-mentioned attack on the Feudal system, and went beyond the legitimation of large land-holding. It is now widely accepted that the *économistes* drew their main ideas from Locke, even though they reread his viewpoints from a very particular way. No matter the strength and appeal that Locke's ideas might have caused, these were precisely the same years in which Hume's sensationism and empiricism began to gain traction among thinkers belonging to different Parisian intellectual circles.[4] In 1754, the second edition of Locke's *Theory of Civil government* was published in French (the preface advised on the many mistakes of the 1724 translation). As one should expect from an order produced by nature itself, it was in man's own nature that the *économistes* expected to find the clue for vouchsafing the roots of ownership.

The natural-law foundations of economic thinking have widely been studied.[5] The foundations of free trade, and more in particular, the grain free trade policies implemented in the 1760s were highly associated with juridical axioms. The laws of the market acquired sense only when they were put into the framework of the natural law. The natural law, such as it had made headway since Grotius to Locke,[6] set the basis for the principles of the market to be disclosed. Quesnay himself wrote the entry on *Droit naturel* in September 1765 at the apex of the debate on evidence.[7] Quesnay's paper had been first published in the *Journal d'agriculture, commerce et des finances*. Later, for instance, Boesnier de l'Orme began his *De L'esprit du gouvernement économique* with a chapter on ownership. Within his understanding, the right of ownership was closely tied to the capacity and right to enjoy one's body and force.[8] In this sense, the fruit ripened on a tree, in a wild country, belongs to nobody. It is then a common benefit of nature. It transferred into the property in the hand of the one who picked it. For Lemercier, in turn, the right to provide for one's own preservation included the right to acquire, by one's own research and work, the things useful to one's existence, and the right to preserve them after having acquired them. Nature itself has endowed human beings with the "exclusive property" of one own's body and whatever thing one acquired with one's work.[9]

Even though Quesnay became a reference for the application of the principles of natural law to emerging economics, he was far from being the only reference in the mid-eighteenth century. Other authors, who are barely mentioned nowadays, regained particular attention. If we consider the length allocated to a review published in 1767, precisely at the height of the discussion, one might be tented to think that Martin Hubner's book on natural law could have played an essential role in the debates. The reviewer reviewed not a new release but an extremely hard-to-find copy of which a new edition was announced. A "matchless landmark oeuvre:" this is how the journal's readers were introduced to *L'essai sur l'histoire du droit naturel*. Hubner has passed mostly unnoticed. Readers, however, read his oeuvre and extracted content from his book in new forms that were much in line with the leads the 1760s debate on the property took.

According to the journal's editors, this book "was by force the precursor" of the school's *Bibliothèque raisonnée des sciences morales et politiques*. It was made up of four parts. The first part thoroughly defined what natural law actually was. The second part minutely disclosed its origins. Finally, the last section tracked down its evolution over centuries. It was precisely this latter part that called the editors' attention in particular. Natural law was conceived of as the compulsory law with which reason had endowed human beings for them to pursue their own happiness. As the editors stated, "The simplest and best-felt truths are almost always the most difficult to express." From Hubner's assumption, readers could deduce that the search for happiness was the only guideline that conducted human actions. This was the very and only axiom one needed in order to understand and explain human behaviour. The reviewer acknowledged that this principle had developed in varying degrees over the centuries. This was precisely the reason why the book was key at that precise moment in which the offering of observable evidence became much essential. Hubner had devoted his attention to disentangling how, over history, natural law (it is, the means of human happiness) had gradually progressed in different historical societies. For so doing, a volume was allocated to ancient times and a second one to the Modern Age.

The reviewer minutiously described the features that Hubner assigned to each one of the societies under scrutiny. The book appropriately recognised that China's government had for centuries been subservient to natural law although great dissatisfaction was shown because of the little room Hubner had allocated to the Asian Empire, at least when compared to the plenty of room allocated to Ancient Rome. This was precisely a point of sharp disagreement among fellows that belonged to circles of intellectuals who sought inspiration in the Classic Age and the *économistes* who insisted on looking elsewhere. The reviewer did not miss the opportunity to warn his readers that a meticulously and well-elaborated analysis of the Chinese government would be in short ready and available for those ones who desired a more detailed assessment; the piece, which would come to complement Hubner's ideas, had been drafted by the "Master" himself. The reviewer was evoking Le *despotisme de la Chine*, which has received a big deal of consideration on the part of the scholars. This is, however, not the case with another paper that also provoked a hot debate among Quesnay's contemporaneous: *Analyse du gouvernement des Incas du Pérou*. Both papers were published in the same year.

The empirical turn took partially the form of a historical turn. My point is that once attacks unceasingly reverberated and the *économistes* laid bare in his incapacity to demonstrate their assumptions, and once discontent boosted their encroachment to a set of assumptions that had been transformed into a faith, the *économistes* sheltered themselves into the lessons that history could teach. Perhaps despite themselves. Foregoing societies were transformed into a dear field through which observing and proving. Poivre's travel account should be read within this context. His observation of Asian societies made more sense when placed into the set of observations that other past societies offered. In particular, Peru and Lacedaemon (Sparta).

## History matters

Ever since the *économistes* (and the economists) have received indictments for their disdain for history. Then and now. In their desperate race for finding universal laws, insights drawn from history were just kept down, let alone simply ignored. This is, however, an assertion that calls for care and one which lacks accuracy. Both Weulersse and Cheney have brought to light how fellows of the sect did resort to history no matter their concern for abstract laws. Weulersse was the first to come up with the idea that the physiocrats blueprinted a new "economic history" different from the "authoritative" classical history: history intended to test and not to ground.[10] In turn, Cheney has recast the key role that the so-called "history of commerce" had among some of the devotees. Physiocrats' attitudes towards history change colours when we move away from theoretical opus to propagandistic means. Cheney accounts 14.4 per cent of the 1,550 articles published in the *Ephémérides* as being part of "historical or exotic demonstration." In the case of the equally renowned *Journal de l'agriculture de commerce et de finances*, at least 14 per cent of 1,280 articles were devoted to history, geography, and voyages.[11]

Only a part of the debates on these uses of history have been brought to the front, the one labelled as the history of commerce.[12] Yet, another substantial debate emerged upon the form of the history of landed property. There were many reasons why to use the past as a way to find solutions to economic dilemmas. On the one hand, history could be useful and singularly effective in reaching a public habituated to narrative rather than abstract ways of thinking. This is a matter which still needs more research. Testing abstract ideas through the uses of historical cases seems to have become trending in the 1760s. The question arose as to whether economic assumptions could be tested through history. This was precisely the case with landed property. The unearthing of evidence left by foregoing societies could help the economists in validating orthodox principles, which many in the Parisian intellectual milieu refused to admit without a critical test. While Poivre demonstrated the validity of the axiom through his observations on China, others, like Quesnay himself, advanced ideas on Peru, but without doubt, it was Sparta the society which received most attention. All these cases were deployed in order to persuade readers that landed property structure was at the very foundation of any society. Let's thus compare some of the trending cases: Peru, Sparta, and China.

## Property and wealth: the Andes

Much less quoted than his often invoked *Le Despotisme de la Chine*, Quesnay's *Le gouvernement des Incas* allegedly stirred a hot debate among his fellows.[13] In particular, the paper sketched how produced wealth circulated through the different social classes. The analysis was perhaps intended to clearly illustrate Quesnay's broadly incomprehensible *Tableau*. The Andean indigenous society became therefore a precious testing field, still more giving the fact that the agrarian structures that prevailed for a long time in South America shared many features with French agrarian patterns.

Quesnay's main assumption was that in the Andean prehispanic world no one possessed the land as his own nor could one inherit it. Arable land was divided into three shares each one allocated and reallocated with the intent to provide for the needs of three specific classes: one third to the priesthood, one third to the farmers (*colons*), nobles and lords of the provinces, and finally, the last third whose output belonged to the king. The two former groups were considered mere tenants. The church's land product was destined to build temples and feed the priesthood. The largest part, however, was stockpiled meant for famine times. The sovereign's land product net was put into service for both public works and war-making. A considerable share was, however, stored to assure the subsistence of peasants when scarcity struck.

In this harmonious Amerindian society, colons could claim the totality of the crop farmed out in their respective strips of lands. It could be affirmed that they obtained "half of the total output" of each harvest. No one, however, had the right to claim ownership. Land was cyclically redistributed in order to match households' ever changing demographic tendencies "the number of subjects was the measure which regulated an equitable division of the plots of land; each one had right to it." Yet, only crops could be claimed as property. Enclosed lands in France somehow resembled this pattern. It was believed that this social order fully complied with the natural one and lasted for centuries until an unexpected fatal event caused its annihilation (Figure 5.1).

In offering evidence on one of the underlying assumptions of his much-misunderstood *Tableau économique*, Quesnay was likely to admit that, in the Inca Empire, the property was nonexistent. It is hard to ascertain whether or not, at that moment, the "European Confucius" was fully aware of the rebuttal that his excerpt would unleash or whether the paper was drafted on purpose. If the property were the main foundation upon which social order was built, how on the earth could it be possible for the existence of a society in which landed property was but unknown? The journal's editors immediately offered a reply to one of the readers who noticed the apparent contradiction. The reason he offered is quite curious: this was a national order.

The paper was titled in a provocative manner: "On the origin and need for inherited landed property." The reply written by Quesnay himself in only a few words could be considered, assured the editor, the sketch of a theory of landed property. The theory indeed recalled the axioms of natural law: above anything else one was compelled to purvey for one's own subsistence. A guide led one in this path: pleasure and pain along with wants, hope, and fear. Purveying for one's own subsistence was the first work any human was endeavoured with. The natural state, before civil society came of age,

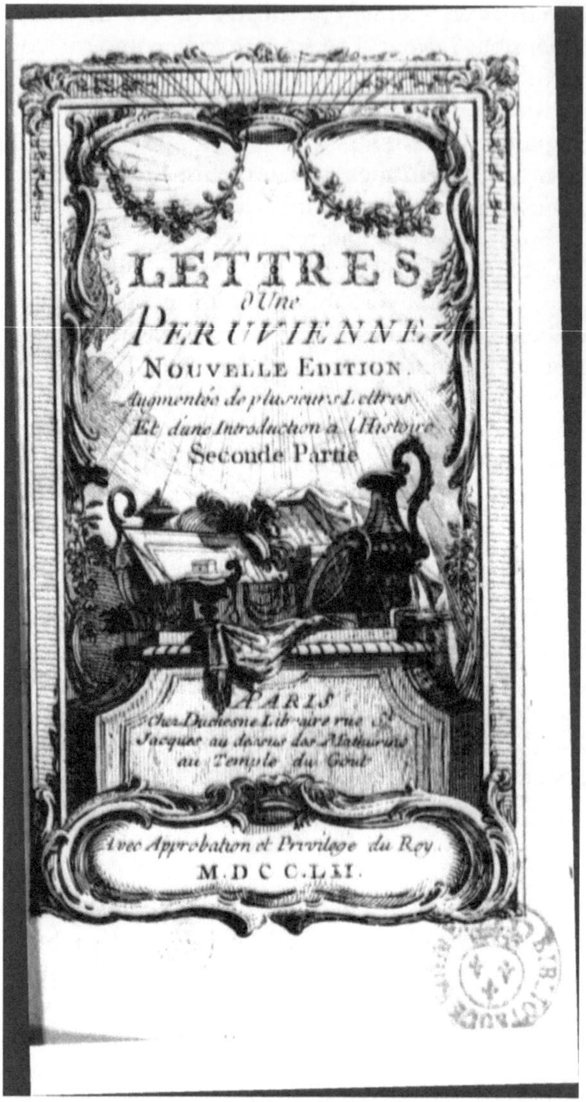




*Figure 5.1* Cover of the Book Lettres d'une péruvienne
Source: Françoise de Graffigny, *Lettres d'une péruvienne* (Paris: Chez Duchesne, 1752)

was one of total peace. As nature itself demonstrated, everybody enjoyed the liberty to care for one's own subsistence. Those who had depicted a natural state of barbaric war should look at the natural world in order to realise how mistakeful this assumption was.

A second stage had followed in which cultivation had led humans to happiness and the species to its natural reproduction. Once people had begun to gradually settle in a place, landed property was the next step to follow. In this regard, a comparison could be drawn between the nomad communities in America and the ancient Germans. The former were only devoted to gathering those fruits that nature offered, the latter, in spite of having more lasting settlements, only claimed the product of the land. In this northern European societies, custom said that land should be cyclically allocated for which reasons "our ancestors were then poor and sauvage."

It would be a great mistake to assume that only an annual amount of labour applied to the ground could be sufficient to yield its full productive capacity. Lands required immense works such as irrigation channels without which fields remained unfertile. These factors partially explained the ultimate emergence of landed property. Somehow mockingly, and in a manner that seems to be a countering against Rousseau's frequently quoted statement, the author recalled that before anyone could have claimed a field as property, "he had first to say I belong to this field, so he can say afterwards, not that this field belong to mine but to us for I would be not the only one to enjoy from its fertility."

Landed property emerged because it had served to guarantee at once "the general well-being and the private prosperity." Through its establishment, humankind had ultimately found a path out of unforeseen and incessant famines. Two social classes with reciprocal interests had then come of age: those who cultivated and those who protected the rights over land. The emergence of landed property should not be understood as a series of "usurpations that some members of the society inflicted to harm the others, as the common people sometimes imagine, and as so-called philosophers have dared to write, all of them accustomed to confuse, blame and destroy every matter." A "tutelar force," however, was required to guarantee landed property. In this sense, "the public power" was a precondition for property to exist. Therefore, the "tutelar force" was in all evidence "the source of diligent and sedentary work." "The right, the want, and the power of enjoying" gave rise to this needed "co-ownership."[14] Inheritance along with the potential commercialisation of the inherited land were means through which owners were encouraged to improve cultivation. Varieties in this order depended, in turn, in the equilibria of power involving the "two co-owner classes."

Those precise interlinks between the safeguarding of property, workforce applied to an owned field, the private interest, and the public well-being were the foundations upon which "social order" had consolidated. Yet, it should be recognised that different "national orders" adapted or modified those principles according to time, place, and circumstances. Two underlying reasons, in turn, explained the variations. On the one hand, geographical and climatic conditions. On the other hand, equilibria of power between the two social classes. Different types of soil required varying amounts of capital, which no doubt had an impact on the emerging social order. This could be the topic of a "beautiful theory that would deserve to be developed in philosophical oeuvres."

Two factors accounted for the peculiarities of the Inca order: no need for public works and the non-existence of money. In those societies in which metallic currency was nonexistent, officials, warriors, and priests allocated themselves portions of land or the crops those lands produced. This was the case in Peru as it had been in Ancient China and Egypt. Once metallic money was introduced, this order had been totally disrupted. Thereafter, everyone coveted only those "representative signs" of wealth. Under the reign of money, "one is dazzled by the efficiency of the universal right of representation which it has as currency" hardly "penetrating beyond the actual wealth it represents." Therefore, it began prevailing the "illusory principle that reduces everything to money, considered not as an image but as a reality in itself."

Quesnay was not alone in holding the assumption that nonexistent property could be even beneficial for the maintenance of social order. A similar argument was advanced in the *Lettere Americane*, a paper published by one of the fellows of the Milanese *Il Caffè* Gianrinaldo Carli.[15] During his Padua university years, Carli had absorbed a particular pleasure for classical studies but also a delight for modern philosophy. His pondering on the Inca government refuted some mistaken assumptions on the Amerindian world, and in so doing, he offered some reflections on inequality.[16]

The letters had been written in Florence and Cremona in the 1780s so more than a decade separated his from Quesnay's paper. Carli disagreed with the perception that the understanding of the Incas' world was a mere Utopia or a pretended invention of European intellectuals. For him, instead, the Inca system "was the best of all the political systems already imagined or followed all over the hemisphere." It was necessary only to mention a reason why this society could be ascribed this feature. In the Andes, "men not only should have been happy but it was impossible for them, even not willing, not to be." Carli further compared the Inca government with the ruling norms implemented in ancient republics in which, according to him, equality was heralded as the quintessential organisational principle. Historical records showed that, in some of these cities, land distribution had been enforced at the dawn of time in an attempt to refrain future inequality. Apart from the policies designed to achieve this goal, it was hard to find among those cities any other policy meant to assure the subsistence of those inhabitants in lack of food. It was very likely that land distribution not supported by subsequent policies could achieve but little in stopping ever-increasing disastrous inequality. The learnings of those ancient cities should be taken seriously. The lack of proper policies led to inequality of heritages to such scandalous and totally inappropriate levels that one can notice "on the one hand the prepotent and insulting wealth, and on the other, the vile and shy indigence and misery." This was the fate all governments could fare.

Only the Incas had escaped this fatal destiny. Quite the opposite happened in the Andes thanks to the particular form of government the Incas had implemented. The government had found a way to keep all the "components" of the society in equilibrium. The achieved success owed not to the fact that their policies had been designed by philosophers or enacted by a perfect government. In the Andes, it was possible to observe certain harmony among private interests. The Incas, recalls Carli, seemed to have been quite acquainted with the difference between natural law property and legal property. The former involved the inalienable human right and need for subsistence and self-existence; the latter, instead, was related to the superfluous, and in consequence, a matter of legal modification. In the Andes, all the subjects were given the necessary for their subsistence but the superfluous was "absolutely forbidden." In the second part of this book, we will further explore mid-century debates on luxury.

## Property, equity and happiness: Sparta

According to Carli, several conflicts had eroded the very foundations of the Spartan society once bans on the property had been brought to bear. His narrative (which diverted from other ones in several points) goes that, in seeking to fulfil the main duty a ruler was responsible for, Lycurgus ended up putting Sparta into a painful path. For the sake of equality, he had forbidden both gold and silver, and further, he had distributed land on an equal foot. There was an agreement on the seemingly consequences this reform unleashed yet explanations greatly differed regarding their actual causes.

Carli, for instance, asserted that Lycurgus' laws enforced property but totally forbade alienation rights. This contradiction ultimately led fathers to ask for reforms as those laws contravened the natural order: they eroded the obedience that descendants owed to their progenitors, a natural acquiescence that partially hinged upon the bound of heritage. The disfiguration of the laws led finally to an increasing inequality and compelled ensuing rulers like Cleomente to make efforts in order to re-enact Lycurgus' forgotten policies. Those rulers, the firsts to have received the title of tyrants, had no choice but to flow the city. The artificially-introduced order broke the natural one and made family ties fragile.

A variant version put the focus on explaining the negative consequences that Lycurgus's laws brought about. In Lacedaemon, property rights had completely been removed and land equitably distributed among all the citizens. This historical process, which Hubner's *Histoire du droit naturel* analysed with due attention, befitted an appealing instance for the *économistes.* They found out that the ancient Peloponnese city could be a captivating case for those intellectuals who reproached the fact that more consideration should be paid to ancient history. Two main lessons could be drawn from Sparta's case. Firstly, no society could ever prosper in which a violation of property rights was enforced. The economists believed that ownership remained as the very foundation of social bounds. This was but a consequence of a natural order of things that placed oneself in the obligation to purvey for one's own existence. Secondly, a perfectly planned and designed equity was but an absurd chimera for no society had ever achieved that pinnacle.

That Sparta aroused great curiosity among mid-eighteenth-century readers is proved by the apparently successful release of two books, not to mention the commonly referred to cases like Mably's, one in 1767 and the second one in 1768: Mathon de la Courts' *Dissertation sur les causes and les degrés de la décadence des loix de Lycurgue* and Abbé de Gourtey's *Histoire philosophique et politique de Lacédémone*.[17] The latter's lengthy subtitle, which in turn recalls the former's title, is telling and throws light on the kind of issues the book dealt with. Indeed, readers could also avail themselves of one of the several editions of Plutarch's *Vies parallèles*.

Gourtey told his readers why Lycurgus had enacted a new set of rules after the advice of the Oracle of Apollo. He also made attempts at explaining the decadence that those rules unfolded. Several causes explained why the Great Rheta had been put into effect yet a preponderant odious inequality was held as the main reason. For Carli, a wish for equality had set the path to reform. For Gourtey, on the contrary, a critical inequality had obliged rulers to implement the reforms. When Lycurgus ventured to radically transform the city's constitution, a hideous inequality carried the day: "All the properties belonged to a few, and an awful indigence was found everywhere." To bring to an end this atrocity, Lycurgus had designed an equal land distribution and had imposed restrictions on any alteration in the years to come.

The legislation had been altered over time, putting Sparta on the road of a despotic government, and ultimately, forcing the republic's path to decadence. Equal land distribution was listed among the main causes of this social chaos. Land equality could not remain unaltered for a long time, Abbé de Gourtey acknowledged. For equal tracts of land to endure unchanged, demographic patterns had to remain immutable. Otherwise, either some citizens would lack land or only a few would reunite the largest tracts. This would no doubt precipitate the tearing down of wealth equality, a matter that worried Lycurgus as much as the "equality of liberty" did. Quoting the poet Tyrtaeus and the Messenian wars, the author held that many poor Spartans petitioned for a new redistribution of land but sedition obliged them to refrain from any reform. Responsibility lies in the Senate whose unrestrained authority disfigured the benefits of allegedly well-intended and sagely-designed laws.[18]

In the review of Hubner's book cited above, Sparta's path to decadence was explained otherwise. By implanting rules that overlooked the nature of property rights, Lycurgus had violated the natural order. His chimerical society of legally enforced and equally allocated rights missed a "legitimate foundation." Many reasons explained the failure of this model but nature itself explained why it was unlasting: soils were differently endowed so yields were necessarily different. Readers were well aware that not only Lycurgus had implemented land reforms in ancient times. A similar situation had happened in Rome, as Montesquieu advanced. Land distribution had happened at the foundation of the city. According to Cantillon, at the dawn of the empire, each citizen had been allotted two acres of land "which he was obliged to cultivated for his subsistence"; over time, however, "by the dispossession of some, the want of oeconomy in others, great inequality arose in such possessions; great possessions began nobility and power is the certain consequence of great property land."[19]

There was a missing piece in this puzzle. Giambattista Vasco, a famous enlightened Piamontese economist who in contrast to his Milanese congeners suffered much from the strictures of censure, discerned a difference between the granting of equal property and the sharing of equal portions of happiness. His book was written in Cremona in 1767 and published in Brescia two years later.[20] A French edition circulated even previously to the Italian one. That the 1760s saw a peculiar concern for property rights is corroborated by the 1767 contest sponsored by the Saint Petersburg Economic Society.[21] In line with some concerns raised by the Empress Catharine, a call for papers was released in journals across Europe in an attempt to find the best solution to a precious and urgent question: "Would it be more useful for society for peasants to own immoveable property or only moveable property, and how far should this right be extended?"[22] The repercussions of the contest were beyond the expectations, even for eighteenth-century standards. The society received 162 papers in different languages. Among the contesters stood renowned French authors like Voltaire, Marmontel, and Du Pont de Nemours. The prize finally went to a Dissertation written by Bearde de l'Abbaye. His paper was published along with the one of another contestant entitled *La félicité publique* written by Giambattista Vasco.

Vasco, like Carli, wrote in the frame of the southern Peninsular Enlightenment. "Happiness is the pivotal concept of Italian economic thinking during the latter half of the eighteenth century."[23] In 1749, Muratori published his book *Della Pubblica Felicità Oggetto dei Buoni Principi*.[24] His ideas found an echo in many young Italians like the Milanese Pietro Vieri who wrote his *Meditazione sulla Felicità*, and also, Beccaria and his much renowned *Dei delitti e delle pene*, both oeuvres being published with only a one-year interval in the 1760s. For Vasco, "a nation's happiness consists of the total sum of happiness of its nationals."[25] In other words, by adding up the happiness of all its members, one could estimate a nation's total happiness. Yet, the matter was not only one of reaching a measure of the quantity of happiness that a country enjoyed. Nothing would be more erroneous, Vasco upheld. It could easily be agreed that happier countries were those ones in which "happiness was more equally shared among the state's members." And he clearly stressed, "notice that I am not talking about wealth's equal distribution but about an equal sharing of happiness." Because "happiness does not consist of mere riches." But there was another reason: if the riches were shared with too much equality, a countries' agriculture and manufacturing sectors would be badly harmed. On the contrary, "an equal proportion of happiness among the members of a state would never harm the community."

His argument goes that equality could be reached in those countries in which peasants farmed their own land. Drawing on Muratori's assumptions, Vasco discerned what happiness was and how it could be estimated: Plenty of possessions and lack of evils. It could easily be agreed that two essentials contributed to achieving happiness. History, according to Vasco, could be seen through the lens of liberty and wealth. In the footsteps of Muratori, he realised that both liberty and wealth were a well-suited alternative to reconcile happiness and reason of state: It was actually in the state's own interest that many of its members enjoyed liberty and accumulated wealth, but as well, that happiness was equally shared among all of them. Vasco goes so far as to design a frame upon which land could be equally distributed, fixing a maximum amount of land for each owner. In his eyes, public happiness and landed property were interlinked. Peasants' right to land assured their happiness, there was no doubt. The opposite happened in a society in which lands were owned by a few and in which "farmers only got a salary." In those countries in which access to the property was assured, one will find greater liberty and wealth and a peaceful well-defended society. In his paper to the Society, he, therefore, altered the question, and instead, recommended its members to ask themselves a totally reshaped question: whether or not the state took advantage of others different from farmers to own the land.

## Property and freedom: China

Disparate as the Incas' and Sparta's cases might at first glance look like, two underlying lessons could be drawn from these instances. As the Incas society could teach the readers, in the Andean world the government intervened twofold, either by distributing wealth and avoiding a large accumulation of property to happen or by allowing the necessary and forbidding the superfluous. One's farming land was not one's own. These incessant redistributions of land had prevented inequality to destroy the very foundations of social order. The opposite situation happened in Sparta where the government's interference tackled the redistribution of the property but without caring about wealth distribution. In committing a breach of the laws of the natural order, Lycurgus' policies led to unrelenting inequality, and ultimately, to social chaos. Demographic trends partially explained both situations. In the Andes, population was the measure of land distribution so in each period tracts were allocated in accordance with households' needs. On the contrary, in Sparta, changes in population led to a disproportionate land concentration. So what seemed at the beginning a well-designed and purposeful policy had no other result but consuming the society itself.

Poivre's observations on China could have been thought as a means to find a midpoint between the above contradictions. The last part of the *Voyages*, before a general comparison was drafted, describes at length what the *philosophe* had observed. "We might remark from these observations, that agriculture flourishes in China more than in any other nation in the world."[26] The reason underlying that robust production of food was essentially a total respect for property and freedom. Let's see how Poivre builds his argument. A basic observation served as his starting point: "by what art can the earth produce subsistence for much numbers?"[27] Three possible answers could be offered. The author proceeded ruling out each one: techniques, knowledge, and technology. The knowledge spread through European agrarian books, both ancient and modern, did not differ from the farming techniques employed in China. One practice seemed to be radically different, though. After having sojourned inland, he had never seen a tract of land left at rest. Here Poivre opposed costume to the system: costume prevailing in Europe found no corroboration in systems of culture practiced across China. This costume, which was widely spread across Europe and which started just to be discredited, was totally unknown in China "Chinese have no meadows, natural nor artificial, and have not the less conception of fallowing." "The Chinese lose not an inch of ground."[28] Gardens of grass were not a need. Fields sawn with grains, as an experience of more than 4,000 years has learned, grown enough to feed both men and animals. Canals and rivers allowed for the avoidance of animal traction; human workforce being always given preference.

Neither different techniques nor farming customs explained the flourishing situation of Chinese agriculture. The explanation for that vigorous agriculture lay in the very foundations of a government that complied with the natural order. Laws that nature gave to the very first men were still enforced all over China. Those were laws engraved not on codes but on the people's heart. Poivre therefore opposed "obscure codes devices by chicanery and deceit."[29] China was a nation of farmers in which, from the dawn of time, emperors had gained fame as farmers. European missionaries and travellers echoed a ceremony performed every year in which the emperor himself disguised as a farmer. In this part, Poivre followed a commonly repeated narrative: Farmers who became emperors, emperors who inaugurated the farming season, and so on.

Surprisingly for a country with that population numbers, and in full contrast to Europe, inequality was almost nonexistent. Yet, it only depended on "merit and talent." Nobility was unknown. Equality among subjects resulted from the very first cause that kept land well cultivated. "The Chinese quietly enjoy their private possessions" so "he who purchases a field, or receives it by inheritance from his ancestors, is consequently the lord and master of it."[30] What an observer could see in China was that "the lands are as free as the people." That essentially means there were no feudal services or even fines of alienation. And here Poivre rose his voice against the tax farmers who for him "never amass more exorbitant fortunes, than when an unfavourable season has destroyed the country."

Precisely, taxation played a key role in preserving this equality. That Poivre's ideas on taxation were largely discussed in intellectual and government circles is proved by a set of questions Turgot wanted to be asked to two Chinese who were expected to come to France. Thirty of those questions concerned issues of wealth and land distribution. The first question regarded the disproportion of fortunes and the existence of wealthy men.[31] Furthermore, Turgot was interested in knowing whether "the large portions of land were farmed by their owners or by tenants who pay rent to their owners? Tenants used to share with owners a portion of the crops, and being the case, should the latter advance any kind of capital?" Specifically, regarding taxation, he commented that he had learned through Poivre and Verthamont that the tenth imposed upon the crops was the main source for the Chinese emperor. According to the former, the share of the tax varied depending on the land fertility: the best lands were charged a tenth while tracks less productive paid only a thirtieth. He wondered whether there was, for each district, a public register in which the tax was stipulated or whether immemorial custom prevailed.

This is exactly the same information Poivre offered to his readers. In China, the only known tax that the emperor charged on his subjects known as tenth was regulated following the nature of land: "in poor soils it is perhaps only the thirtieth part, and so in proportion." Furthermore, subjects knew that the emperor "would never in the least think of enlarging in it, nor his subjects have the least fear of such augmentation." Collected not by particulars but by governors, the amount of the tribute, no matter how small it was, produced the emperor a huge revenue. Subjects faithfully paid it because they were well aware of how the collected taxes were used. Part of it was destined, as in the Inca Empire, to supply the subjects in times of famines "when there is a scarcity, these magazines are free to all."

In the mid-century, discussions on property transformed into a battlefield. Pushed by antagonistic intellectual circles (particularly the ones affiliated to the *Encyclopédie*), the *économistes* were compelled to prove their assumptions not by evidence (as they assume that scientific knowledge must), but by observation. In taking up the challenge, history unexpectedly became a key matter. Opposing intellectuals pushed once more and compelled the *économistes* to integrate a large palette of societies beyond the small set of ones with which they pretended to reductively frame their analysis. Observations cannot any longer be based upon almost exoticised and highly romanticised overseas societies like China. Yet, a debate which was supposed to test the foundations of an imagined social physics supported on natural law ultimately unleashed in an unexpected discussion in which property was linked to liberty, happiness, and equality.

## Notes

1 Pierre-Joseph Proudhon, *What Is Property? Or an Inquiry into the Principle of Right and of Government* (Cambridge: Cambridge University Press, 1994); Harold Demsetz, 'Toward a Theory of Property Rights', *American Economic Review* 57, no. 2 (1967): 347-59; Geoffrey M. Hodgson, 'Much of the "Economics of Property Rights" Devalues Property and Legal Rights', *Journal of Institutional Economics* 11, no. 4 (2015): 683–709; Douglass North, *Institutions, Institutional Change and Economic Performance* (Cambridge: Cambridge University Press, 1991).

2 Albert O. Hirschman, *The Passions and the Interests.*

3 *Éphémérides Du Citoyen, Ou Bibliothèque Raisonnée Des Sciences Morales et Politiques*, Vol. II, 117.

4 Michel Malherbe, 'Hume's Reception in France', in *The Reception of David Hume in Europe*, ed. Peter Jones (London: Thoemmes Continuum, 2005), 43–97.

5 Catherine Larrère, *L'invention de l'économie*; Istvan Hont, *Jealousy of Trade*; Arild Saether, *Natural Law and the Origin of Political Economy: Samuel Pufendorf and the History of Economics* (New York: Routledge, 2017).
6 Stephen Buckle, *Natural Law and the Theory of Property: Grotius to Hume* (Oxford: Clarendon Press, 2002).
7 François Quesnay, *Le Droit Naturel* (Paris: s.n., 1765).
8 M. Boesnier de l'Orme, *De l'esprit Du Gouvernement Économique* (Paris: Chez Debure, freres, libraires quai des Augustin près la rue Pavée, 1775), 27–32.
9 M. de la Rivière, *L'ordre Naturel et Essentiel Des Sociétés Politiques.*
10 Georges Weulersse, *Le Mouvement Physiocratique*, Vol. II, 129–30.
11 Paul Cheney, *Revolutionary Commerce*, 150.
12 Paul Cheney, 87–116.
13 Auguste Oncken, ed., *Oeuvres Économiques et Philosophiques de F. Quesnay Fondateur Du Système Physiocratique Accompagnées Des Éloges et d'autres Travaux Biographiques Sur Quesnay Par Différents Auteurs* (Paris: Jules Peelman & cia, 1888), 555–62.
14 Pierre Du Pont de Nemours, *De l'Origine et des Progrès.*
15 Franco Venturi, *Settecento Riformatore* (Torino: Einaudi (edizione speciale per il Giornale), 1998), Vol. II, 700–37; Sophus Reinert, *The Academy of Fisticuffs*, 199–201; Till Wahnbaeck, *Luxury and Public Happiness: Political Economy in the Italian Enlightenment* (Oxford: Clarendon Press, 2004), 92, 146, 147, 160.
16 Sophus Reinert, *The Academy of Fisticuffs,* 82, 137–38, 145–46, 151–54, 178, 375–77. Boesnier de l'Orme held that a certain degree of land inequality made commerce rise. A larger inequality set the foundations for the refinement of arts and the emergence of foreign trade. Yet, "an excess of inequality on land and wealth unchained the decadence of the arts and commerce." Manufactures could not prosper without the existence of a certain number of owners whose rents entertained a number of workers. Consequently, it could be expected that the more refined arts arose there where some owners dispose of large rents.
17 Mathon de la cour, *Dissertation Sur Les Causes et Les Degrés de La Décadence Des Loix de Lycurgue. Par Quelles Causes et Par Quels Degrés Les Loix de Lycurgue Se Sont Altérées Chez Les Lacédémoniens Jusqu'à Ce Qu'elles Ayent Été Anéanties* (Lyon: Chez Durand libraire rue Saint-Jacques, 1767); François Antoine Étienne de Gourcy, *Histoire Philosophique de Lacédémone, et Des Loix de Lycurgue, Où l'on Recherche Par Quelles Causes & Par Quels Degrés Ces Loix Se Sont Alterées, Jusqu'à Ce Qu'elles Ayent Été Anéanties; & Se Précipita Ver Sa Ruine, Par Les Mêmes Causes & Les Mêmes Degrés* (Nancy & se trouve à Paris: Chez Delalain, Libraire, rue Saint Jacques/ Chez Valade, Libraire, rue de Parcheminerie, maison de M. Grangé, 1768).
18 François Antoine Étienne de Gourcy, *Histoire Philosophique de Lacédémone*, 48–50.
19 Philip Cantillon, *The Analysis of Trade, Commerce, Coin, Bullion, Banks, and Foreign Exchanges Wherein the True Principles of This Useful Knowledge Are Fully but Briefly Laid down and Explained, to Give a Clear Idea of Their Happy Consequences to Society When Well Regulated Taken Chiefly from a Manuscript of a Very Ingenious Gentleman Deceased and Adapted to the Present Situation of Our Trade and Commerce* (London: Printed for the author, 1759), 8.
20 Giambattista Vasco, *La Felicità Pubblica Considerata Nei Coltivatori Di Terre Proprie* (Brescia: Presso Giammaria Rizzardi, 1769).
21 Colum Leckey, *Patrons of Enlightenment: The Free Economic Society in Eighteenth-Century Russia* (Delaware: University of Delaware Press, 2011); Michael Confine, 'Les Enquêtes Économiques de La "Société Libre d'économie de Saint-Petersbourg" (1765–1820)', *Revue Historique* 227, no. 1 (1962): 155–80.
22 Colum Leckey, *Patrons of Enlightenment*, 66.
23 Luigino Bruni and Pier Luigi Porta, 'Economia Civile and Pubblica Felicità in the Italian Enlightenment', *History of Political Economy* 35, no. Supplement 1 (2003): 361–85.

24 Lodovico Antonio Muratori, *Della Pubblica Felicità, Oggetto de Buoni Principi* (Luca: s.n., 1749).
25 Giambattista Vasco, *La Felicità Pubblica Considerata Nei Coltivatori Di Terre Proprie*, 13.
26 Pierre Poivre, *Travels of a Philosopher*, 150.
27 Pierre Poivre, 133.
28 Pierre Poivre, 135, 144.
29 Pierre Poivre, 150.
30 Pierre Poivre, 162.
31 Gustave Schelle, ed., *Oeuvres de Turgot*, Vol. II, 462.

# Part II

# "A universal warehouse of workforce"

## Reindustrialisation, delocalisation, deurbanisation, and the propagation of economic maxims

# 6 Ange Goudar

## Does the republic of economists need transgressive authors?

### An iconoclast

"Travellers who write, do not set down things in precise order but as they see them. This variety, being nature itself, is preferable to art, the slave of rule and method."[1] This was the mind of an anonymous writer who availed himself of the much-used figure of the fictitious traveller in an attempt to denounce the corrosive symptoms of the mid-century European society. The book, titled *L'espion Chinois*, reached the public around the same years in which Poivre sent to print his observations on Asia.[2] The book seems to have at full tilt drawn the public's attention, becoming immediately a best-seller. The imagined traveller claimed to be a Chinese envoy who had been tasked to report back to Pekin about the undergoing European state of affairs. A claim was also made that the book was actually a compilation made up of letters dispatched from different cities in Europe. In the preface, readers were told that the letters had been handed on to the editor in the hope that they could be published and that anything more had been added.

The book listed among the bestsellers written by an eighteenth-century highly renowned yet nowadays forgotten author: Ange Goudar.[3] While Poivre's *Voyages d'un philosophe* offered his readers observations on China, Goudar's *L'espion Chinois* narrated a Chinese envoy's impressions during his European continent-wide visit. This was somehow a reversed mirror. The book was written not in a travelogue format but the form of brief letters, all of them signed and dispatched from each one of the cities the spy had allegedly visited. The first three volumes intercalated letters dispatched from Paris with the ones sent from Turin, Venice, Milan, and Naples. The fourth volume began with the arrival of the envoy to the British island, a nation to which the following volumes were allocated.

This was by all its features a demolishing book. One written with the mere intention to scandalise. A manuscript purposely drafted to appal some readers and meant to wreck the foundations of a European order ill for wars and luxury. In a style that resembled many other eighteenth-century scandalous manuscripts that fared censorship or that were clandestinely printed, the Chinese spy mocked all aspects of European behaviour.[4]

DOI: 10.4324/9780429028199-9

The spy's criticism stretched six whole volumes. Rulers, elites, fellows of the republic of letters: no one was spared satirical condemnation. The book portrayed kings consumed by power and maddened for wars whose appetite required a lot of wealth and great paraphernalia to be satiated. Moreover, a pernicious society obsessed with sexual desires and hazardous games was depicted. Into the narrative were integrated prostitutes turned into ennobling lovers who during their routinary walks fashioned futile luxuries. Young maidens willing to fulfil the desires of courtiers at Versailles were also mentioned in the book. A rapacious church whose sins were scandalous and whose wealth endless was not left out. Particular attention was paid to Londoners who spent a lot of money on opera plays and who learnt by memory Italian scripts just to pretend they knew a few words of the Tuscan language. Not to mention walks across London that proved the rudeness of its inhabitants and the dangerousness of a city crowded with coaches.

The spy echoed a ferrous dislike for, and reproval against a fully discredited intellectual elite. He was flabbergasted by the censorship imposed by lazy censors, but still more, he remained wordless before the astonishingly unreasonable number of printed books: "There is nothing easier at present in Europe than book-making. Genius has little or no part in it, it is merely a business of memory." For the Chinese envoy, a modern writer could be compared to a gardener who collected "trees from all parts of the world into a piece of ground of some acres, without any merit of his own but the labour."[5] Most of those books barely deserved the merit to be brought to public notice.

The republic of letters was dismissively depicted. It appeared as a humdrum intellectual world in which an author gained fame "if he exhibits in a new light what everybody knows." This ridiculous practice granted writers the consideration of being "an original writer."[6] Still worse than the insignificance of all those books were the ideas they conveyed. Notorious efforts had been carried at building a science whose maxim was "to doubt of everything." "Great labour was required to demolish all principles, and accustom the imagination to float continually between truth and falsehood."[7]

In spite of the booming book market, authentic authors were rare to find. The world of letters was fully influenced by a pernicious spread of widely voiced yet impressively questionable and tedious ideas. The absence of true authors did not mean that "the kingdom is in want of book-makers;" all the contrary "never did it abound so much in writers, but small is the number of those who deserve that appellation."[8] A simple reason explained why those commonplace and vacuous oeuvres could have regained fame. Renowned authors gained this title not because of the quality of their oeuvres but thanks to the faulty workings of a defective circle of intellectuals and the pernicious activities of engagé and sectarian journalists who, without any regard for the actual qualities of a book, filled up many pages with reviews merely with the intent to destroy or extol authors depending on whether they agreed or hated their arguments. Furthermore, wallets and not the search of truth remained the actual stake for those corrupted and biased makers of public opinion.

Consequently, those who owned the money and were ready to disburse huge sums were the ones who reached fame. In an analogous way, the envoy told his readers about his experience in a London bookstore. There, patrons in search of novelties should be recommended those new releases that matched their political likes and preconceived ideas. This was the only matter that really mattered. Many owned impressive libraries yet an observer could wonder whether or not owners actually read all those books that were rather meant to embellish their houses.

To search for authentic authors in an ocean of pretentiousness was a waste of time. A handful of conceited minds had even imagined it possible to arrange all the existing knowledge in grammatical order.[9] "Five or six men, who know but little, are to fill it with knowledge. Every leaf will be fraught with taste and erudition: there will be only genius wanting."[10] The spy admitted he would likely purchase the volume for the letter C, out of curiosity for "such absurdities in the article of China." It was evident that there was an illness for dictionaries all across Europe, the spread use of which could account "for the decline of sciences." Thanks to the common use of those defective libraries, people knew "a great useless things" but were ignorant "of more that are necessary." The spy recommended that no permission be given to any "bonze" to teach that scientific method in China for "a mind, once habituated to these sudden transitions, becomes unfit for that methodical and connected study, necessary to the abstract science."

Readers could find some enthralling economic reflections interweaved in the threats of all these sarcasm and criticism. The spy explicitly disparaged the transformation of France into "a universal warehouse of manufactures" (as the English translator put it), or in French a little different "a magazine universel de main d'oeuvre." Alongside, criticism was cast towards a hilariously deranged society obsessed with luxury. A world in which one finds a distressingly coexistence of luxe amid the lack of the essential goods.

Ange Goudar, like Pierre Poivre, is barely quoted and studied nowadays. Their works now in the shadows, however, enjoyed a wide circulation among the fellows of the eighteenth-century republic of letters, in general, and the republic of economists, more in particular. Poivre's observations, as has been shown in the first part, took part in a set of intellectual discussions regarding property and evidence in the making of a new science whose supporters fondly believed in the existence of universal laws. In turn, Goudar, whose bestsellers were printed around the same years, could be considered a propagator of economic ideas. Different from the closely-tight clique of physiocrats based at the Parisian court whose ideas remained highly incomprehensible for many of their coevals, Goudar's books (written in different forms and formats) contributed to the spreading of economic reflections to the large public.

Goudar was a transgressive writer/author of economic matters in the republic of economists yet he could hardly be associated with any of the three most famous mid-eighteenth-century cliques: neither fellow of the physiocrats nor member of the encyclopaedic circle nor friend of Goudar's friends.

He was rather an outsider. Apparently, this feature offered him the freedom to write in an open-minded manner. This second part will bring to the front Goudar's economic reflections. Five chapters will compose this section. It will basically concentrate on the interconnections between social existence and theoretical thinking.

To begin with, I will unveil Goudar's existence and the social dilemmas he underwent along with the intellectual debates he faced while he lived in-between societies. His social experience was marked by a non-stop motion between northern and southern Europe. He untiringly travelled across the continent, and that experience robustly impacted both the books he wrote and the outlooks he offered. One of his books, *Les intérêts de la France mal entendus*, reached great success, being immediately translated into German,[11] and lately, into Spanish.[12] Another manuscript that offered some explanations on, and recommendations for Naples's backwardness was condemned by the Neapolitan officials.[13] I have found an Italian translation that proved that the book circulated in manuscript form.[14]

Secondly, I will shed light on a specific way of building logical reasoning about economic matters. A logical way of organising the ideas that has so far been overlooked. While great endeavours have so far been made at disclosing the emergence of the universal laws that governed the market or to uncover the assumptions that guided free trade, less attention has been granted to the inquiry of a way of forming judgement about economic matters, one which, doubtless, was prevalent in the mid-century. This "will to know" took the form of maxims. Goudar's ways of reasoning reflected this logical way of approaching the economy and the patterns that organised the mechanisms of market economies.

Finally, room will be given to the main discussions Goudar advanced, in particular, his transnational approach to economic dependence and his explanations for England's rise and the pervasive poverty that prevailed in South Europe, especially Portugal and Naples. Further, I will analyse one of Goudar's core ideas: a universal magazine of workforce. He was maybe one of the first to have spoken about delocalisation and deurbanisation. Therefore, we will focus on the geometries and geographies of production, as he called it. One assumption underpinned Goudar's understandings of economic life: a tightly global commercial interdependency could put countries in the path of dependence. Therefore, it was necessary for any country to first assure what was necessary, the subsistence. Nothing was more dangerous than to be fed and clothed by other nations.

## Social existence and theoretical concerns

Living Europe madly. This thought could easily illustrate Goudar's lifestyle. In spite of having left but a few archival traces, Goudar's lifetime has been studied in some detail. Biographies exist on his private life in which he is predominantly featured as an adventurer of the Enlightenment.[15] This attribute owes much to the adventures he shared with his much renowned friend Casanova, an Italian expert on music.

Goudar himself would rather have self-identified as an "author" (perhaps an authentic one). A transgressor who faced a faulty republic of letters. An author whose books were intended to generate hassle. An author who gained his life writing on economic matters. The scope of his whole oeuvre was vast and encompassed several topics among which music, games, history, politics, philosophy, etc. In spite of the alleged repercussions and wide circulation of his economic books, Goudar remains totally unknown to the "republic of economists" nowadays.

He was born in the outskirts of Montpellier at the turn of the eighteenth century into a merchant and manufacturer family. Early in his youth, he worked in Turkey overseeing the quality of textiles shipped from Marseilles, the Mediterranean French city-port, and from 1662 free port, which enjoyed the monopoly to export clothes to the Levant markets. By chance, one of Goudar's first books dealt with the issue of Mediterranean free trade.[16]

Goudar's trajectory was stamped by singular situations and events. It could be said that he faced harsh times. As happened with many European intellectuals who dreamed of perpetual peace, Goudar underwent the fate of dynastical and international disputes that provoked much conflict. "During the last century, fights, sieges, and battles have prevailed."[17] Born in the midst of the Spanish war of succession, the outbreak of the war of Austrian succession happened when he was 37 years old. During those years also took place the war of Polish succession, the war of Jenkin's ear, and the outbreak of the conflict in Silesia. Later, just around the same years in which the first volume of his *Les intérêts de la France* had been sent to print, the seven-year war broke out.

France faced fierce international competition overland and overseas. Overland, a preposterous and pointless quest for the universal monarchy (as Montesquieu entitled his 1730 book which was penned in the footsteps of his considerations on the Roman Empire) had led the Bourbons to perpetually engage in wars with the Habsburg dynasty. In the 1740s, Italy became one of the war stages. Goudar travelled across the peninsula and lived there for two years in Venice and eight years in Naples. One of his books precisely focused on the latter's city's economic backwardness; the other one told the history of the Genoese revolution. Translated into English in 1752 and authored by an "envoy from the Genoese to the Infant don Philip," the book appraised why the Genoese had revolted against the senate and the noble class following the apparently surreptitious help in money and soldiers that the Ligurian city-state offered to the French-Spanish alliance. Siding with the Bourbons, the city was surrounded by the Austrian army and compelled to negotiate a truce. Once the enemies reached the city's wall, a popular revolution broke out.[18] Right after the end of the conflicts, Goudar moved out to Lisbon. This was an opportunity for him to learn about and give some thoughts on economic theoretical matters. In particular, the Lisbon experience offered him the occasion to articulate readings and debates proper to the French intellectual environment and to take them out of context in an attempt to explain the rise of England. These reflections prefaced a historical relation to the 1755 Lisbon earthquake that completely ravaged the city.[19]

Overseas, France had witnessed the rise of England to maritime dominion. In a few decades, the country had achieved dominion in both the northern and Atlantic trades. Those were also the years in which a certain Anglophilia got French intellectuals into madness.[20] Both Voltaire and Montesquieu visited the island. Like these French philosophers, Goudar lived in London in the 1760s, and again at the end of his life.[21] In one of his books, an imagined spy criticised the fact that the Chinese envoy had rudely lambasted the country which had allowed him to speak with no constraint.[22] Like many other French nationals, both Voltaire and Montesquieu raised questions about England's apparently unstoppable success; the former in a more positive way, the latter with some reserves.

Many were astonished by the formal and informal institutions through which English domestic and international affairs were conducted. Many were disturbed by the very fact that both the fate of a nation and its public well-being could be discussed and ultimately decided upon in London coffee shops. Out of doubt was the fact that the English navy had already overcome the Dutch contest so English merchants were no longer customers in search of, but instead, suppliers of freight. The mercantile contest in the Mediterranean markets had been conducted under the auspices of a monopolistic company, even though in those waters, many acknowledged, French traders and manufacturers were ahead in the race. During the seven-year war, alliances radically changed and France's everlasting enemy sided with the Bourbons against the English-Prussian alliance. The war overflew the European scenario, and the colonies around the world suddenly became a theatre of battles. This was a global war carried out to assure imperial dominion, one which sought to definitively set whether England or France should have global command in the years to come.[23] For France, the war meant the loss of a colonial empire in North America and the Caribbean.

## Notes

1 Ange Goudar, *The Chinese Spy; or, Emissary from the Court of Pekin Commissioned to Examine into the Present State of Europe*. Translated from the Chinese (London: M. A. McGuire, 1765), Vol. I, VI.

2 Ange Goudar, *L'espien Chinois, Ou l'envoyé Secret de La Cour de Pekin, Pour Examiner l'état Présent de l'Europe. Traduit Du Chinois*, 6 vols (Cologne: s,n., 1765).

3 Alessandro Ademollo, *Un Avventuriere Francese in Italia Nella Seconda Metà Del Settecento* (Bergamo: Fr. Cattaneo editori, 1891); Gianfranco Dioguardi, *Un Avventuriero Nella Napoli Del Settecento* (Palermo: Sellerio editore, 1983); Jean-Claude Hauc, *Ange Goudar: Un Aventurier Des Lumières* (Paris: Honoré Champion, 2004).

4 It is well known that nothing could be better for an author than censorship and to get a book burned into ashes see, Robert Darnton, *The Forbidden Best-Sellers of Pre-Revolutionary France* (New York: W W. Norton, 1995).

5 Ange Goudar, *The Chinese Spy*, Vol. II, 164–65.

6 Ange Goudar, Vol. II, 164–65.
7 Ange Goudar, Vol. II, 235–36.
8 Ange Goudar, Vol. III, 81.
9 Robert Darnton, *The Business of Enlightenment: A Publishing History of the Encyclopédie* (Cambridge, MA: Belknap press of Harvard university, 1979).
10 Ange Goudar, *The Chinese Spy*, Vol. III, 48.
11 Ange Goudar, *Staatsfehler Der Mehresten Höfe Im Französischen Gemählde. Eine Uebersetzung von Johann Albrecht Philippi* (Berlin und Leipzig: Rüdigerischen Buchhandlung, 1766).
12 Ange Goudar, *Los Intereses de La Francia Mal Entendidos: Destierro de Errores Comunes En La Agricultura, Industria, Comercio, Población y Navegación: Plan de Sistema Económico. Traducción Del Francés Por D. Domingo de Marcoleta* (Madrid: Oficina de Blas Román, 1772).
13 Ange Goudar, *Naples Ce Qu'il Faut Faire Pour Rendre Ce Royaume Florissant* (Amsterdam: s.n., 1771).
14 Archivio di Stato di Salerno, Anonymous, Cio Che è Utile Farsi Per Lo Bene Del Regno Di Napoli Neli Anno, 1797.
15 A. Ademollo, *Un Avventuriere Francese*; Gianfranco Dioguardi, *Un Avventuriero Nella Napoli Del Settecento*; Jean-Claude Hauc, *Ange Goudar: Un Aventurier Des Lumières.*
16 Ange Goudar, *Questions Sur Le Commerce Des François Au Levant* (Marseille: Chez Carapatria, Libraire près de la loge, 1755).
17 Ange Goudar, *Los Intereses de La Francia Mal Entendidos*, Vol. I, 65.
18 Ange Goudar, *A General History of the Late Revolution of Genoa* (London: Printed for the Author, 1752).
19 Ange Goudar, *Relation Historique Du Tremblement de Terre à Lisbonne Le Premier Novembre 1755. Avec Un Détail Contenant La Perte En Hommes, Eglises, Convents, Palais, Maisons, Diamands, Meubles, Marchandises, &c.Précedée d'un Discours Politique Sur Les Avantages Que Le Portugal Pourrait Retirer de Son Malheur. Dans Lesquels l'auteur Développe Les Moyens Que l'Angleterre Avait Mis Jusques-Là En Usage Pour Ruiner Cette Monarchie* (Haye: Chez Philanthrope, à la vérité, 1756).
20 Jean-Claude Perrot, *Une Histoire Intellectuelle de l'économie Politique* (Paris: EHESS, 1992); Arnault Skornicki, *L'économiste, La Cour et La Patrie. L'économie Politique Dans La France Des Lumières* (Paris: CNRS Éditions, 2011); Loïc Charles, Frédéric Lefebvre, and Christine Théré, *Le Cercle de Vincent de Gournay: Savoirs Économiques et Pratiques Administratives En France Au Milieu Du XVIII* (Paris: Institut National d'Études Démographiques, 2011); Paul Cheney, *Revolutionary Commerce: Globalization and the French Monarchy* (Cambridge, MA: Harvard University Press, 2010), 37, 72, 105, 128, 256, 257.
21 Jean-Claude Hauc, *Ange Goudar: Un Aventurier Des Lumières.*
22 Ange Goudar, *Lettres D'un Allemand à L'auteur De L'espien Chinois* (Geneve: Au dépens de l'auteur, 1764).
23 For a recent overview see, John Shovlin, *Trading with the Enemy: Britain, France, and the 18th-Century Quest for a Peaceful World Order* (New Haven, CT: Yale University Press, 2021).

# 7 The will to know

## The praxis of economic maxims

A mania for economic books. This hallmark clearly characterised the eighteenth century, an age that preceded any other in the profuse number of printed books. Contradictorily, there was no other epoch in which public opinion was so misguided about economic matters. This is how Goudar introduced his book on the means to re-establish the Neapolitan economy. Only in the last decade, he stressed, many more books have been published on population, agriculture, commerce, and the arts than all those published in Europe since the breakdown of the Roman Empire.

"I have read all those books, or quite all, and I have found but words. Once I applied those words to things, they all vanished." Goudar was convinced that ideas remained diffuse when books overwhelmed public opinion. He analogised that mania for economic books with the obsession that a king had for a time. This monarch was so anxious about the exact "time of his existence" that he ordered fifty clocks to be hung in his apartment: "Thereafter, he had no idea about the exact minute of his existence."[1] Authors believed that an increasing number of publications along with the multiplication of ideas would ultimately enlighten the royal administration. They were totally mistaken, Goudar maintained. For a reason: "profusion is a sign of vice in the spirit." Therefore, clarity of mind needs no rambling: "there is only one path to truth, and when many are shown, the tendency is to head in the wrong direction."

A rigorous revision of the contemporaneous literature evinced a penchant for words. In his preface, agriculture, finance, and commerce opera were criticised indistinguishably. In an attack on the *économistes*, Goudar told his readers that in the library shelves, agrarian books were emplaced beside revered theoretical oeuvres on agricultural production. As a consequence, readers would find productions of the spirits where those of the land were supposed to be located. On the other hand, an incomprehensible jargon was conveyed in finance books, compelling curious and neophyte readers to leave books half read. In addition to that mania for exotic words, explanations on commerce were rather bizarre. After a million pages had been written on the balance of commerce, authors had solved the matter using a simple and meaningless statement: "the balance of commerce is the balance of power."

DOI: 10.4324/9780429028199-10

That was all that a reader was supposed to know. Amid all this confusion, no concern was shown for the "principles of the things themselves." In a phonetic play of words, Goudar affirmed that books were about "sound but not meaning." Balances of trade were in fashion so authors now devoted much time to estimate numbers with accuracy. Hard efforts had been conducting at estimating all the riches of a country: real estate, agriculture, and industry productions, luxuries. Sadly, this was a will that could prove rather disappointing for all those plucky authors obsessed with balances of trade. For one reason: riches changed endlessly and there was no certainty to find them in the exact condition once estimated.

Like the Chinese spy, Goudar dared to condemn the book production of his time, in particular those publications authored by the so-called *auteurs économiques*. Goudar was right on the apparently boosted number of new oeuvres. As we have already seen, the mid-century witnessed an impressive increase in the number of books. Topics expanded and translations multiplied. Economic matters were apparently discussed as never before. Both agrarianists and botanists regained large attention. In a similar way, physiocrats emerged as the sect that reclaimed the merit of having unveiled in the laws of the market the final solution to social mechanics. Gournay along with his group of friends published and translated extensively, and further, backed *laissez-faire* policies; one of them, Forbonnais, being in charge of writing the headword *commerce* for the *Encyclopédie*. This was no doubt the high time of the *Encyclopédistes*, and furthermore, the moment of the Montesquian turn in political science. Notice should be made of the impact that Montesquieu had on the emergence of the political economy, as Du Pont himself recalled.[2] While Quesnay laid down the foundations of an understanding of social behaviour and government that differed from the Montesquian model, Goudar affiliated with, and admired some of the ideas that Montesquieu had put forward. He made free use of Montesquieu, though.

There is no doubt that Goudar was impressively knowledgeable in economic matters. He mastered both formerly and recently published oeuvres. Fully in line with one of the criticisms voiced in the *Chinese Spy*, Goudar duly quoted and recognised his debts *vis-à-vis* other authors "it is much better to copy than to plagiarise."[3] He cited at length and avoided repetitions on topics he considered already profusely studied. Methodologically speaking, and at least in connection with economic ideas, two rules seem to have commanded the production of his pieces of writing. Firstly, know as much as possible and endeavour to unveil links in-between clashing ideas. Irreconcilable ends offer good chances to test new ideas. Secondly, indeed in a Cartesian vein, doubt of everything. No idea, no author (even the dearest one) should spare criticism.

It was thus crucial to master the inherited and recent intellectual production. Goudar's command of the printing, however, recalled less the number of books (or not only the quantity of) and more the capacity to masterfully command former and recent publications, but above all, the skill to consistently put them into dialogue. Throughout his oeuvre, one can immediately realise that Goudar read with an open mind, seeking in the authors what he could perceive by experience. Reading and writing were manners of destroying one's own prejudices and common ideas and an occasion for, through the implementation of sure principles, capturing the world. Writing only with the intent to reinforce one's own preconceptions served but little. Goudar seemingly refused any kind of dogmatism. He opened wide his eyes to observe the world and his mind to read thoroughly. His use of authors in a rather eclectic manner could lead one to think that his oeuvre was merely a patchwork of irreconcilable and conflicting ideas.

Goudar carefully drew on different concepts and principles and sought for those ones that offered consistency to his arguments no matter what their affiliations were. We should be careful of the fact that such a multifarious use of ideas could in any way indicate a lack of originality. Neither can we ascertain that Goudar was totally misled in his understanding of economic matters. As I will demonstrate, his thoughts show total logical coherence.

A commitment was crucial: to cast doubt on any author. Not even the most highly held writer, whose work one finds worthy of admiration, should spare criticism. Any idea should be put into doubt. "To doubt of everything" and avoid "to accustom the imagination to float continually between truth and falsehood." As the Chinese spy put it. No idea could be endorsed without a previous critical test. Even the much appraised Montesquieu was submitted to the first rule of the method. Consequently, only principles present in mind as evidence could be accepted.

It is quite easy to identify the authors who helped Goudar in organising and building his ideas. In his books, one finds a combination of references to both old and more recent publications. In *Les intérêts de la France*, for instance, Melon is cited five times,[4] Plumard de Dangeul seven times,[5] Forbonnais two times,[6] and Herbert one time.[7] Among the authors who are mentioned in other books appeared Mirabeau, Muratori, Hume, and Voltaire. The only classic author referred to was Suetonius. Strategically, Goudar seemingly incorporated either recent publications or authors known to the local audiences to which he addressed his books. For instance, while Forbonnais and Dangeul were mentioned several times in *Les intérêts de la France*, Muratori was cited in *Naples ce qu'il faut faire* along with Mirabeau and Hume, the latter authors being targets of criticism and derision.[8] Plumard de Danguel, no doubt, is one of the most quoted authors yet his book was mainly used to draw data or facts that supported Goudar's arguments. Strangely, Forbonnais' extensive quotes are related to agricultural and not to commercial matters, as one could expect. Melon remained at the very core of the book. He, in fact, provided Goudar with the kernel thesis: agriculture was the main source of state power. Montesquieu and Nicolas Dutot are quoted three times each. Either for the number of quotations or their length, Montesquieu and Dutot remained at the very core of Goudar's writing. The former, indeed, needs no introduction. The latter, instead, like Goudar and Poivre, fared the shadows of memory.[9] It seems to me that Dutot was the author who exerted most influence on Goudar, and not only in regard to his economic ideas. While Melon provided the main argument on agriculture, Dutot provided the main argument on money and population.

Nowadays, Dutot might be familiar only to a handful of specialists on mid-eighteenth-century fiscal matters. For the most part, and for the Enlightenment movement as whole, he remained rather in the shadows. Even his name was only recently unearthed.[10] In the 1730s, however, Dutot was widely known due to the hard criticism he cast on Melon, who, in turn, replied with the 1736 second edition of his *Essai sur le commerce* by adding new chapters that were expressly drafted to counter Dutot's refutations: Chapter 19 "observations on money" and Chapter 21 "on agio." In the first moment, Dutot addressed the dispute through a set of public letters; nonetheless, after Melon's second edition was already in circulation, he decided to rearrange his ideas and published two years later in two volumes his *Réflexions politiques sur les finances et le commerce*. The actual impact this book had on the French intellectual milieu is still to be correctly appraised. The book knew at least three editions in the first half of the century: 1738, 1743, and 1754.[11] It means that, when Goudar wrote his books, *Réflexions politiques* was still demanded on the market of ideas.

The Melon versus Dutot debate did not emerge out of nothing but on the ground of the monetary crisis unleashed by Law's financial laboratory. In fact, Dutot was involved in Law's experiment, having worked in his company. He was the son of a shipwright who, surprisingly, reached the top of the French intellectual world. An accurate observer and participant of the most dramatic financial crisis Europe had gone through in the first half of the century. We now dispose of more details about Dutot's life. The huge impact he had on Goudar's ideas and way of writing makes it necessary to depict a little more in detail his library.

Dutot's library was undoubtedly huge, holding 1,662 titles and a total of 3,279 volumes. It accounted for 40 per cent of his wealth at the moment of his death, high above many of his contemporaries. The large share of books belonged to history and geography topics (around 60 per cent); French history being 41 per cent. Travelogues appeared to be worthy for someone who collected descriptions of European countries and the West and East Indies alike (30 volumes). Translations of classic historians were found in a library in which classics were rather rare. Velde held that Dutot found in some seventeenth-century writers a particular fondness for "independent minds:" Guillaume du Vair, La Mothe Le Vayer, Naudé, Patin, and Richard Simon. All of them are rather unknown to us. In the field of mathematics, measurement and observation along with navigation, fluid dynamics, shipbuilding, were represented. As for philosophy, without doubt, Descartes was the favourite with six titles in a library in which Malebranche, Bacon, Locke, Pascal, and Bayle found a place. Spinoza was absent although Dutot owned a biography of him. Leibniz and Newton were equally present. Montaigne,

La Rochefoucauld, La Bruyère, and Gracián were "well represented." As for philosophy, it could be said that "Dutots' philosophical tastes, not surprisingly, were analytical and moral rather than purely metaphysical, with a strong tinge of criticism and empiricism."[12] As for political economy properly, the following authors were owned: Montchrestien, a 1700 French Translation of Thomas Mun, Le Pelletier's *Mémoires pour le rétablissement du commerce en France*, the French translation of Law's *Money and Trade*, and indeed, Melon's *Essai sur le commerce.* Books on finance, coinage, and prices dating to the sixteenth and seventeenth centuries were present. Dutot drew from these books the quantitative data for his *Réflexions politiques.* English authors like Locke, Child, Petty, Grount, among others are also found. More astonishing was his collection of journals which reached 680 volumes. Velde concludes that Dutot was rather a "man of the seventeenth century," 70 per cent of his books having been published between 1610 and 1715 and that "he found certainty in numbers, but he loved history and what we now call social sciences." A bibliophile and a *libertin*, a "free thinker" who hoped "that truth might be attained through reasoned argument."

Hume cited Dutot in his *Political discourse.* The Scottish philosopher used Dutot's book as a source of data for his "Early Memoranda."[13] Hume had lived in France in the heights of the Melon versus Dutot debate, and both Dutot's and Melon's books were rapidly translated into English in 1739 in London and Dublin respectively. Further, the *Scots Magazine* published fragments of both books as well as the rebut of an English author. Hume availed himself of the French debate and French crisis in his repel of Law's ideas on the allegedly positive effects caused by paper money and banks. Hont remarked that the use Hume made of Dutot was rather on date-drawing although Dutot's impact on Hume's thinking on money should be revisited.

Law endorsed the assumption that the artificial injection of money could bring growth to an economy.[14] While a shortage of money provoked underemployment, money issuing could generate growth by employing many more workers than otherwise expected. Paper money could substitute metallic one, the former being even much more preferable. It could be expected that inflationary trends would slow down because of the impacts of prosperity. In the second volume of his *Les intérêts de la France*, Goudar opposed the mistaken but widely echoed idea that the money stock had little impact on an economy, in other words, that 500 million and 1,000 could give the state the same "degree of power." On the contrary, he argued, "the larger the monetary stock, the wealthier and opulent the state."[15] Citing Dutot, Goudar called to mind the fact that state power owed to the number of its inhabitants, and that those numbers, in turn, were always proportional to the circulating money. Briefly said, the larger the monetary stock, the larger the number of workers employed, and consequently, a steady population growth. As we will see, Goudar added a few caveats related to the geometry and geography of monetary circulation, as he called it.

Yet, Dutot's influence on Goudar surpassed the fact of having been a mere source of data or a fountain of reflections on prices and the actual impact of monetary injections. Goudar's *Rélation Historique* and Dutot's *Réflexions politiques* followed a very similar structure. Dutot settled a series of maxims and dismantled each one in a subsequent manner. Goudar resorted to the same strategy, discussing 14 maxims. In his oeuvre, Goudar reconciled the positive effects of money issuing with Montesquieu's conception of gold and silver as mere "signs." Furthermore, in the same line with Montesquieu, Goudar maintained that mine-endowed countries barely profited from the bullion they exploited.

Montesquieu is said to have written the best book on luxury ever written. From the *Spirit of the Laws*, Goudar drew the distinction between *commerce d'économie* and *commerce de luxe*.[16] Nonetheless, he cautiously took distance from the underlying tripartite division of virtues and governments that Montesquieu vindicated. This author, Goudar contended, was a "great genius," who, erroneously, classified people according to the form of government. In this fashion, Montesquieu assigned a virtuous behaviour only to the Republic form of government (the government of many), leaving readers with the impression that people living under other forms of government were guided purely by vices.[17]

Goudar was in contention with the assumption that virtues could ultimately determine whether fiscal policies should be decided upon a republican manner (the opinion of many) or by ministerial discretion (the monarchy and the balance of power involving the king and the intermediate powers). In other words, it was hard to ascertain that "because of their different constitutions, those governments should be guided by opposing principles." Conversely, he maintained that in all countries ("even in the most absolutist ones") this branch of the administration should be guided by republican principles, which does not mean diminishing a ruler's power or corrupting a nation's constitution. Such a rigid Montesquian notion of government disregarded the maxim that should guide any government: it was advisable to emulate those countries which performed the best without any regard for virtues or vices.[18]

## Bewitched by maxims: a Cartesian economics

It goes without doubt that the most prominent economic book Goudar elaborated was his *Les intérêts de la France*, first released in 1756 and at speed translated into German and Spanish. His *Rélation Historique*, which was printed a couple of years before, was also translated into Spanish, and from this edition later into Portuguese.[19] This book offered an explanation on Portugal's dependence and on its backward economy. His book entitled *Naples ce qu'il faut faire* was immediately censored yet it circulated in manuscript form, some extracts being added to a compilation published in Switzerland. It somehow complemented and added new reflections regarding southern Europe's backwardness.

*Les intérêts de la France* was straight away publicised and reviewed in a Parisian journal, being advertised as having been written by a Montpellier merchant.[20] This fact seems to confirm that the book received immediate appeal among the fellows of the local Parisian republic of letters. His introduction as a "merchant" leads to think that he was yet far from being appreciated in the intellectual Parisian circles as a famous writer on economic matters, precisely the fashion in which Galiani would depict him ten years later.[21] Despite that, in the eyes of the scathing reviewer, the author deserved far more fame than the "crowd of beautiful subaltern minds" whose only merit was to know how to exasperate and irritate readers with their frivolous and disproportionately overrated oeuvres. Potential patrons should be aware of the likelihood to find a set of disparate assumptions drafted by a "fool" author. Goudar's mind and arguments seem to have been hard to frame. The reviewer further asserted that the author could not be considered as either of the following: profound politician, great philosopher, good writer, or someone with moderate and methodical spirit. Here, it appears crystal clear why *L'espien chinois* was so enraged with the Parisian journalist milieu. No matter all these shortcomings, the sceptical reviewer recognised that "there are but a few books on these matters more enlightening than his." This was a "golden book for ministers and all those who rule the country." The author was particularly informed and skilful to find the main problems although most of his recommended remedies seemed to be violent or just impracticable.

The oeuvre, however, is said to have been badly praised. In the preface to the third volume, Goudar himself bitterly complained of what he considered unfair criticism, more devoted to form than to substance. For him, fault-finders had placed too much attention to style and language, content having for the most part been disregarded: "Criticism was cast on the terms, the words, and prepositions; the merit of the book lessened by an apparently abuse of prepositions." He raised his voice against the existing mania for diction of which many French readers were fully impregnated. Fitting in with this unwise flavour of the age, books were read because they "follow a certain taste" and at all because of their actual utility.

This was an epoch in which everybody seemed to be eager for words, things, on the contrary, being unworthy of any due attention. To make things even worse, "great authors" had invented a fashionable jargon. In this world of words, the form prevailed over the substance "the mechanics of the book having become the book itself." One is tempted to think that the reference to a fashionable jargon was a direct attack on the emerging group of physiocrats. Apparently, the "free and unknown manner" in which Goudar had shaped his economic reflections caused much discomfort among many readers. It is hard to state what exactly a "free and unknown manner" of writing on economic matters actually meant. Further, the question arises as to the "mechanics of the book" itself, as Goudar named it.

When reading Goudar's books, a reader could at first glance have the impression of being dealing with a set of rather disparate and unrelated topics as well as unsound assumptions. A further deep reading, nonetheless, offers support for a strong logical coherence and a clearly chosen methodical approach that reverberated in each one of Goudar's books.

Maxims along with general rules assisted the author in shaping the thinking. They gave form to the thoughts. As no clue is given on the actual definition of maxims and general rules or what exactly differentiates one from another, it is hard to set an accurate explanation of their meaning or the exact intent with which maxims and rules were set forth. Maxims are sometimes twinned with what seems to be a deduced general rule. Sometimes, nonetheless, general rules appeared on their own, no maxim preceding or following them. In his *Réflexions Historique*, a total of 14 maxims were established (many of which designed for a local economy) and brought into play for explaining Portugal's backwardness. In spite of the unsettled definition, it remains plain that both ways of reasoning or giving shape to the ideas lay at the very core of Goudar's way of writing. Further, they shed light on a methodical approach that was usually employed in the mid-century to write on economic matters yet now largely disregarded.

Consistency and logical coherence characterised not only the 1756 book but also the former and latter ones. It is hard to find contradictions in the ensemble of Goudar's oeuvre from a logical point of view. This fact is quite more surprising given that, as we have already seen, Goudar read with an open mind a vast palette of authors and carefully incorporated their arguments when building his own. In that sense, Dutot's interlinks between monetary theory and population growth could go hand in hand with Melon's basic premise on agriculture and subsistence as the very foundation of any economy. In this regard, we should take Goudar's insistence in appraising form and matter differently. In this chapter, I will thus put much more attention to form.

Historians of economic thinking have profusely enquired about the natural law foundations of the new science.[22] Another branch of the scholarship has further highlighted commercial humanism, tracing its origins back to Machiavellian times.[23] In this approach, republicanism merged with this long-centuries tradition of renaissance political thinking that regained attention among intellectual circles in the mid-century.[24] Content along with context but not form, both aspects have already been objects of full consideration. As happened to many intellectuals in mid-eighteenth-century France, maxims were the particular form upon which the economic order was given coherence. Goudar was far to be alone. Quesnay, for instance, wrote the Maxims on government.

The philosophical foundations of this new-born political economy have remained a little in the shadows in comparison to its natural-law and humanist ones. By philosophical foundations, I mean rather the form than the matter of the thinking: the shape through which the mind is told and truth disclosed in a consistent manner. A conjunction of means of intuition and means of deduction came into play to apprehend the mechanics and geometry of the world. As if the world could be deconstructed and then projected in a new logical order. As if the world could be disassembled and remoulded. This entailed syntax (an order of words and enumeration), and further, training of the mind upon the rules of a method.

To frame the mechanics of the economy into an order of maxims demanded efforts carried out in order to shape the geometry of the world into a set of assertions and prescriptions. Indeed, the exercise of deducing maxims evokes a very ancient Greek philosophical technique. Foucault, in one of his later seminars, appraised them as "an exercise of thought on the truth."[25] Thinking through maxims was a form of philosophical reasoning quite common to philosophical thinking. They work simultaneously as "statements of truth and the pronouncement of a prescription."[26] Epicurus expressed his learning in both the form of maxims and statements. Stoicism was also expressed that way, an instance being the letters Senec wrote to Lucius. Perhaps the most famous maxim was the one found in the Oracle of Delphi: "know yourself."

Indeed, Goudar was one among many who synthesised his economic reflections in the form of maxims. The practice seems to have broadly been used in the mid-century even though it has regained little attention. Properly in the field of commerce, Melon advanced many maxims. In comparing the policies and institutions employed in England and Holland to promote trade, he asserted that the opposed policies were nevertheless "based upon the same principles and were determined by each country's circumstances." Melon even expressed a few of his maxims through Latin sentences. He invoked the Ciceronian maxim *salus populi suprema lex*; the fundamental maxim that should guide any government, a maxim of which, unfortunately, all the governments had abused.[27] *Panen et circenses* was another maxim mentioned in his book. As for commerce, "the greatest of all maxims, and the best understood" was that the only thing commerce needed was liberty and protection. Yet, if one of these had to be given preference, it would be much better to lift protection in favour of liberty "for with liberty, the power of commerce alone, can hold the place of protection."[28]

The logical coherence of Goudar's arguments stands in a more net manner when we analyse them from a Cartesian perspective. In his *Rules*, Descartes gives the following piece of advice "we first reduce complicated and obscure propositions step by step to simpler ones, and then, starting with the intuition of the simplest ones of all, try to ascend through the same steps to knowledge of the rest." We find therefore a path to logical concreteness of reasoning when the first maxim is incontrovertibly distinguished.

Any country should endeavour to produce "*le nécessaire physique*" (the basic needs). This maxim was highlighted as the foremost of all the maxims and could be deduced from the nature of things themselves. Further, this is in fit with the notion that, for correctly ruling a country, the first principles of the things themselves should be always present in mind. In other words, "it is enough to look after a unique principle."[29] This principle could be reached through deductive means: producing the basic goods was the only means a country needed to stand by itself. This was a truth on which no doubt could be cast. A sure foundation upon which to build a set of statements. From this point, a series of maxims could thus be deduced: "a country's degree of weakness increases as its dependence on the production of basic goods does."[30]

On that account, agriculture seemed to be the first source of state power. One can wonder whether the idea of subsistence is drawn from natural law or not. We have already seen that Locke's conceptions of one's own survival impacted discussions on property. This might lead one to think that Goudar also operated in a natural-law framework. Nonetheless, it seems to me that, regarding specifically the maxim on subsistence, he draws on the axioms of force and motion, it is, on mechanics. The question is posed in an indistinctly manner: Whence does state power stem? The answer: in finding its own source of motion inside itself.

Maxims and general rules could be logically arranged without setting contradictions among them. Yet, their logical interconnections remain invisible to an unaware mind. Agriculture was the true source of state power. If subsistence were the very source of power, agriculture should be the first activity to be encouraged. Agriculture improved through the enactment of wise policies, as a consequence, the most powerful of all nations were those ones that designed the best suited agrarian policies.[31] Whether a country could stand by itself depended on the force of their farmers so it could be deduced that farming should be granted preference over the industry. Moreover, within a country, an equilibrium should exist among those who were fed and those who provided the means of subsistence. Luxury drew peasants away to cities and disproportionately multiplied the number of servants, provoking also distorting prices. An increase in the number of those devoted to liberal arts generated a disequilibrium. Singles were deeply obsessed with luxuries, and furthermore, they "see nothing in the world beyond their own existence."[32]

A similar method was followed in order to unveil the principles that command population growth. A large population was a source of strength for a great state (even though this was a relative force and should be considered *vis-à-vis* other states). This force, however, stemmed from the available degree of subsistence, an assumption that, in turn, recalls the first maxim. Both maxims allowed one to deduce that a large population could be found only in those countries where farmers were a flourishing class. Therefore, food supply actually depended on the "*aissance*" of the farming class. This, in turn, implied an equilibrium in prices, the different economic sectors, and the number of workers allotted to each sector. Again, in line with the first maxim, it was assumed that the power of the state depended on this equilibrium between professions, which produced the "total of general work" upon which the wealth of the "republic/commonwealth" ultimately relied.[33]

The arts should always tread on the heels of the production of basic goods. Manufactures could generate happiness only in those countries in which they were set up on a consistent production of raw materials. Another reason explained why the industry should walk behind agriculture: while nature was already given, the arts were not. Industry harmed rather than benefited a country in which the manufacturing sector found its foundations elsewhere and not in the national agriculture. In this sense, it was held that industry could not be founded upon commerce since luxury varied over time. Luxury altered incessantly and was guided not only by insatiable and fortuitous tastes and inventions but also by *moeurs*, religion, and costumes proper to each society, which were hard to be modified from outside.[34] This accidental nature of luxury and industry compelled a nation to cement its prosperity upon non-accidental foundations such as the ones agriculture provided with. For agriculture to prosper, a geometrical distribution of both habitants and monetary stocks should be sought. Gold and silver being the only means that "contribute to form more riches." In consonance with the above two maxims, the means of exchange should be necessarily in proportion with circulating goods.

As we will see more in detail later, this set of maxims offered Goudar the framework within which three different economies were assessed: Portugal, France, and Naples. Portugal had failed to support luxury on its national production so the country should first avoid luxury, and above all, should promote the production of the "basic goods." France, on the contrary, was a country with a mania for extravagant goods. The country's privileged international position in the creation of fashions and tastes offered no opportunity to capture huge masses of bullion. Manufactures were supposed to attract larger quantities of bullion since large stocks of money benefited agriculture. Finally, there was Naples, a country that fulfilled all the conditions for industry to flourish but which remained in a terrible decadence.

## Apologists of machines

One of the most radical forms of criticism that Goudar raised was cast on the promoters of machines or what he called "*systèmes de machinistes*." Many foresaw that a time would come in which machines could work automatically, human workforce no longer being needed. In this regard, Goudar showed his disagreement with Melon who thought in an opposite manner and held that technology increased productivity without harming population growth. Those who supported that system and aggressed human workforce have barely deduced the principles of the nature of things and their only concern was for accidents in themselves. "I have carefully read the apologists and have found out that, for the most part, their support relied merely on vague reasons."[35] Three main criticisms could be raised. To begin with, supporters failed in seeing the differences between two contrasting goals: on the one hand, the need to give subsistence to a large number of workers, and on the other hand, the desires of a few well-off citizens for getting richer and richer. In addition, no one had enquired about the very origins of the arts. Finally, accidents in things were confused with things in themselves.

Manufactures should serve to accomplish the first of all maxims: to feed and clothe as many workers as possible. Diverting from this principle meant to violate the nature of things. Those who aligned with Melon and supported the spread use of machines were wrong by mingling industry's productivity and its capacity to employ the largest number of workers: "Two completely different things whether in principle or in goal."

Let's suppose, affirmed Goudar, a branch of manufactures that employed 10,000 workers and another one that yielded the same output with only 500 machines. There is no doubt that the former would provide subsistence to a larger number of workers and "by those very means reached a greater goal." Workers' consumption would in turn reverberate in the form of "small industries." An alternative explanation was commonly advanced merely with the intent to mislead public opinion. Apologists assumed that once those workers were substituted with machines, they could easily be allocated to other branches of industry or being in the position to effortlessly change their profession. Those wise authors were totally deluded because a learned art required a high degree of specialisation and too much time to be earned, and therefore, for jobless people life was too short to acquire the necessary training in a new branch. Once one lost one's job, one remained hopeless to find another one. Finally, the apologists wanted everyone to be convinced that a reduction in labour further enriched a country. No one, in contrast, paid attention to the way in which that new wealth was distributed: "no one cares about the fact that those riches are precariously distributed." Much of that wealth ended up in the pockets of "a few" who owned those machines. Yet, "it is possible to demonstrate geometrically that 10 million in the hands of 50,000 craftsmen enriched the state much more than 100 in the hands of 1,000 men."[36]

## Notes

1 Ange Goudar, *Naples Ce Qu'il Faut Faire Pour Rendre Ce Royaume Florissant*, 25.

2 Jean-Claude Perrot, *Une Histoire Intellectuelle*, 68; Paul Cheney, *Revolutionary Commerce*, 52–86; Céline Spector, *Montesquieu: Pouvoirs, Richesses et Sociétés* (Paris: Presses Universitaires de France, 2004); Catherine Larrère, *Actualité de Montesquieu* (Paris: Sciences Po, 1999).

3 Ange Goudar, *Los Intereses de La Francia Mal Entendidos*, Vol. II, 48.

4 Jean-François Melon, *Essai Politique Sur Le Commerce. Nouvelle Édition. Cette Édition Est Augmentée de Sept Chapitres, & Les Lacunes Des Éditions Précédentes y Son Remplies* (s.l.: s.n., 1736).

5 Plumard de Dangeul, *Remarques Sur Les Avantages et Les Désavantages de La France et de La Gr. Bretagne, Par Rapport Au Commerce, et Aux Autres Sources de La Puissance Des État. Traduction de l'anglais Du Chevalier John Nickolls* (Leiden: s.n., 1754).

6 François Véron Duverger de Forbonnais, *Eléments Du Commerce*, 2 vols (Leyden, 1754).

7 Claude Jacques Herbert, *Observations Sur La Liberté Du Commerce Des Grains* (Amsterdam: Michel Lambert, 1759).

8 Lodovico Antonio Muratori, *Della Pubblica Felicità, Oggetto de Buoni Principi* (Luca: s.n., 1749).

9 Nicolas Dutot, *Réflexions Politiques Sur Les Finances, et Le Commerce Où l'on Examine Quelles Ont Été Sur Les Revenues, Les Denrées, Le Change Étranger, & Conséquemment Sur Notre Commerce, Les Influences Des Augmentations & Des Diminutions Des Valeurs Numéraires Des Monnoyes*, 2 vols (Haye: Chez les frères V. Aillant & Nicolas Prevost, 1738).

10 Antoin E. Murphy, 'Nicolas Du Tot and John Law', in *Economic Development and Social Change: Historical Roots and Modern Perspectives*, eds. George Stathakis and Gianni Vaggi (New York: Routledge, 2006), 171–89; François R. Velde, 'The Life and Times of Nicolas Dutot', *Journal of the History of Economic Thought* 34, no. 1 (2012): 67–107.

11 Simone Meyssonnier, *La Balance et l'horloge. La Genèse de La Pensée Libérale En France Au XVIIIe Siècle* (Paris: Éditions de la passion, 1989), 95–96.

12 François R. Velde, 'The Life and Times of Nicolas Dutot', 94.

13 Istvan Hont, *Jealousy of Trade: International Competition and the Nation-State in Historical Perspective* (Cambridge, MA: Harvard University Press, 2010), 275.

14 John Law, *Money and Trade Considered: With a Proposal for Supplying the Nation with Money* (Glasgow: Printed and sold by R. & A. Foulis, 1750).

15 Ange Goudar, *Les Intérêts de La France Mal Entendus, Dans Les Branches de l'agriculture, de La Population, Des Finances, Du Commerce, de La Marine, & de l'industrie. Par Un Citoyen*, 3 vols (Amsterdam: Chez Jacques Coeur, à la corne d'abondance, 1756).

16 Monstesquieu distinguished between *commerce de luxe* (luxury trade) and *commerce d'economie* (carrying trade). The former was more suited for monarchies and the latter for republics. "Luxury trade concerns goods of fashion and ostentation, befitting nations given to vanity and pride" in contrast carrying trade involved "law profit margins and high volume" which required "scrupulous attention to bourgeois thrift and honesty, which are rewarded with larger absolute profits over the long term." (Paul Cheney, *Revolutionary Commerce*, 67.)

17 Ange Goudar, *Naples Ce Qu'il Faut Faire Pour Rendre Ce Royaume Florissant*, 210.

18 On emulation see, Istvan Hont, *Jealousy of Trade: International Competition and the Nation-State in Historical Perspective*; Sophus Reinert, *Translating Empire: Emulation and the Origins of Political Economy* (Cambridge, MA: Harvard University Press, 2011); Sophus Reinert, 'The Empire of Emulation: A Quantitative Analysis of Economic Translations in the European World, 1500–1849', in *The Political Economy of Empire in the Early Modern World*, eds. Sophus Reinert and Pernille Roge (New York: Palgrave Macmillan, 2013), 105–30.

19 Ange Goudar, *Profecía Política, Verificada En Lo Que Está Sucediendo a Los Portugueses Por Su Ciega Afición a Los Ingleses: Hecha Luego Después Del Terremoto Del Año de Mil Setecientos Cincuenta y Cinco* (Madrid: Imprenta de la Gaceta, 1762).

20 *Correspondance Littéraire, Philosophique et Critique de Grimm et Diderot, Depuis 1753 Jusqu'en 1790. Nouvelle Édition, Revue et Mise Dans Un Meilleur Ordre, Avec Des Notes et Des Éclaircissements, et Ou Se Trouvent Rétablies Pour La Première Fois Les Phrases Supprimées Par La Censure Impériale* (Paris: Chez Furne, librairie quai des augustins, n. 37 et Landrage, même quai, 19, 1829), Vol. I, 457; II, 40–44, 46–51.

21 Gianfranco Dioguardi, *Un Avventuriero Nella Napoli Del Settecento*, 64–65.

22 Istvan Hont, *Jealousy of Trade*; Catherine Larrère, *L'invention de l'économie Au XVIIIe Siècle. Du Droit à La Physiocratie* (Paris: Presses Universitaire de France, 1992); Arild Saether, *Natural Law and the Origin of Political Economy: Samuel Pufendorf and the History of Economics* (New York: Routledge, 2017).

23 J. G. A. Pocock, *Virtue, Commerce, and History: Essais on Political Thought and History. Chiefly in the Eighteenth Century* (Cambridge: Cambridge University Press, 1985); Steve Pincus, 'Neither Machiavellian Moment nor Possessive Individualism: Commercial Society and the Defenders of the English Commonwealth', *American Historical Review* 103, no. 3 (1998): 708–36; Istvan Hont and Michael Ignatieff, eds., *Wealth and Virtue: The Shaping of Political Economy in the Scottish Enlightenment* (Cambridge: Cambridge University Press, 1983).

24 John Shovlin, *The Political Economy of Virtue: Luxury, Patriotism, and the Origins of the French Revolution* (Ithaca, NY and London: Cornell University Press, 2006); Arnault Skornicki, *L'économiste, La Cour et La Patrie.*
25 Michel Foucault, *The Hermeneutics of the Subject. Lectures at the Collège de France, 1981–1982* (New York: Palgrave Macmillan, 2005).
26 Michel Foucault, 261.
27 Jean-François Melon, *Essai Politique Sur Le Commerce. Nouvelle Édition. Cette Édition Est Augmentée de Sept Chapitres, & Les Lacunes Des Éditions Précédentes y Son Remplies*, 140, 156.
28 Jean-François Melon, *A Political Essay upon Commerce.* Written in French by Monsieur M. Translated, with Some Annotations, and Remarks by David Bindon (Dublin: Printed for Philip Crampton, 1738), 39.
29 Ange Goudar, *Les Intérêts de La France Mal Entendus*, Vol. II, 22.
30 Ange Goudar, Vol. I, 16.
31 Ange Goudar, Vol. I, 13.
32 Ange Goudar, Vol. I, 52.
33 Ange Goudar, Vol. I, 200.
34 Ange Goudar, Vol. III, 199.
35 Ange Goudar, Vol. III, 274.
36 Ange Goudar, Vol. III, 278.

# 8 The will to write

## North and South Europe in transnational perspective

Following the end of the war of Austrian succession, Goudar moved out to Lisbon. In his book, he told his readers that the "providence" had transferred him to the city in 1752. Yet, archival records show that he arrived at the Portuguese imperial port in July 1751.[1] It is believed that Goudar could have acted as an informant for the French monarchy, which was highly interested in surveying the English stakes in the peninsula.[2] A letter, however, supports the fact that he moved to Lisbon with the intent to establish a factory of cotton textiles. He convinced the Portuguese envoy in London about his capacity to master the secrets of the dyeing industry, being an expert on imprinting clothes with the red pigment that European customers demanded. He had acquired that know-how during his travels in Turkey, for the acquisition of which he had spent a lot of money. It is hard to give credit to the supposed exclusive skills that Goudar asserted to have yet it is true that he had spent some years in Istanbul. True or not, the Portuguese envoy bought the idea and offered Goudar the opportunity to establish what should have been the first fabric of cotton textiles in Lisbon. He even received some monetary rewards and wrote a memoir on how to settle a fabric. Whether or not Goudar worked as an informant for the French service is hard to determine.[3]

What remains beyond doubt is that his squashing survey of the first half of the mid-century Portuguese economy sought to overthrow the very foundations of the English–Portuguese alliance. His thoughts were expressed in the introduction to a history of the earthquake that ravaged the city on 1 November 1755. He told his readers that apart from some buildings and many lazy people, the great losers of the natural disaster had been the English merchants along with their venture capital. Nature itself had provoked a valuable occasion for Portuguese people to get free from that horrible economic dependence.

In 1767, the providence again pulled the threads of destiny and transplanted Goudar to Naples. It is very likely that he could have moved out to the southern Italian city in order to offer his manufacturing know-how. On this occasion, he was joined by an Irish ex-waiter whom he had met in London and married. Sarah became the envy of the Neapolitan king himself and the regret of his friend Casanova.

DOI: 10.4324/9780429028199-11

There is no doubt that the mid-century Neapolitan intellectual world enjoyed a much more ebullient atmosphere than the one Goudar could have found in Lisbon a decade earlier.[4] In a letter, the Neapolitan expert in economic matters, Ferdinando Galiani, told Madame d'Epinay that a "renowned economic writer" had just published a "terrible and bloody" work against the Neapolitan administration. Galiani had just returned from Paris after having spent some time in London. During his Paris stay, he had been a recurrent guest in the fashionable Parisian salons. He was embedded in ongoing economic debates,[5] having written himself a much provocative book on the grain market that enraged many French economists. Besides, Galiani collaborated in the drafting of an opera whose Socratic evocation recalled the style of his dialogues on grains.[6] For all those reasons, it is at the least appealing that Galiani regarded Goudar as a "famous economic writer." This label results out of the blue given the customary mockery with which he treated the *économistes.*

The alluded book was titled *Naples ou ce qu'il faut faire pour rendre ce Royaume florissant.* As happened with the book on Lisbon written by Goudar, this one was also condemned by the censorship. A decade separated both oeuvres. *Réflexions historiques* portrayed the underlying reasons of the Portuguese backwardness whereas *Naples ou ce qu'il faut faire* advanced a set of accurate policies that could improve the Neapolitan languish state. Goudar sought to appraise the southern European economies as an ensemble. Perhaps, he was not the first to do that yet his was an attempt to offer a series of theoretical explanations on south Europe. Precisely, by intermingling the two oeuvres, it becomes possible to delve into the evolution of Goudar's economic existential concerns and to unveil the factors that, according to him, explained the southern European backwardness.

## Lisbon's earthquake: natural disasters are opportunities for new economies

Portugal had since the seventeenth century been a natural ally of England. The Methuen Treaty, signed in the times of Bourbon-Habsburg conflict in 1703, came to bolster the already close English–Portuguese alliance. There were more than dynastic or political stakes at issue. The discovery of gold mines in Brazil, and consequently, the arrival to Portugal of tons of gold further strengthen the political friendship. In the first half of the eighteenth century, Portugal went through the craziness of a gold boom cycle.[7] By the arrival of Goudar to the capital of the empire, nonetheless, the Brazilian mineral deposits had already drained. Even though the issue has received a great deal of attention, it is still far from clear whether or not the fall of gold inflows unleashed a crisis that profoundly hit the Portuguese economy. In the midst of downturn times, reforms were implemented by a high-powered minister, Marquês de Pombal, who had been trained in London.[8] The Marquês is said to have conducted huge efforts in order to promote the consolidation of a merchant national elite through the promotion of colonial re-exports and the creation of monopolistic companies. By the same token, manufactures were given particular care, and plenty of projects emerged on how to promote the national industry. New institutions were created to channel the voice of merchants and to solve mercantile suits in a more efficient and timely manner. Some blamed Pombal for his supposed anti-English bias. Others, instead, believed that accusations were merely part of a campaign against the powerful minister and that England merchants continued to enjoy favour.

On 1 November 1755, a cataclysmic earthquake left the city in ruins. A tsunami further ravaged the ruins and terrified the survivors. The curiosity that the natural disaster arose across Europe was as strong as the earthquake itself. Many pamphlets were published. One of the scenes of Voltaire's Candide precisely happened in the city. Goudar, who had already left Lisbon by the moment the earthquake happened, published, apparently in Avignon, a book that narrates the history of the event. Actually, much of the book was a sedulous survey of the Portuguese economy, which would later be censored by Portuguese officials.

The book explained Portugal's path to decadence and England's great enrichment. Goudar held that both phenomena were tightly interlinked. England had put Portugal into a situation of total dependence and had impoverished the country. For Goudar, dependence meant a situation in which a country was supplied with the basic goods or what he called the "*nécessaire physique*." This is a consistent idea throughout Goudar's oeuvre. There was a difference between the nations that "can stand on their own," and those that "are supplied the basic needs by foreigners."[9] By providing Portugal with foods and clothes, it is, by feeding and clothing its people, England had put the country under dependence. In 1754, at least two-thirds of the essential goods had arrived at the Portuguese ports carried on English vessels.

Goudar told how England obtained huge sums of bullion through a particular cycle of the capital venture. In the Brazilian gold mines, enslaved workers unearthed the mineral. Even the clothes those enslaved Africans wore were advanced by English merchants' capital. Further, for the barter of enslaved workers in Africa, a total fund of 50 million *livres tournois* was necessary. This capital should produce an interest of 2.5 million *livres tournois* that should be taken from the extracted gold. England provided also the goods for the living of 100,000 whites and slaves in Brazil as well as all the luxury goods. In total, gold remittances reached 60 million but imports worth 70 million with an imbalance of 10 million *livres tournois*.

Portugal had gradually destroyed its agricultural and manufacturing production persuaded that its climatic conditions were unfit for the promotion of food growing and the processing of raw materials. Many were fallaciously convinced that it was much better to purchase all those commodities abroad. In any case, huge amounts of gold were at their disposal. Goudar contended that the Portuguese ministers had been misguided by a set of maxims learned from English merchants. He listed and refuted 14 maxims. For him, those countries which took no account of their own subsistence would fare Portugal's destiny. This unique principle demonstrated why, in spite of having absorbed tons of gold, the economy had failed in developing its industry and agriculture. Unsound maxims had misguided Portugal's government and led the country into poverty.

England had trapped Portugal into the worst of all possible dependencies: that of the necessaries of life. Some pretended that the nation actually benefited from importing cheap commodities. "This was a national safe," ministers blindly reiterated. What a mistaken principle, though. "This ruinous saving economy had in a sense bewitched the ministers who accepted no other explanation." When attempts were conducted at implementing any factories, the order of the day was always to first corroborate whether or not the commodity could undersell the made-in England or whether the more expensive domestic salaries made it dearer. No minister had even realised that "the price of the national worker was but a chimera," and that, on the contrary, "an increase in wages further increased the circulation of money."[10]

Five *livres* paid to a national worker on daily basis could be "combine in infinite ways," the opposite happening when five *sols* were paid to a foreign craftsman "causing an actual lost." Being provided with all the basic goods by others meant being in a situation in which "civil freedom is but a name."[11] In any case, it would be much better to be conquered by the weapons since, at least in this case, opportunities might happen for breaking the shackles. When the conquest was achieved not through the weapons but through the dependency on the basic needs, freedom was much harder to be regained. History was full of instances in which a conquered nation rebelled against its warrior conquerors yet in no instance a nation had freed itself "from those who had conquered them by destroying their arts and commerce."[12]

## England's great enrichment

Portuguese decline was hand in hand with England's ascendancy. In full contrast to most authors of his time, Goudar acknowledged that Brazilian bullion had propelled the island's economic growth. This was the very "force" that explained England's rise. He rebutted all those who asserted that the very peculiar and unmatched political English institutions were at the roots of all the achievements the country had reached from the turn of the century. A combination of civil and political institutions had made England rich: this idea had found an echo in most contemporary accounts. "It is barely seen," Goudar objectionably sustained, that a small state had reclaimed the control over the "key of the richest treasure of the universe." The Brazilian gold: "here is the enigma of this greatness that has surprised so many until now."

Most eighteenth-century authors in France and elsewhere held the English political constitution in high regard. There was no doubt, Goudar considered, that it was one of the best-suited political systems to have ever been designed yet its notability owed much to the inferior quality of the continental forms of government than properly to the praiseworthy nature of the English government. A much praised system had actually had a little impact on the conduction of governmental affairs. "It is the ideal republic of Plato which never came about except in the imagination of this philosopher." For Goudar, the English government "was the most beautiful show of theory."

On the one hand, those who commended the nature of the English government had envisaged a system in which the common well-being was granted priority. They presupposed the existence of a nation in which the private interests were sacrificed for the sake of national prosperity socially pursued. This set of assumptions turned a blind eye to the "human core," and disregarded "the force and extent of the human passions." Time has come for the legislators to consider the true nature of the human being and "once and for all" to make those imagined systems fit the weakness of the human passions. On the other hand, those who celebrated liberty's merits should first acknowledge that this was but the figment of the imagination upon which "the most beautiful buildings of political reasoning had been built." Said more clearly, in much of the prevailing literature, liberty had turned into "a shadow without a proper body."

Once the putative institutional foundations of England's ascendency were discarded, Goudar proceeded to settle how bullion inflows had propelled the British economy. No one could cast a shadow of doubt on the English agrarian advancements yet "without the golden Brazilian mines all of this would have been a chimera."[13] Any improvement in agricultural output without the gold inflows would have served to make "wealth to circulate, but not to increase it at a certain rate." Goudar assumed that "grain does not produce gold yet gold does produce grain." Large monetary injections had propelled households' consumption therefore increasing the demand for agricultural staples; a level of demand that the author supposed was non-existent "in the absence of the bullion." The same could be said of the English manufactures even though most of them found a sure market in Portugal. Let's suppose a recently created country, Goudar hypothesised. A money supply of 5 million would make agriculture grow to this ceiling. If this fund were increased twofold, the land output would increase in the same proportion. The continuous arrival of Brazilian bullion and the rapid circulation of money had several effects: (i) agriculture output had known a certain increase; (ii) a larger stock of money had lowered interest rates; (iii) farmers now disposed of cheap money to invest; (iv) the subsequent increase in production had further increased the wealth and the need to put into cultivation more portions of land.

In fit with this rationale, the rise of England could be explained otherwise. An increase in money stocks had impacted households' consumption ultimately leading to the commoditisation of agriculture. Once staples had been transformed into marketable commodities, a demand in tonnage had in turn made the marine thrust. It was eventually upon this powerful navy that England had set the foundations of its great power. As we will see in the next part, the 1661 Navigation act was thought to be the ground upon which the English navy became the master of the seas. In his *Les intérêts de la France*, Goudar himself advanced that this was the main cause of England's might. Yet, according to his *Réflexions Historique*, this was rather an epiphenomenon that had resulted from the enlargement of money supplies.

People should not be shocked at not finding all that gold on the island. It was precisely due to the fact that much of it had been spent abroad that England had climbed to world dominion. A part of that money had served to afford all the wars that had made England powerful. Another share had been disbursed in the purchase of raw materials needed to propel the manufacturing sector. Not to mention that silver and not gold was carried eastward to defray Asian imports. Silver mined in America had provided the needed money to pay for the high demand for Asian goods. European ships barely transported gold to China and India. Therefore, it was dubious that the Brazilian gold was "lost in Asia as the English systems reported."[14]

Furthermore, Goudar advanced some estimations on the impact that an increase in the money stocks could have on a given economy. France served as an instance. In particular, he sought to unveil "the proportion between an increase in a country's wealth and the relative increase of prices." He found that in a country like France whose money stock could roughly be estimated to be around 900 million *livre tournois*. When this fund was augmented to 100 million, *ceteris paribus*, salaries would augment a fifth.[15] This "political thermometer" (an expression taken from Dutot) could be used to calculate the level of a nation's wealth. Further, the estimates could serve to determine to what extent bullion had been exported from England to Asia causing no impact on its domestic economy. Had the Brazilian gold caused no benefice to the island, "an inalterable equilibrium in salaries" should be evident.

Goudar was much less concerned with the hoarding of bullion and inflation and much more attentive to the impacts that the circulation and the enlargement of money supplies had. His interpretation was not merely one that overstated a quantitative monetary theory as an all-encompassing and fit-for-all explanation. Portugal's and England's cases were read through the lenses of the intellectual debate that had taken place in France decades earlier, involving both Melon and Dutot. Further, through the English case, Goudar seems to cast evidence on the ideas advanced by John Law at the turn of the century. It is hard to ascertain whether or not Goudar had read Law's *Money and Trade* although his ideas were filtered through a detailed and careful reading of Dutot, an author quoted repetitively in all his books. Law ascertained that "domestic trade depends on the money, a greater quantity employs more people than a lesser quantity." It implies that "an addition to the money adds to the value of the country." In foreign trade "more money, by employing more people, will make an overplus to export." A country achieved but little by just lowering the interest rates legally. This measure had no actual impact in those cases in which law interest rates were not in relation to money supplied to households.

Several accounts have since long been offered for the great eighteenth-century English enrichment, which allegedly put the country on the path of the Industrial Revolution. Institutions, ideas, factor endowments, and salaries, this assorted set of factors have been held as the actual underpinning conditions that brought economic growth and set apart the destiny of the island from the rest of the world. Neo-institutional economists have assumed that the country's ruling representative institutions framed a market in which the executive was under the rule of the law, therefore, setting the foundations of a market in which property rights were appropriately safeguarded.[16] Both conditions ultimately laid the foundations for the workings of an efficient credit and investment market. This institutional guarantor framework emerged or consolidated with the Glorious Revolution, and for instance, supported a patent system that decades later, it is assumed, positively impacted in the inventiveness of technological machinery.

"Idealist" accounts have sought to explain in a more accurate way why technological change would have first happened in England and not anywhere else. An enlightened intellectual revolution anticipated technological innovation for decades. A belief that reason and observation should be applied to the transformation of the social and natural worlds in a perpetual search for progress and happiness had been the quintessential condition upon which the forthcoming take-off had taken shape.[17] Within the field of cultural and idealist accounts, the search for dignity and liberty preceded and paved the way for the configuration of radically more open societies and efficient institutions.

The enlightened intellectual and idealist roots of social evolution came to contest accounts that, on the contrary, overstressed material incentives. Economic historians have advanced an alternative explanation according to which the sudden explosion of growth resulted from a contradiction involving high relative prices of labour and cheap and easy-to-access coal deposits.[18] In this vein, it is assumed that the inversely proportional prices of human and natural energy compelled capital investors to gradually replace the human workforce with machinery, therefore, settling the path to the take-off.[19] Attempts made at comparing real wages across time and space offered evidence that, by the eighteenth century, England was a high-wage economy. Real wages, what a worker could actually afford with the daily wage, were much higher in England than in the continent or China and India.

Wage estimates and the framing of accurate methodologies for determining the high standard of living had received more attention than explanations on why English wages were higher both in terms of a basket of commodities and money. The assumption, nonetheless, is much in line with Goudar's interpretation. A large and sudden circulation of money that resulted from the arrival of the Brazilian bullion positively impacted the English economy. The idea seems to have been rather overlooked. Some decades ago, historians estimate that Atlantic colonial markets had been rather small for having a considerable quantitative impact on Britain's economic growth rates.

Empirical data seem to further support Goudar's explanation. A coin stock index shows that available money almost doubled when compared to the last years of the seventeenth century, increasing from 200 to 400 by the 1730s and 500 by the years Goudar wrote his books. It means that, at a constant pound of 1700, per capita coin increased from two to five.[20]

## Naples: journeying to the Vesuvius

In his forbidden *Naples ce qu'il faut faire*, the money supply almost vanishes from the book. Or at least, the matter is downplayed at the expense of the manufacturing sector, which, now, claimed all the attention. There are many reasons why money stocks might have been a pointless topic when it comes to Naples.

In southern Italy, there was a long-lived intellectual tradition that dated back to the sixteenth century which placed manufactures at the core of the argument. This tradition explained backwardness and decline as a consequence of the deterioration of the national industry.[21] So, a likely argument could easily resonate in the ears of the targeted audience. Monetary theory had widely been discussed in Naples as is proved by the 1751 publication of the obstreperous Galiani's *Della Moneta*. By the same token, in his *Lezioni di commercio*, Genovesi discussed monetary issues at length. Framed within the Melo versus Dutot debate, Genovesi offered an interpretation that resembled the one Goudar had already advanced for Lisbon: an injection of money generated a real increase in consumption and not merely in prices. On the other hand, it could be supposed that political French interests were not any longer at stake so Goudar could disregard political concerns and write in a more free manner. The goal now was to convince the Neapolitan king of developing the textile industry. Apparently, Goudar offered his manufacturing know-how to the Neapolitan officials as well.

None of the above reasons, nonetheless, seem to explain why Goudar now emphasised industry as the true motor of a national economy. In the preface, he himself announced "one will be surprised that all my thoughts lay on the arts and that no thought is given to commerce." To him, a utopian geographical distribution of manufactures came hand to hand with a much desired European equilibrium.

To provide all his subjects with all the basic needs was the most basic ruler's task. Therefore, luxury and opulence were not to be encouraged in a country in which people lacked subsistence. Goudar critised the Colbertian illness for luxuries in a country in which famines happened recurrently. The inverse situation was found in Naples where poverty was a direct consequence of the lack of, and government's neglect for manufactures. At the first glance, there seems to be a contradiction. However, a deep reading shows how the ideas had gradually evolved, and why encouraging the manufacturing industry resulted necessarily.

The 400-page book included a long theoretical introduction which, not surprisingly, began with Goudar making fun of the ongoing mania for economic books, most of which, he made clear, were but of little utility. The question remains as to whether this lengthy and philosophically grounded introductory piece was meant to please the tastes of a brawny local intellectual circle or whether it was inserted in an attempt to call the attention of a group of intellectuals updated on international book releases. Bartolomé Intiere had trained a generation of young scholars in the new foundations of scientific knowledge and the applicability of Newtonian conceptions of the world to social life.[22] Genovesi himself had made a transition from metaphysics to mechanics, and then, from mechanics to economics.[23]

This closely-tied group of friends was tasked with the translation of a number of books from English and French into Italian. So it could be said that Intierie's group in Italy was the counterpart of Gournay's circle in Paris. Genovesi himself had participated in the translation of Montesquieu's *L'esprit de lois*. As already mentioned, Goudar showed in all his books a critical, but at the same time, admiring engagement with the French author. As if having a high regard for an author forced one to partially refute his thoughts. Besides, Genovesi used the French translation of Cary's *On trade* to make his own version into Italian, adding a large set of notes and disproportionately increasing the book's length.[24] Only a few years later, Genovesi published his *Lezioni di commercio sia d'economia civili*. In the summer of 1764, a manuscript was in preparation whose first volume went to print in 1766 but was delayed until 1767 when the second volume was finally printed.[25]

Goudar's book was somehow under the pressure of what came to be later known as a highly celebrated oeuvre. Genovesi's method was featured by a logical-historical analysis or "historically determined abstractions." This implies a combination of deductive and inductive reasoning, the former intended to establish general relations and the latter meant to shed light on the diversity and peculiarities of the world itself.[26] Only a couple of years later, Galiani published his daringly burlesque, anti-partisan, anti-*économiste* refutation on grain-free trade. One of Galianis's points precisely pointed out the inversely proportional returns of agriculture and manufactures.[27]

Publishing a book intended for this local although highly well-informed intellectual circle could be hazardous. Perhaps much more compelling than censorship itself. Goudar's ideas were, as he accustomed, frameless yet astonishingly knowledgeable. The proposals he came up with were challenging and controversial, and at the latest, caused discomfort and compelled some to reposition their own mental foundations. Similar to Genovesi, Goudar's framework combines luxe and decadence in an attempt to explain the need for, and the lack of manufactures in Naples. The prospective positive impacts of fabrics in Goudar's account, however, surpassed local explanations and sought to place the issue into a larger global perspective. For him, the promotion of manufactures should lead to the emergence of a utopian universal society, not serving merely national interests. He was fully convinced that the search for a universal equilibrium should guide the location of manufactures so as to set an evenly geographical distribution of wealth and the arts.

## "A balance of the arts"

Universe. Universal. Universal society. These are words that are recurrently referred to in Goudar's pieces of writing. Indeed, the resort to this conceptual apparatus is owed in part to the impact of the introduction of mechanics in the understanding of the social world. Mid-eighteenth-century philosophical and political debates had also a huge imprint in Goudar's reflections.

Goudar advocated that any industrial improvements should ultimately lead to a European equilibrium. He was convinced that the expansion of the industrial production should serve not to fulfil national cravings for world dominion. Not surprisingly, his thoughts were much in line with philosophical and legal texts widely read at the time. Around the 1750s, the expressions European equilibrium, system of equilibrium, and European system were all common languages in political books. In 1752, Hume himself published his *On the balance of power.* Previously, in the same year in which the European powers signed the Utrecht Treatise, a book was printed in that city titled *Projet de paix perpétuelle.* The book reached a wide audience, especially in the second half of the century, being widely read, particularly by philosophers. The oeuvre discussed the prospective ways out of the path to universal monarchy: either by the law or by military force: through the signing of peace treaties with no arbitrage enforcer or through the force of an equilibrium of armies.[28] By reconciling political and economic distinctive theoretical approaches, Goudar set the foundations for an interpretation of commerce and manufactures that hardly fit within either the *doux commerce* thesis or what Hume labelled as jealousy of trade.

When one assumed that differences across countries brought prejudices or well-being only for their own inhabitants, one was left with no choice but to envy the fortune of a few and pity the misfortune of many. However, the truth was that any implemented economic policies impacted all the members of what Goudar called the "universal society."[29]

Through a historical analysis, Goudar sought to demonstrate that a formerly prevailing equilibrium in the arts had vanished, being followed by a perpetual state of war. Following the fall dawn of the Roman Empire, isolated countries had for long enjoyed their own national industries in an age in which no country had dared to seize its neighbours' productive power. Nonetheless, once rulers found out that the promotion of manufactures could turn into a machine of money with which to defray continuous wars and to strengthen their power, manufactures had caused a greater revolution than the one formerly carried by the weapons. Both Greeks and Romans had, through their wars, transformed only the "known world." The modern industry had gone much farther extending itself over the whole universe: "The arts had united all the parts of the globe."

Goudar approached international competition not from the supposed positive social and moral refinements of a much more integrated commercial society. The focus was put on the arts rather than on commerce, as was usual for many authors at that moment. The idea of *doux commerce* had been brought to the front for many in the first half of the century, Montesquieu himself being one of its main supporters. The prevailing conception presumed that the emergence of a universal commercial society might deviate the world from the current path of everlasting wars. Commerce would eventually relieve humanity from conquerors and would ultimately lead humankind to the achievement of a much higher level of civilisation. Commercial interdependence would release humanity from a dramatic history of soul-destroying violent subjugation. Commerce was expected to act as a "moralising agent." As Montesquieu put forward, everywhere commerce could be found, sweetness and soft manners accompanied it.[30] In his essay, *On the jealousy of trade*, Hume attacked those who backed old-fashioned ideas according to which rich nations should look with suspicious eyes at the progress of their neighbours. Conversely, the Scottish philosopher maintained that "the increase of riches and commerce in any one nation, instead of hurting, commonly promoted the riches and commerce of all its neighbours." Emulation was at the very core of Hume's argument. "The emulation among rival nations serves rather to keep industry alive."

In contrast, Goudar anticipated a rather pessimistic future that differed both from Hume's jealousy of trade and the *doux commerce* theory. This was a dissimilar interpretation that dialogued with, but differed from, the humanistic republican tradition and the moralising theory that overemphasised the unexpected benefits of the emergence of a global industrial society: "One will be surprised that all my thoughts lay on the arts and none to commerce."

The discovery of mines in America, the narrative went on, unchained a revolution that had toppled a former European equilibrium. Since the dawn of ancient times, three historical stages had unfolded. The implosion of the Roman Empire had settled the foundations for a new equilibrium in which the arts were "geometrically" distributed. In the second stage, nonetheless, princely contests provoked intense competition and the boosting of manufactures. The industry was at service of rulers' territorial ambitions. Finally, more recently, bullion inflows had come to radically transform the European equilibrium. Suddenly, two "poor nations" found themselves endowed with the deposits of metals, it is, "the power itself." This wealth rather hammered the interests of both Spain and Portugal, having enriched three or four nations that supplied those countries and their colonies with both the luxurious and the necessaries of life. This had provoked a situation in which "the arts and jobs had been lost in different kingdoms" while they had concentrated "in a corner of Europe."

At this moment, humankind witnessed the rise of a "new power set by the arts."[31] This era had come to replace an imagined golden age in which the arts had proportionally been distributed. Industry was not just a matter of emulation, as Hume aspired it to be. It had, on the contrary, exacerbated international warfare. Not to say that jealousy of industry had acted as an impetus to the invention of "infernal machines," which had been designed to kill millions of people with a simple shot. "Infernal machines," Goudar remarked, for "only the devil could have imagined them." Prior to the renaissance of the arts, wars had had a rather local reach, thereafter, however, wars had spread to all the corners of the world, not even a retreat having been left sheltered. Those who championed all these nonsense battles justified the war paraphernalia upon the lawfulness of the rights of peoples and the balance of commerce. Goudar even mocked Hume's *Balance of Power*, accusing him of voicing England's interests and blaming him for aspiring to see his country as "Europe's tutelary angel."

"New forms are incessantly given to the matter" just with the intent to leave countries into the dependence of a boundless use of labour force. A formerly non-existent luxury had drastically reconfigured the European equilibrium. A lack of universal perspective was evident in many authors whose systems showed no care for a true underlying assumption: "the combination of the advantages of each nation could form a common good." Many had even raised their voices in favour of the instability of the universal republic. All of them were misled, and the time has come once and for all to show that the illnesses that affected any of the countries of the universal republic ultimately reverberated in all of its members. Put another way, all those illnesses were "stored in a universal magazine full of political and civil disorders."[32] The idea should be finally embraced that, such as happened in the physical world, forces hit with a similar intensity all the members of the universal republic. Therefore, policies that had not in sight the universal republic in the first moment only degenerated a part but sooner than later marked the end of the whole body.

This new equilibrium had put the "universal industry" upon the control of a few countries. Those ever-enriching states had gradually been destroying their neighbours unaware that their own actions had set the path to their razing. In order to avoid such illnesses, industrial production should be allotted according to each country's estimated labour force. In this regard, an estimate was offered on the number of jobs to be created across the continent: Russia needed more than 140,000 jobs, Germany 110,000 jobs, Italy, Spain, and Portugal 80,000 jobs. As we will see, deurbanisation was key to making the fabrics boost. "This is the void." And Goudar was convinced that "as long as it is not filled, there will be nations that will impoverish others, and with their wealth will agitate our world."[33] Goudar prevented those sceptics who remained unconvinced of the unattainableness of "a relative industry" (as he named this evenly distribution of the arts) that not long ago the arts were evenly distributed in the world. This was a balance of the arts, the proper way to attain a balance of commerce.[34]

## Underselling: history, competition, and the state

A geometrical distribution of the arts. This was at a time a retrospectively projected utopia and a contemplated future. This account should offer support for Naples's aspirations to finally break the shackles of dependence. In the pursuit of this new equilibrium, Neapolitan policymakers should encourage merchants to tap into eastern markets where a contest with Holland, England, and France was to be faced. History showed that those countries had in due course taken control of the Turkish market. A gulf separated the three northern countries from the Kingdom of Naples, though. In accordance with Goudar's maxims, the Italian kingdom possessed the raw materials needed for the textile industry to be well cemented. Cotton, wool, and silk all grew in the realm plentifully. While France was compelled to import wools from Spain, Naples could weave its own wools. England was supplied with expensive and excellent Italian silks and Indian cottons. Naples had, on the contrary, upon the same sky, the three most coveted fibres any country could dream of.

Tapping on an oversupplied market meant essentially to undersell. Goudar had both practical and theoretical knowledge of the Levant trade. On the one hand, he had worked for years overseeing the quality of French textiles introduced into Turkey. In his book on Naples, he wrote extensively on how to improve woven fabrics. On the other hand, his first book on economic matters sought to condemn monopoly and ceiling prices on clothes exported from Marseilles and destined to eastern Mediterranean markets.[35] He came to the conclusion that private privileges should not be granted preference over state interests. It was in the interests of the state to export far many pieces of cloth at much lower prices. Merchants might be of a different mind. Exporting larger quantities benefited the country since many poor people could be employed and larger quantities of money put into circulation.

A history of the Levant trade served to illustrate how markets actually worked. Formerly warriors, thereafter peaceful people, and much recently a nation prone to luxe and voluptuousness. This was how Goudar depicted the Turkish people. This was a country that had never endeavoured to re-establish its arts, no matter that their land was endowed with plenty of workers and all sorts of natural materials. Dutch traders had been the first to profit from the Turkish inertia and disdain for the arts. They had navigated to the Levant and set the production of the peculiar clothes demanded in the far-flung eastern markets. English merchants had subsequently conducted great efforts to profit from the opportunities the eastern Mediterranean offered and had rapidly overcome Dutch contesters. Not for a long time, until Louis XIV decided to take part in the contest. France was in a bitter situation since woven clothes manufactured in the northern countries had already reached a certain degree of perfection; a degree of perfection the country would be unable to reach in the short run. Therefore, to compete in terms of quality was highly unlikely for French weavers. All endeavours were then conducted to induce customers with different tastes. It means, giving to the matter new forms of luxe. In order to reach that goal, Colbert had promoted the design of textiles "extremely fine, light wooled, but highly colourful." Dying became the only matter that actually mattered. Low-priced fashions had the last say in the contest.

History demonstrated, Goudar contended, that markets could only be taken through a slow gradual process of competition. France had fastly supplanted Holland and England in the Levant, though. The latter countries had required a long time to improve the quality of thick woollen textiles sold in the eastern markets. Conversely, France had quickly developed the capacity to produce 10,000 bales of light woollens yearly, which is 7,000 more ones than England did. Prices explained the success. Goudar was of the mind that when customers can change clothes without spending more "they consume all the more willingly." The success of new fashions hinged on cheap prices. Customers could now purchase 10,000 bales of French textiles with the same amount of money they purchased 7,000 ones from English merchants.

To increment productivity as to rapidly being in the position to export 10,000 bales of textiles had required the efforts of at least 200 entrepreneurs and 20,000 workers. A solution had been also found to this issue. Gratifications became the order of the day. Colbert was well aware that investors could barely profit from new branches of fabrics. And that for a reason: "experience always unveiled expenses that theory had barely forecast."[36] Gratifications were no doubt the most appropriate means to encourage the production of new manufactures. Goudar harboured suspicions about the public administration of fabrics; being more advisable than rulers devoted their efforts to encourage the arts and not to become artists themselves. Those gratifications had been accompanied by tight regulations that sought to oversee the quality and to make feasible the tracking down of origins.[37] All these factors (innovation in tastes, low prices, gratifications, and tight regulations) explained how France had overcome England, becoming the dominant provider.

Goudar seems to have been quite accurate in his historical account. Available statistics give support to his interpretation. Between 1666 and 1683, France exported on average 280 bolts of fine woollen cloth yearly. This is a time in which annual Anglo-Dutch imports reached 12,000 bolts. At the turn of the century, the pattern had already been set: 3,200 bolts in 1698 and 10,300 ones on average in the first quinquennium In the 1730s, spectacular growth happened as Turkish customers abandoned English fashions in favour of French tastes. Around those years, 58,650 bolts were exported to the Levant yearly. When Goudar wrote his book, woollen exports had reached their apogee yielding 85,300 bolts. In total, France's exports to the Levant had expanded from 6.7 million *livres tournois* to 25 million in the 1730s. While at the turn of the century only 95 ships were involved, the number had increased to 150 by the mid-century when Levant trade made up 10 per cent of French trade.[38]

## Notes

1 José Barreto, 'O Discurso Político Falsamente Atribuído Ao Marquês de Pombal', *Revista de História Das Ideias* 4, no. 1 (1982): 385–422.

2 Jean-Claude Hauc, *Ange Goudar: Un Aventurier Des Lumières.*

3 José Barreto, 'O Discurso Político Falsamente Atribuído Ao Marquês de Pombal'.
4 Franco Venturi, *Settecento Riformatore. De Muratori a Beccaria* (Torino: Giulio Einaudi, 1969); Eluggero Pii, *Antonio Genovesi: Dalla Politica Economica Alla 'Politica Civile'* (Florence: Leo S. Olschki, 1984); John Robertson, 'The Enlightenment above National Context: Political Economy in the Eighteenth-Century Scotland and Naples', *Historical Journal* 40, no. 3 (1997): 667–97; John Robertson, *The Case for the Enlightenment: Scotland and Naples, 1680–1760* (Cambridge: Cambridge University Press, 2005); K. H. Stapelbroek, *Love, Self-Deceit and Money: Commerce and Morality in the Early Neapolitan Enlightenment* (Toronto: University of Toronto Press, 2008).
5 Paolo Amodio, *Il Disincanto Della Ragione e l'assolutezza Del Bonheur. Studio Sull'Abate Galiani* (Naples: Alfredo Guida, 1997); Augusto Bazzoni, ed., *Lettere Ferdinando Galiani al Marchese Bernardo Tanucci* (Florence: Gio. Pietro Vieusseux, 1880).
6 Ferdinando Galiani, *Dialogues Sur Le Commerce Des Bleds* (Londres: s.n., 1770).
7 Virgilio Noya, *O Ouro Brasileiro e o Comércio Anglo-Português* (São Paulo: Companhia editora Nacional, 1979); Leonor Freire Costa, Maria Manuela Rocha, and Rita Martins de Sousa, *O Ouro Do Brasil. Lisboa* (Lisboa: Imprensa Nacional, 2013).
8 Maxwell Kenneth, *Pombal, Paradox of the Enlightenment* (Cambridge: Cambridge University Press, 1995).
9 Ange Goudar, *Relation Historique Du Tremblement de Terre*, 15, 23, 68, 83, 86–87.
10 Ange Goudar, 108.
11 Ange Goudar, 68.
12 Ange Goudar, 68.
13 Ange Goudar, 48.
14 Ange Goudar, 97.
15 Ange Goudar, 100.
16 Douglas North and Robert Weingast, 'Constitutions and Commitment: The Evolution of Institutional Governing Public Choice in Seventeenth-Century England', *Journal of Economic History* 49, no. 4 (1989): 803–32; Douglass North, *The Rise of the West World: A New Economic History* (London: Cambridge University Press, 1973); Douglass North, *Institutions, Institutional Change and Economic Performance* (Cambridge: Cambridge University Press, 1991).
17 Joel Mokyr, *The Enlightened Economy: An Economic History of Britain 1700–1850* (Princeton, NJ: Princeton University Press, 2012).
18 Kenneth Pomeranz, *The Great Divergence. China, Europe, and the Making of the Modern World* (Princeton, NJ: Princeton University Press, 2009).
19 Robert Allen, *The British Industrial Revolution in Global Perspective* (Cambridge: Cambridge University Press, 2009); Robert Allen, 'The High Wage Economy and the Industrial Revolution: A Restatement', *Economic History Review* 68, no. 1 (2015): 1–22.
20 Nuno Palma, 'Money and Modernization in Early Modern England', *Financial History Review* 25, no. 3 (2018): 231–61; Nuno Palma, 'Reconstruction of Money Supply over the Long Run: The Case of England, 1270–1870', *Economic History Review* 71, no. 2 (2018): 373–92.
21 Sophus Reinert and Robert Fredona, 'Political Economy and the Medici', *Business History Review* 94, no. 1 (2020): 125–77.
22 Franco Venturi, *Settecento Riformatore*; Till Wahnbaeck, *Luxury and Public Happiness: Political Economy in the Italian Enlightenment* (Oxford: Clarendon Press, 2004).
23 Antonio Genovesi, *Lezioni Di Commercio o Sia d'economia Civile* (Bassano: Spese Remondini, 1769); Eluggero Pii, *Antonio Genovesi.*
24 Sophus Reinert, *Translating Empire.*

25 Maria Luisa Perna, 'L'edizione Delle Lezioni Di Commercio Di Antonio Genovesi', in *Genovesi Economista*, eds. Bruno Jossa, Rosario Palatano, and Eugenio Zagari (Naples: Istituto Italiano per gli studi filosofici, 2007), 59–66.
26 Eugenio Zagari, 'Il Metodo, Il Progetto e Il Contributo Analitico Di Antonio Genovesi', *Studi Economici* 92 (2007): 5–32.
27 Ferdinando Galiani, *Dialogues Sur Le Commerce Des Bleds.*
28 Bruno Bernardi, 'L'idée d'équilibre Européen Dans Le Jus Gentium Des Modernes: Esquisse d'histoire Conceptuelle', in *Penser l'Europe Au XVIIIe Siècle: Commerce, Civilisation, Empire*, eds. Antoine Lilti and Céline Spector (Oxford: Voltaire Foundation, 2014), 19–46.
29 Ange Goudar, *Naples Ce Qu'il Faut Faire Pour Rendre Ce Royaume Florissant*, 51.
30 "It is not very clear in Montesquieu whether the douceur-inducing effect of commerce is supposed to be brought about by the changes commerce works among the people engaging in trading activities or, more amply, among all those who use and consume the commodities made available through commerce. In any event, the term in its widest meaning had a successful career outside France." Albert O. Hirschaman, *The Passions and the Interests: Political Arguments for Capitalism before Its Triumph* (Princeton, NJ: Princeton University Press, 2013), 60; Anoush Fraser Terjanian, *Commerce and Its Discontents in Eighteenth-Century French Political Thought* (Cambridge: Cambridge University Press, 2016).
31 Ange Goudar, *Les Intérêts de La France Mal Entendus*, Vol. III, 181.
32 Ange Goudar, *Naples Ce Qu'il Faut Faire Pour Rendre Ce Royaume Florissant*, 79.
33 Ange Goudar, 86.
34 Ange Goudar, 88.
35 Ange Goudar, *Questions Sur Le Commerce Des François Au Levant.*
36 Ange Goudar, *Naples Ce Qu'il Faut Faire Pour Rendre Ce Royaume Florissant*, 311.
37 Philippe Minard, *La Fortune Du Colbertisme: État et Industrie Dans La France Des Lumières* (Paris: Fayard, 2014); Jeff Horn, *Economic Development in Early Modern France. The Privilege of Liberty, 1650–1820* (Cambridge: Cambridge University Press, 2015).
38 Jeff Horn, *Economic Development in Early Modern France. The Privilege of Liberty, 1650–1820*, 149.

# 9 Industry's geometry and geography

## A chimerical wealth

Both agriculture and luxury were placed at the very core of Goudar's oeuvre. His *Les intérêts de la France* was written in the midst of a wave of intense debates on agriculture and agronomy. The mid-century was precisely the time in which Quesnay and his followers reinforced their influence on, and practically dominated public discussions on political economy. Among the famous books published by one of the sect's fellows stood Mirabeau's *L'ami des hommes*, which reached a great reception across the continent. Not for Goudar who, in his *Naples ce qu'il faut faire*, gave the book a bad press.

Sharing the assumption with many other authors, and in line with the physiocrats, Goudar considered agriculture as the first source of state power. Perhaps, there is a subtle difference in apprehending agriculture output as a source of state power instead of a pure source of wealth. The ideas were already discussed in Melon's 1730 book. Melon hypothesised three islands, each producing a particular commodity. According to his prediction, the islands would exchange surpluses as to the point that "the wants, and the exchanges or permutations, will be equal, and consequently the Balance of trade will be so too." In this rationale, the island devoted to corn cultivation would improve the most "as the inhabitants of the other three islands cannot subsist without corn, the first step they will take, must be to quit their island, and go to work in the island of corn, in order to earn bread." Melon maintained that "corn is the basis of trade, because it is the necessary support of life, and the providing thereof, ought to be, the first care of the legislature."[1] As we have already seen, Goudar's thinking acquired coherence in the form of maxims. The assumption that agriculture was the source of state power hardly lined him along the members of the sect no matter his unrestricted support for agriculture.

Only agriculture "could give a country rule over the whole world."[2] Four main reasons explained why this basic economic activity remained as the original foundation of state power: (i) its self-standing; (ii) it was a creative everlasting power that enriched the state; (iii) agriculture's outputs were real; (iv) temporal and changing tastes and prejudices barely affected its yields.

DOI: 10.4324/9780429028199-12

Cultivation could be considered as both a real and relative source of power. To be in a position to supply one's neighbours with the largest share of food meant at the same time to enjoy a relative power over the others. Only agriculture created this kind of power. Agriculture was a source of power in that it freed a country from any sort of dependence. In other words, this was a non-accidental form of power.

A reader should be surprised, Goudar found out, to discover that a country like France endowed with roughly 150 million *arpens* could barely feed its own people, a population estimated at 17 million. Available arable land would be enough to feed at least 25 million inhabitants. The greater the degree of dependence to grow its own food, the weaker a country was in itself and *vis-à-vis* other nations. England, having smaller numbers and enjoying far less arable land, could survive without procuring food outside the island. This was proved by the fact that only in the years 1715–55, France had imported from England roughly 21 million *septiers* of *froment* worth 200 million *livres tournois*.

Another debate left its imprint on the book. *Les intérêts de la France* shaded an anti-Colbertian fanaticism for industry and an obdurate reproval of luxury. Relative and real wealth were in consonance with luxury and subsistence. Goudar traced a deep line that separated luxury commodities from the basic goods. A country that imported luxury commodities could refrain from purchasing them at any time in accordance with temporal and changing tastes and fashions. The opposite went for food as no country could abstain from importing the basic goods. From this perspective, England was far more powerful than France, as it was the "first subsistence" that decided upon the question.[3] Goudar brought to the front Portugal's terrible situation and applied the same logic to France. Let's suppose, says Goudar, that France enjoyed a fund worth 1,000 million whose returns could be estimated at 50 million, or what is the same, 59 *sols* per cap. This was far below the sum each person needed to cover the basic needs, a cost of life estimated at least 160 *livres*.

## Opulence amid deprivation

The debate on luxury remained at the very core of Goudar's arguments, not only in *Les intérêts de la France*, but also, previously in his *Réflexions historique*, and later, in his *Naples ce qu'il faut faire*. The issue (considered a hot one over the whole century) remained at the very foundations of Goudar's thoughts and the assumptions and maxims he upheld. Notwithstanding, he distanced himself from a polarised intellectual dispute that either praised luxury as the main motor of economic growth or condemned it from a moral and republican viewpoint.[4] Indeed, many of Goudar's assumptions on *bon luxe* or *mauvais luxe* hinged on the widely held notion that luxuries set the ground for corruption, and therefore, made societal decadence to germinate. Montesquieu was complimented even though he was not left out of criticism. If Goudar extensively drew on the intellectual tradition, at the same time, he formed an opinion of the topic from a totally different angle.

Luxury was appraised from a more "mundane" perspective. For once. An observational instead of a logically-deductive outlook was privileged. Three different economies (each quite differently endowed) allowed the author to assess luxe's unexpected salutary impacts or its apparently disturbing disintegrative consequences. Goudar attempted to prove luxe's pernicious or stimulating effects on the ground. Each one of the places Goudar had lived in offered him a valuable field to observe consumption's impacts and the arts' harmful or positive effects: a bullionist Portugal, a post-Colbertian land-endowment France, and a languishing but potentially rich Naples.

Luxury was far from being seen only in the light of the republican and humanistic tradition although it remained a weapon to fight back absolutism. In France, superfluous and excessive luxes resulted from Colbertian economic policies, which had been set with the only intent to set the path to European hegemony. As Hont has distinctively put it "It was Colbert, not Mandeville, who was the standard-bearer of the luxury party in France."[5] A special concern was shown for poverty and subsistence. The alleged benefits manufactures brought had not been realised in a country like France whose streets remained crowded with deprived people; those were countries in which, the experience showed, famines frequently hit an already starving population. Goudar's was a more down-to-earth outlook yet one that built strongly on logical deduction.

Goudar's approach is in full contrast with the way in which the debate has commonly been explored. Eighteenth-century disputes over luxury have overall been researched as an engaging and learned discussion that involved many and which unfolded in a rather linear and teleological manner. Essentially, the dispute involved a paradigmatic change in mindset that could be abridged using Mandeville's book's subtitle: private vices produced public benefits. An allegedly more accurate conception of human behaviour read that passions could counterbalance each other and spontaneously generated public well-being.

Mandeville was widely read, being considered a ground-breaking figure for those interested in unveiling new conceptions of the human nature.[6] When the main tracts of the discussion are revealed, a genealogical and teleological line takes shape which begins with Fenelon's *Adventures of Telemachus, son of Ulises* and goes down to the mid-eighteenth-century publications. The luxury debate is somehow propounded as a self-embedded and autopoietic discussion that gradually unfolded over time. Therefore, a timeline emerges in which one subsequently sees Fenelon, Mandeville, Shaftesbury, Hutcheson, Berkeley, Montesquieu, Melon, and Voltaire to emerge.

Telemachus raised his voice against a Colbertian madness for fashion. Luxe was said to poison a society and to disintegrate the very foundations of its social order. For two reasons. Living in an ostentatious society incites poor people to hide their poverty through the consumption of vanities that rapidly become out of fashion or that are gradually transformed into necessities. Wealthy people, in turn, compete in a wasting display of wealth trying to differentiate from one another. In this society, yesterday's superfluities convert into today's necessities.[7] Many gave credit to the assumption that the never-ending invention of superfluities contributed much to the wealth of a nation for in this manner the poor were maintained "at the expense of the wealthy people."[8] Telemachus, on the contrary and in consonance with what Goudar would later held, held that urbanisation and manufactures ultimately led to the "neglect of agriculture, the decline of the rural population, and the collapse of royal revenues."[9] Essential for the ensuing debate was the distinction set by Fenelon, and then by Boisguilbert, between superfluities and the basic needs.

In the 1730s, the debate took wing once more again with the publication of Melon's *Essai sur le commerce.* Inspired by Mandeville's hive, Melon became one of the manufactures' most tenacious advocates. Agriculture should be considered the true source of wealth yet national power relied on the industry. Successful countries were those which exchanged superfluities for basic goods. Industry should depend on agriculture and an equilibrium should exist regarding the number of workers allotted to each sector. As we have seen above, Melon was involved in a monetary debate with Dutot in which luxe remained a substantial element of the discussion.

Later, taking the debate out from narrower economists' circles, Voltaire gave mass-market appeal with his *Mondain* and the defence of worldly pleasures. His was an anti-Telemachus defence of pleasures against the virtuous, patriotic, and moral promises of a paradise: "whatever is, is right." In his defence of the *Mondain,* Voltaire presented the king Salomon as the model to be emulated. He exceeded any other king in intelligence yet nobody equalled him in his excess for luxury. The question arises (as Voltaire put it in his dictionary) as to whether one would wish to live in an austere and virtuous Rome whereas Paris offered all the luxes on the earth.

In the 1750s, the debate continued. There was an elevated number of authors who published on the topic and many definitions were commonly offered so conceptual confusion remained the order of the day. Nobody seemed to assert what luxury exactly meant. This is how Forbonnais began the Chapter XI of his *Élements du Commerce.* "The only party that one can really take" is to assume the vagueness and indetermination of such a word luxe. Forbonnais summarised at least five definitions. After having reviewed at length each one, the idea was advanced that an accurate definition would define luxe as the use that one could make of anybody else's labour in order to exist pleasantly.[10] After having taken stock, however, Forbonnais took distance from the tradition. He assumed that luxury "is good in itself" yet consideration should be given to the fact that the nature of the circumstances upon which it had been introduced could generate a negative balance of illnesses. Luxury should be founded upon commerce otherwise "the useful effects would be felt only by a few" and "as the crowd is more inclined to feeling than to reasoning, luxe would become the bitterness of the complaints."[11] When luxe failed to filter down to the low social classes or when it barely corresponded to the outcome of national wealth, "disorders will happen capable of destroying the political body itself."

Goudar proposed a quite different outlook. It was possible to overcome narrow erudite debates on luxury. There was no need to deep into all those discussions that politicians usually entertained with in order to prove that luxury produced differentiated effects according to each country. Goudar also contended that "modern writers" had spilled much ink in determining whether luxury was an evil or a heaven. History showed, Goudar held, that luxury remained the main cause of the empires' decadence. Rome found itself subjugated to luxury after having subjugated the world. Authors could affirm that modern governments were unlikely ancient ones. In any case, "men have always been the same." Ancient peoples were unaware of the "art" of disdaining essential goods. They had strictly regulated fashion so one's status could be notorious in the public space. When decadence hit the Roman Empire, "everyone who dressed in purple was held as an emperor," which proved that "veneration was given to clothes rather than to persons."[12]

Goudar distanced himself from Montesquieu and his rigid tripartite classification. Luxe could be the dorsal spine of a monarchy, and in consonance, seen as an affair of state. However, even under this form of government, proper circumstances should prevail in order for luxury to be encouraged. In England, for instance, the foundations of luxury lay on the farmers' work. Fitting in with one of his maxims, Goudar asserted that manufactures reached better outcomes in the nations that grew their own raw materials. In line with this thought, manufactures should be encouraged only in those countries in which the inhabitants were already provided with the "*nécessaire physique*" for "if this first subsistence lacks, luxe should be forbidden." In opposition to Montesquieu, therefore, Goudar upheld that setting as a general rule that luxe was intrinsic to Monarchies was rather to advance an absurd.

Goudar also displayed disagreement against the Mandevillian-side of the argument. Criticism was cast towards those who were persuaded that vices might generate advantages for they failed to see that "corruption never contributes to the greatness of a nation."[13] In opposition to Forbonnais, Goudar believed that those in charge of producing the "*nécessaire physique*" should be banned from luxury. For one reason. Once luxe regained the core of the "*bas peuple*" "everything was lost."[14] In that, Goudar recalled Dutot and his conception of luxury as a "poison." When luxury reigned, the harmony among the classes was ruined. Luxury caused disequilibrium between farmers, craftsmen, and those devoted to the liberal arts; farming always being abandoned at the expense of urban jobs. Luxury should not be fixed in the minds of those who produce the basic goods. In other words, they should be freed from the corruption that luxe always caused. For instance, as long as Portugal was incapable of growing its own food and manufacturing its own clothes, all sorts of luxe should be forbidden.

Neither a mere vice nor a counterbalance of passions that promote well-being. There were still more reasons why luxury caused illnesses rather than benefits. Previous to the luxury revolution, gold, and silver circulated as coins. Over time, they had been transformed into symbols of lavishness. No one could have ever imagined that "poverty could exist amid kings' luxe and magnificence." Rulers should attempt not to empower their neighbours' industries by promoting imports. In that sense, luxe was relative because it enriched one side while impoverished the other one. Luxe should be encouraged in countries in which the arts and manufactures already flourished whereas it should be forbidden in those ones in which laziness and inaction prevailed. It was astonishing to see that luxury was rampant precisely in kingdoms like Naples in which it should be banned "it is out of this borrowed magnificence that resounds a public voice asking for bread."[15] In a country like Naples, profusion in gold and silver items of crockery was a mark of poverty rather than a symbol of wealth, "metals piled up in the houses of the nobles provoked indigence in the streets."[16] "As if these metals remained still underneath." Every year high-interest rates gnew this sumptuousness for all those tablewares collateralised credits, and therefore, banks ended up accumulating wealth. Gold and silver were supposed to circulate. This inclination toward luxuriousness affected all the members of the republic because "when money lacks, all the classes suffer."

## Reindustrialisation

In France, industry was a fashionable language, manufactures being the very concern of the day.[17] Ministers would have voluntarily transformed every household into a small fabric. Commonly, pieces of writing that avoided industry and focused on agriculture were given no attention, being considered as "erroneously drafted or non useful at all." Shortly, "we will have no bread but a lot of clothes," Goudar forewarned.[18] Moreover, luxury had grounded the depopulation of the countryside. Peasants had migrated to the cities in order to join an army of workers. Labourers were hard to hire in the rural areas since in the overpopulated cities there were at least 300,000 different classes of jobs that entertained several million people. Luxe had given birth to superfluous professions, therefore, breaking a necessary equilibrium.

The government was, however, totally misled in believing that luxury should be promoted at any cost. Precisely, this was one of the main arguments that Goudar attempted to dismantle. Several geographical and cultural conditions should prevail for the industry to be promoted. Climate and soil's fertility had a huge impact on the arts. Frugal countries like England and Holland had been those in which the manufactures had steadily flourished. Goudar compared the total amount of labour required to sustain the level of French and English luxury, and found that at least sixfold more workers were needed to sustain French madness for luxury "any proportion of length and population taken into account."[19] For this reason, one of France's advantages (its law wages), which Goudar estimated at least a fifth cheaper than in England, turned into a lost opportunity.

Indeed, both England and Holland envied Frances' fascination for fashions. Both countries desperately sought to reach the same level of perfection in the arts. France had obtained little from this advantage, though. France's clothes were consumed in countries whose negative balance of commerce was not necessarily paid on bullion. Consequently, the industry should adjust tastes and fashions in order to fit the patterns of metal-extracting economies. This implied reindustrialising the country, readapting the production from a domestic to a foreign market.

Furthermore, France should cut back commercial exchanges with Cadiz and should try to further promote closer commercial relations with Lisbon. The Spanish port provided France with silver, which was a commodity, while Lisbon provided England with gold, which was a currency. As we have already mentioned, Goudar grounded England's great enrichment in the huge injections of gold that its economy had received from Portugal in the first half of the eighteenth century. In France, on the contrary, the monetary stock had known no increase, regardless of the country's descommunal growth of exports.[20] Promoting an industry of luxury that chased no coins resulted purposeless.

"Ideal values" should be exported in exchange for gold. When this was unlikely to be the case, it would be much better to receive "intrinsic values" in exchange for "ideal" ones. Labour force was conceived of as an ideal value whereas raw materials were seen as having an intrinsic one. In this line of thought, "it was better to exchange forms for the substance."[21] Exchanging fine commodities for raw materials caused a loss. For this reason, it seemed better to export superfluities in exchange for essentials or raw materials. Industry's main goal was to provide a country with large quantities of bullion.[22]

Manufactures' prospective positive impacts should be estimated in general and in a relative manner. Using the balance of commerce as a barometer served but little for this measure only accounted for exchanges. It was believed that an increase or decrease in the balance of commerce shed light on the arts' progress. Yet, little attention was commonly paid to the fact that a country could be a creditor and still have an advantage in its industry since imported goods served to acquire larger quantities of labour force.

## Delocalisation and deurbanisation

France's main unfavourable economic condition resulted from its disparaged geometrical distribution of population and stock of money.[23] Goudar sided with those who recognised a stagnation in the level of injected money and the need for a proportionality between the stock of money and adequate levels of employment; both phenomena being appraised as true drivers of economic growth. At the same time, he asserted that manufactures provoked disequilibria in the geographical distribution of the population and with it a concentration of money. He advanced three main solutions to solve this issue: reindustrialisation, deurbanisation, and delocalisation.

Reindustrialising France meant to readapt the offer to suit the tastes of foreign markets at the expense of a domestic madness for fashions. This measure was, nonetheless, insufficient due to the pervasive effects of high wages and high rates of urbanisation which provoked a loss of competitiveness. Compared to England and Holland, in France workers were paid a fifth cheaper although the country could hardly undersell its manufactures abroad. This disadvantage derived from a disproportionate geographical concentration of its population. Politicians usually cared about the number of occupied workers but no concern was shown for the actual patterns of their spatial distribution.

"One million craftsmen" might enrich a country upon the condition that the labour force was evenly distributed on its whole surface. Geographical overconcentration, on the contrary, provoked dearer wages and high prices. For the economy to growth, money should circulate widely both spatially and socially. Only when riches circulated proportionally, they "bring life to the many parts of the political body." Any government should particularly care about this geographical proportionality. This principle was contravened in France where most fabrics had been located within or surrounding the great cities. Paris had absorbed the largest share. The selected locations, indeed, sought to match the emplacing of wealthy customers who could afford the expensive goods. Consequently, cities drew from the countryside a large number of peasants who became domestic servants. Servants were so devoted to luxury that they barely cared about having a progeny. To make things worse, laws were enforced in order to ban servants from marriage.

Governments should be guided by a general rule that reads: overpopulated capitals necessarily meant an underpopulated countryside and food underproduction. Ministers who left Versailles to visit Paris found an overcrowded city in which all kinds of arts boomed, and because of that impression "they believed that the state was extremely powerful." They had no idea of the vacuum countryside that this migration left behind.

All the above reasons led Goudar to endorse deurbanisation. Fabrics should be delocalised to the rural areas where a cheaper workforce could propel them. Manufactures were supposed to make money circulate nation-wide and to generate a positive balance of trade in bullion. Both goals depended on transport costs, which, in turn, hinged on the localisation of the fabrics. As a consequence, industries should be located along the coastline or close to the rivers and navigable routes. Some objections could be raised, though. Port cities already enjoyed the advantages of maritime trade, and further, in those spots wages tend to be dearer than in the countryside where high unemployment prevailed. Yet, the reduction in transport cost inclined the balance. In England, the tendency was for industries to be emplaced close to the coastline. It was advisable that France move the fabrics as close to the cost as possible.

## Notes

1 Jean-François Melon, *A Political Essay upon Commerce.* Written in French by Monsieur M. Translated, with Some Annotations, and Remarks by David Bindon (Dublin: Printed for Philip Crampton, 1738), 2–5.
2 Ange Goudar, *Les Intérêts de La France Mal Entendus*, Vol. I, 10.
3 Ange Goudar, Vol. I, 21.
4 Albert O. Hirschman, *The Passions and the Interests*; Istvan Hont, 'The Early Enlightenment Debate on Commerce and Luxury', in *The Cambridge History of Eighteenth-Century Political Thought*, eds. Mark Goldie and Robert Wokler (Cambridge: Cambridge University Press, 2006), 379–418; Simone Meyssonnier, *La Balance et l'horloge. La Genèse de La Pensée Libérale En France Au XVIIIe Siècle*, 61–93; John Shovlin, *The Political Economy of Virtue*, 18–26; Anoush Fraser Terjanian, *Commerce and Its Discontents*, 26–67; Till Wahnbaeck, *Luxury and Public Happiness*, 20–54; Audrey Provost, 'Le Luxe Publié Au Dix-Huitième Siècle: Questions de Formes', *L'atelier Du Centre de Recherches Historiques* 8 (2011).
5 Istvan Hont, 'The Early Enlightenment Debate on Commerce and Luxury', 382.
6 Albert O. Hirschman, *The Passions and the Interests*, 18, 25, 112, 119, 130. On Mandeville's influence on Melon, and therefore, indirectly on Goudar, see, Simone Meyssonnier, *La Balance et l'horloge.*
7 "les hommes s'attachent à de nouvelles commodités, qui lui deviennent aussi nécessaires que les premières" Ange Goudar, *Les Intérêts de La France Mal Entendus*, Vol. III, 180.
8 Istvan Hont, 'The Early Enlightenment Debate on Commerce and Luxury', 384.
9 Istvan Hont, 384.
10 François Véron Duverger de Forbonnais, *Eléments Du Commerce*, Vol. II, 295.
11 François Véron Duverger de Forbonnais, Vol. II, 302.
12 Ange Goudar, *Naples Ce Qu'il Faut Faire Pour Rendre Ce Royaume Florissant*, 136.
13 Ange Goudar, *Relation historique Du Tremblement de Terre à Lisbonne*, 121.
14 Ange Goudar, 123.
15 Ange Goudar, *Naples Ce Qu'il Faut Faire Pour Rendre Ce Royaume Florissant*, 141.
16 Ange Goudar, 142.
17 Ange Goudar, *Les Intérêts de La France Mal Entendus*, Vol. I, 28.
18 Ange Goudar, Vol. I, 30.
19 Ange Goudar, Vol. III, 235.
20 Ange Goudar, Vol. III, 195.
21 Ange Goudar, Vol. III, 207.
22 Ange Goudar, Vol. III, 208.
23 Ange Goudar, Vol. II, 314.

# 10 Materialising ideas

## A chamber of agriculture

The economic policies that Goudar supported sounded a little bit radical. As already said, this criticism was already raised by some contemporaneous unconvinced readers. Radical as those measures seemed, they fit flawlessly the maxims Goudar had deduced in order to give a sense to the economic reality in which he lived. Alongside those allegedly violent reforms, Goudar proposed the creation of a particular institution meant to promote agriculture.

In France, at that moment, there was a council of commerce but no body of government had yet been set to promote agricultural matters. In accordance with his maxims, Goudar maintained that commerce should be founded upon commercial agriculture, and in consequence, farming was the first activity to be improved. In other words, *commerce d'économie* should precede *commerce de luxe*. The opposite happened in France where the ministers were merely concerned with the division of substance while no care was given to its creation. The manufacturing process only entailed the division of intrinsic values, on the contrary, agriculture entailed the creation of wealth. All these reasons led Goudar to recommend the establishment of a chamber of agriculture, which should promote know-how on the field in the same way the council of commerce supervised the betterment of the arts and commerce.

The council of commerce had been settled at the turn of the eighteenth century. Previous attempts had been made in the seventeenth century to create committees responsible for offering advice on commercial matters with rather unlasting results. Finally, in 1700, a council had been created which operated over the whole century. The institution had essentially been designed as a royal initiative. Indeed, the body suffered changes over time, and it seems that it was especially active in the 1710s and 1720s but not later.[1]

The chamber could be modelled after the council so no innovation was needed. The institution's success in achieving a perfection in the arts could be held as a proof of how useful such institutions seemed. France's manufacturing achievements could in no way be attributed to entrepreneurial individual endeavours. The degree of perfection that its arts had lately achieved derived from the activities of a myriad of provincial and Parisian officials who carefully oversaw both quality and the production process. In all these matters, a pervasive confusion had prevailed until the council had begun its

DOI: 10.4324/9780429028199-13

works. Colbert had reformed the industry giving form to a formerly "chaotic mechanics." The council came to "methodically" deal with commercial matters through the implementation of multiple regulations. Once the council was settled, every step of the manufacturing process began to be carefully and minutiously regulated: wool qualities, number of threats, the length and width of textiles. A number of decrees were issued in order to determine all those matters. Every fabric had its specific regulations. Further, local inspectors enforced them and oversaw the quality of the local production.

A chamber of agriculture should strive to reach the same goals. The kingdom should be divided into forty departments each headed by a director of agriculture. Within one year of the appointment, each director would address to the chamber a memoir on the state of local cultivation. All these papers should offer a general overview of the state of agriculture and serve as the base upon which the economic policies should be modelled. The chamber should instruct ploughmen and farmers alike and should help them to abandon all kinds of old and futile cultivation practices. Special attention should be paid to households and peasants in order to teach them new practices. For this task to be successfully accomplished, translations should be encouraged for most peasants in the countryside neither spoke nor read French. Practice has shown that priests used to evangelise in those local dialects for otherwise their teachings were totally incomprehensible. If priests could not teach the gospel in French, it was much more unlikely that innovative agriculture techniques could be read in that language. Of 10,000 ploughmen, merely 100 could read and understand the new principles of cultivation Duhamel offered in his *Traite de la culture des terres*. This famous book had rather served to embellish the libraries of some "curious" in the cities or to fulfil the likes of some *gentils hommes* who indeed devoted their attention to agriculture. These books became completely useless when they failed to filter down to the peasants "upon which the building of agriculture is founded."[2] The nation gained but nothing from the improvements carefully conducted by a hundred farmers. For these reasons, the chamber would be tasked with translating all these agricultural manuals into the local dialects and would print them. Copies would freely be distributed among ploughmen, farmers, peasants who were unable to purchase those kinds of books. Households that could not afford them would pay only production costs.

The chamber, like the local societies of agriculture, was projected as a counterpoint institution to the Academies of science. Goudar especially proposed to cut off prefaces, introductions, forewords "and all superfluity" with which books were embellished. Readers in the countryside should find only "the essential to the cultivation." New techniques should be spread in the form of "precepts simple to understand and facile to keep in mind," most minds being unable to "hold long details." For this reason, it was better to supply the targeted readers with "short maxims easy to range in mind." Goudar recognised that books were not enough to make the land reach higher levels of production. Tools and machines should also be freely distributed.

If the state supplied the soldier with all the equipment needed to sustain its power, why would it be unthinkable to supply peasants with the tools needed to seed the true sources of state's power and enrich the peasants.

Minds could only be convinced through practice, the sight being much more convincing than the words. No authors or *academiciens* should be appointed at the departmental level. Only cultivators could be appointed as deputies. They were supposed to conduct all sorts of experiments to be emulated by the ploughmen. Deputies' main task should be to increase land productivity. For this to be successfully carried out, they would be entitled to the right of enlisting all sorts of land in their districts and assigned them to specific crops. Special attention should be paid to determine the more fertile and appropriate lands and destined them to the farming of corn, being strictly forbidden for particulars to alter the crops or transform these fertile lands into grazes. Goudar already heard the critics' voices who defended the individual freedom to allocate the land according to their particular interests. Two replicas could be advanced. On the one hand, any regulation that sought the public well-being was already a foundation of liberty. On the other hand, the same system had been enacted for the arts without much complaint. Indeed, it could also be applied to agriculture. The small losses caused to some individuals were worth the advantage caused to the public. One more task of the chamber would be the granting of prizes and recompenses. The same strategy had been displayed to promote the arts. "This is maybe the only means that we had to make agriculture flourish." Goudar listed several prices and gratifications.

## Notes

1 Thomas J. Schaeper, *The French Council of Commerce 1700–1715: A Study of Mercantilism after Colbert* (Columbus: Ohio State University Press, 1983); David Kammerling Smith, 'Structuring Politics in Early Eighteenth-Century France: The Political Innovations of the French Council of Commerce', *Journal of Modern History* 74, no. 3 (2002): 490–537.

2 Ange Goudar, *Les Intérêts de La France Mal Entendus*, Vol. I, 126.

# Part III

# "A universal intercourse of traffic as is desired"

## Free ports, fairs, and institutional evolution in a global perspective

# 11 Free ports

## The idol of all economists

In a very short allusion to free ports, the prominent Neapolitan economist Antonio Genovesi dubbed them the "idol of all economists." The remark illustrates without ambiguity the negative image that the holder of one of the first political economy chairs had on this peculiar institution. By the time the Neapolitan scholar wrote his *Lezioni di comercio*, free ports had come to be a century-long, highly mutable and extremely adaptable, multifaceted, and worth-emulating institution, which had been designed with the intent to promote international trade.

The story goes that the institution had first emerged in the Tyrrhenian Sea from whence it swiftly spread all across the Mediterranean Sea, and later, to the Atlantic Ocean. First created in 1591–93 in Livorno, the model was speedily emulated and copied once and again in several cities across the Italian Peninsula; sometimes with the intent to achieve the same goal for which it had been designed, sometimes with the intent to imitate because there was no alternative left. Genovesi, who found his sources of inspiration in a long-lived Italian economic tradition (and from Broggia in particular), firmly discouraged policymakers to declare free ports. At the same time, however, he bitterly regretted that "if all or most of a country's neighbours set up free ports, there is no way not to have one, because the country would rest alone.[1]"

This third part will thus track down the making and unmaking of free ports in the early modern times. It will unravel the institution's evolution and persistence. It will focus on the innovation versus imitation debate, and what I have called "innovation in persistence.[2]" I will approach this particular evolutionary path from the perspective of an enduring trading institution in the *longue durée*, since the latter half of the seventeenth century all across the eighteenth to the first two decades of the nineteenth century. Yet, no monographic-like approach is attempted in the chapters that follow. Many scholars have already carried this task judiciously.[3] The main endeavour assumed throughout the next five chapters is therefore not to narrate when, how, and why each one of the settled free ports saw their day. Here, on the contrary, I grasp with the transformations and continuities that made that an institution be altered or kept over centuries. In other words, the way in which

DOI: 10.4324/9780429028199-15

commercial regulations and intellectual debates shaped and reshaped a very specific model over a long time. Instead of unfolding singular local processes of emulation one after another, the chapters will rather disclose particular waves of imitation and innovation. The chapters will in particular unveil the main results achieved in each one of those waves in which free ports became trending and were branded as the main solution to economic and commercial downturns. They will be organised chronologically.

To begin with, I will define what a free port was. As we will see, this is a hot issue about which much ink has already been spilled. I will, nonetheless, deviate from prevalent explanations and will advance an alternative account for free port's emergence and design. Fundamentally, I will alter the framework within which the question is commonly asked. Accordingly, my efforts will be conducted at repositioning a rather overlooked phenomenon that has to do with the nature and emergence of commercial exchanges: how markets emerge in space and time. The spatial dispersion or concentration of exchanges, capital, and labour, along with the temporal conditions upon which markets took form call to mind a candent eighteenth-century debate: fairs versus markets. I will propose the idea that through the refashioning of centuries-old medieval juridical norms, Renaissance rulers transformed fairs from sporadic, seasonal-held meetings into perpetual markets: free ports. I will then approach each one of the three waves that happened over the eighteenth century.

By all accounts, Livorno had first settled the path to free ports' continental-wide renown in the sixteenth century.[4] My analysis will, however, specifically tackle processes that happened at the turn of the eighteenth century onward. One of the oddities of this modern institution is that, at first glance, it seemed to have gained rather little or no support in the allegedly most advanced northern countries like England and Holland. In the 1660s, France created a couple of free ports, one at the Manche Channel and the other one in the Mediterranean basin. Yet, the refashioning of these two city ports (Dunkirk and Marseilles)[5] into free ports brought about certain innovations that profoundly modified the institution's main features, somehow setting it apart from the sixteenth-century original.

Italian cities like Florence and Genoa had created their respective specific models of free ports in a strive to redirect international or corn trade upon their rule. In lieu, in France, the institution was thought of as a means to propel manufacturing urban emporia.[6] In England, the strict uphold to the Navigation act led many to argue the impracticability of settling a free port. There, discussions on whether to create or not a free port lasted for the whole century. England somehow gave this institution a new dimension by metamorphosing free ports into an imperial project. Earlier in Tanger (1662),[7] a failed attempt, and later, in Gibraltar (1706),[8] more successfully, or at least, more lasting. In the eighteenth century, many in the continent and the island asserted that England had devised a substitutive institutional model, which, by calibrating tariffs, could achieve exactly the same goals that free ports could achieve. In that sense, free ports and the drawback system could be seen as interchangeable, or at least, contestant institutions.

As an outcome of the above along with other policies introduced in Genoa at the outset of the eighteenth century, free ports became trending once again in the 1740s. As we have already seen, these were hard times for those who dreamed of eternal peace. I will demonstrate that during these first decades, the institution was once again reshaped. From being mainly an overseas-deserving route, free ports were transformed into a new silk road. This scheme was very likely to have been mapped out in Turin whose enlightened officials got inspiration from previous measures implemented in Genoa. In the 1760s, contests in the Caribbean Sea led Nordic European rulers with small dominions to bring into play free ports in an attempt to redirect colonial commerce into their islands, therefore, transforming the rosary of small Caribbean spots into an aqueous road for illegal trade.[9] The wave impacted England and Spanish powers alike, obliging them to enact particular policies. The results could be no more contrasting. Whereas England was compelled to open up Jamaican ports upon the rules of the free port Act,[10] Spain opposed to do so but instead put into practice a set of reforms called *Puertos libres* (free ports).[11]

The last wave took place after Smith's fight against the mercantile system of privileges. We will follow a failed but obstinate and unsuccessful attempt to settle a free port in Lisbon at the dawn of free trade. A very location, halfway the Mediterranean and the North and South Atlantic. The project entertained many authors and officials for at least four decades, the debates being framed in a large intellectual discussion that happened in a time in which no one was seemingly to back a mercantilist-like policy. Sismondi in fact did.

## "A universal intercourse of traffic as is desired"

Over the seventeenth and eighteenth centuries, free ports awoke the envy of many across Europe. The institution's alleged benefits captured the imagination of many policymakers and intellectuals who dreamed of its advantages. Its incessant shaping and reshaping over centuries ended up leaving lots of records. So, paradoxically, this is a topic over which a large panoply of multivariate records exists. Of still more interest is the way in which knowledge on free ports accumulated, creating many overlapping chronological sedimentary layers.

In a nutshell, free ports were commonly linked to at least one of the following interlinked policies: (i) tax-exempt marketplaces; (ii) multicultural and diasporic marketplaces; (iii) marketplaces where merchant communities could apply their own costumes and laws.

Likeliness of the establishment of a free port unchained vivid discussions, both in the public sphere or in the narrower intellectual or bureaucratic circles. All these discussions were at the origin of publications, manuscripts, or reports. Occasionally, free ports were settled as a result of previously held theoretical discussions. Intermittently, debates were rather held as a reply to the alleged damages or disorders the institution was being blamed for. It is hard to conjecture why the model was often brought back from the edge of death in specific moments in history over the last three centuries. For instance, in France, first in the first decades of the nineteenth century, and then again, at the turn of the twentieth century.[12] In the last century, free zones grew out of the idea of free ports even though a similar model can already be found in eighteenth-century Marseilles.

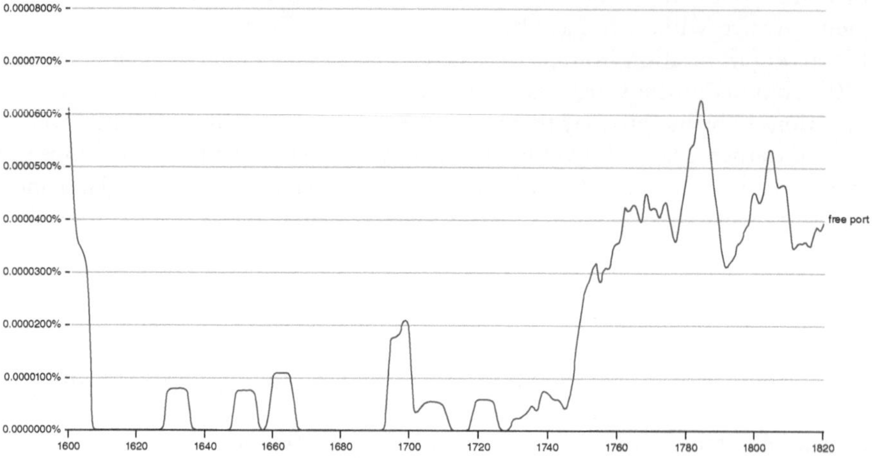


*Figure 11.1* N-gram Google. Free port

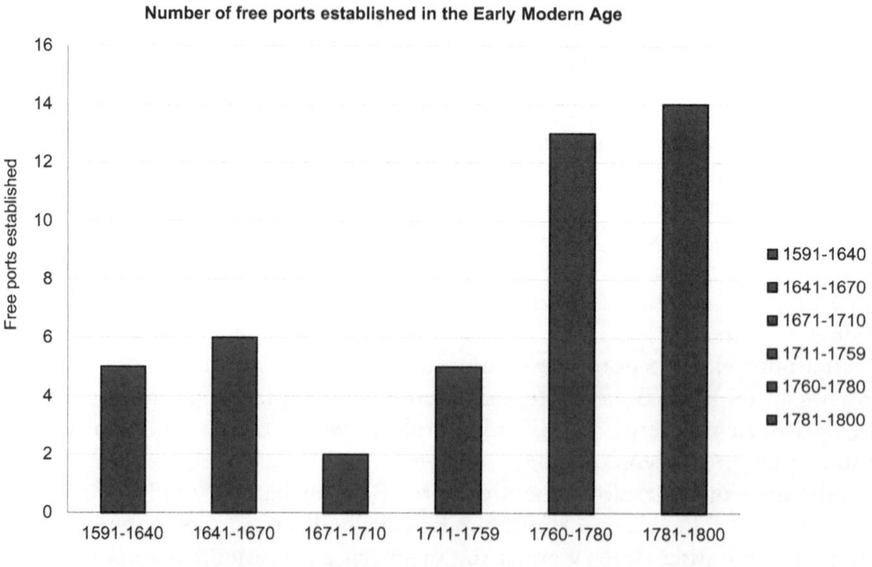


*Chart 11.1* Number of free ports established in the early modern age
Source: Tazzara, "Managing free trade"

What is settled is that overlapped layers coincided with debates held on whether to settle or not free ports. Assisted by N-gram google, we can broadly approach the specific moments in which debates were most likely to have happened. We can in turn contrast this information with the data on the years in which free ports were created over the seventeenth and eighteenth centuries (Figure 11.1; Chart 11.1).

Data on the English printing sphere show that free ports seem to have regained some appeal in three specific junctures: the 1660s, 1690s–1700s, and 1760s–80s. These stages roughly coincided with the enactment of certain policies in both Tanger and Gibraltar in the 1660s and the turn of the century, and later, with the settlement of free ports in a few Caribbean islands in the mid-century. At least in England, it is seemingly that the word began to lose track in the 1780s yet it was at this very moment that many supported the establishment of a free port at home in order to transformed London into a "universal market." Specifically, the first wave began in 1662 when Tanger was converted into a free port. This happened around the same years in which Venetian authorities agreed to modify the city's tariffs in order to accommodate the institution, which lasted only for a few years.[13] Later, the English's takeover of Gibraltar winded up with the settlement of a free port within the borders of Spain, in the lane that connected the Levant and northern markets, a move that triggered great repercussions across the Mediterranean Sea.

The question arises as to what actually a free port was, on the one hand, and whether there was a fixed model upon which emulators could build their copies once and again, on the other hand. As a matter of fact, in the seventeenth and eighteenth centuries, there were many definitions of free ports although officials and functionaries were so much inclined to draw on the one included in Savary's dictionary.

In spite of that, outlooks differed radically. Some saw free ports as a promising institution while others blamed them for their adverse repercussions. They were conceived of either as an innovation or an old model. Either a powerful policy that served to syphon international trade or a harmful device that destroyed commerce and the national navy alike. Most dreamed of free ports. Others, instead, feared they could unexpectedly turn into a nightmare.

Another branch of the discussion has to do with free ports' pretended innovation. In other words, whether they were a true invention or rather a refashioned old model. The question remains as to whether the institution was a Medieval-inherited model or a creation of early modern times.

In the eighteenth century, Broggia alerted policymakers to free ports' harmful effects. Writing from Naples and deeply concerned about a declining manufacturing industry, and particularly, about the re-establishment of the silk industry, Broggia singled out several reasons why not to settle a free port. They provoked an adverse effect on the state, commerce, and the merchants alike. They not only ruined manufacturers but also dismantled the national navy. Foreigners ended up controlling all branches of trade, such as had happened in Livorno. Smuggling was also to fear. Dockers and storehouses located within free ports made it easier for smugglers to conduct their illegal activities and for merchants to fraud the customs house. In conclusion, a Toscan manufacturing canton was much more valuable than many thousands of Livornos.

More recently, in his lengthy and centuries-encompassing study on free ports, Dermigny brought forth the fact that ports like Dunkirk and Bayonne often purported their Medieval privileges, a kind of propaganda that should be taken with a grain of salt. In contraposition, he conceived of free ports as a radically new institution, a modern "reality" designed by modern central states. For him, they were an offspring of the modern states' mercantile practices. In consonance, the institution should be understood as a modern model created to promote trade in a new changing environment.

Diversity remained at the core of the model so, over the centuries, it had gradually evolved. Dermigny paid little or no attention to the set of factors that underpinned such an evolutionary path to diversity. Yet, some of his conclusions are worth mentioning. He linked free ports to the idea of scales and narrow seas. Dermigny also raised the question about free ports' performance; in other words, why some of them reached a strong influence while others just languished or remained in the shadows. For him, two conditions were necessary for free ports to yield success: warehousing and transit rights should be enhanced by powerful diasporas. This was the key. In Livorno, there were the Jews. In Trieste, there were the Greeks. In Singapore, there were the Chinese. Maybe this explained Tanger's failing attempt. The East India Company managers recommended the transformation of Bombay into a free port and asked that Hindu merchants were invited into the city.[14]

Livorno, the first free port ever, has recently deserved a fascinating, lucid, and rigorously documented study, which encompasses three centuries. Tazara fully agreed with Derbigny in that free ports were a radical new invention; still more, for him "The free port was the most notable invention of the seventeenth-century Italian political economy."[15] His approach is, nonetheless, different in several ways from Dermigny's. For him, this "most notable invention" would in large part be the outcome of bottom-up solicitations that gradually transformed the framework into which free ports operated. In other words "a system of supplications was responsible for elaborating the theory and practice of the free port."[16]

A nineteenth-century Italian author envisaged free ports as a measure that had been implemented by Italian cities in order to reposition themselves in the international arena once the African route to Asia was circumvented. Livorno was the first port to have been ever engineered as a free port. Even though many measures were gradually implemented during the latter half of the sixteenth century, scholars have considered with much care the so-called *Livornina*, a set of laws issued in 1591–93. Livorno's apparently radical transformation should be attributed to a series of regulations and not to a single measure.[17] Essentially, those regulations made a call for merchants of any nation and practicing any religion to move over to the emerging Toscan port.

Besides, they authorised foreigners to move over without being levied any taxes, and further, allowed them the possibility to renegade the honouring of debts outside Toscany. These privileges that targeted particular national communities (and particularly the Jews who later reached 10 per cent of a burgeoning population) complemented a set of tax reductions extracted on storage and transit trade.

By enacting all those new rules, the Dukes of Toscan transformed a bleak swampy fortress, which had been bought from the Genoes in 1401, into an allegedly multiconfessional marketplace where commodities could be stored and reshipped paying light taxes. Partially, Livornos' pre-eminence owed to the fact of its having emerged out from nothing to rapidly become an international port that attracted ships from the Levant and the northern sea. By the same years, Genoa rearranged its customs house's guidelines in order to draw trade to its coast.[18] The measures were enacted in the midst of a hard famine and with the hopes that Dutch vessels would supply inhabitants desperate for corn. Ships carrying two-thirds of the cargo in corn without having called at another port (especially Livorno) were granted lower duties.

From the very beginning, two models were put into contest. One the one hand, Livorno's model, which is overall framed as an emporium, and on the other hand, the Genoa's one, which is assumed to have given shape to an *entrepôt*. In other words, freedoms and privileges granted either for people or goods or for both of them.

In Savary's dictionary, two specific privileges defined a free port. In those privileged-granted ports, merchants from all nations were allowed to unload their merchandise and reship it elsewhere "without being levied any tax whatsoever." In this sense, the institution was linked neither to a city's whole urban area or its harbour, but specifically to a narrow-circumscribed warehouse area. Genoa was a case in point. However, free ports, according to a second definition, referred not to within-bonds warehousing footprint but to the specific kind of tax exemptions that cities offered to merchants interested in exporting or importing, no spatial connotation being attached. This double-faced notion has generated too much confusion.[19]

## Notes

1 Antonio Genovesi, *Lezioni Di Commercio o Sia d'economia Civile* (Bassano: Spese Remondini, 1769), Vol. I, 288.

2 Gabriel Tarde, *The Laws of Imitation* (New York: Henry Holt and Company, 1903).

3 F. L. A. Ferrier, *Essai Sur Les Ports Francs* (Bayonne, Bordeaux, and Paris: Messidor an II); Paul Masson, *Ports Francs d'autrefois et d'aujourd'hui* (Paris: Hachette, 1904); Georges Musset, *Les Ports Francs. Étude Historique* (Paris: Ernest Leroux éditeur, 1904); Louis Dermigny, 'Escales. Échelles et Port Francs Au Moyen Âge et Aux Temps Modernes', in *Les Grandes Escales. Période Contemporaine et Synthèse Génèrales*, 3 vols. (Bruxelles: Éditions de la librairie encyclopedique, 1974), Vol. 3, 213–644; Alberto Caracciolo, 'Il Dibattito Sui "Porti Franchi" Nel Settecento: Genesi Della Franchigia Di Ancona', *Rivista Storica Italiana* 75, no. 3 (1963): 538–58; Thomas Kirk, 'Genoa and Livorno: Sixteenth and Seventeenth-Century

Commercial Rivalry as a Stimulus to Policy Development', *History* 86, no. 281 (2001): 3–17; Corey Tazara, *The Free Port of Livorno and the Transformation of the Mediterranean World* (Oxford: Oxford University Press, 2017); Corey Tazara, 'Managing Free Trade in Early Modern Europe: Institutions, Information, and the Free Port of Livorno', *Journal of Modern History* 86, no. 3 (2014): 493–529; Guillaume Calafat, 'L'indice de La Franchise: Politique Économique, Concurrence de Ports Francs et Condition Des Juifs En Méditerranée à l'époque Moderne', *Revue Historique* 686, no. 2 (2018): 275–320; Guillaume Calafat, *Une Mer Jalousée. Contribution à l'histoire de La Souveraineté (Méditerranée, XVIIe Siècle)* (Paris: Seuil, 2019); Jespers Meijling, 'La Lenta Diffusione Di Un Modello: Il Porto Franco Da Livorno a Marstrand Nel Settecento', *Nuovi Studi Livornesi* 17, no. 2010 (2010): 95–120; Victor Wilson, *Commerce in Disguise: War and Trade in the Caribbean Free Port of Gustavia, 1793–1815* (Abo: Abo Akademis förlag, 2015); Antonio Iodice, *Il Porto Franco, Diffusione Di Un Modello Economico: Politiche, Attori, Ideologie, Mito. Due Realtà a Confronto: Genova e Marsiglia (1590–1817)* (Aix-Marseille, 2017); Christopher Denis-Delacour, *Entre Normes et Pratiques. Les Étrangers Des Trafics Maritimes Romains (1742–1797)* (Aix-Marseille/Istituto Italiano di Scienze Umane, 2012).

4 Corey Tazara, 'Managing Free Trade'; Corey Tazara, *The Free Port of Livorno*; Guillaume Calafat, *Une Mer Jalousée*, 309–59; Guillaume Calafat, 'L'indice de La Franchise'.

5 Antonio Iodice, 'Il Porto Franco'.

6 Jeff Horn, *Economic Development in Early Modern France. The Privilege of Liberty, 1650–1820* (Cambridge: Cambridge University Press, 2015), 135–42.

7 Tristan Stein, 'Tangier in the Restoration Empire', *Historical Journal* 54, no. 4 (2011): 985–1011.

8 José Ignacio Martínez Ruíz, 'De Tánger a Gibraltar: El Estrecho En La Praxis Comercial e Imperial Británica (1661–1776),' *Hispania* 65–3, no. 221 (2005): 1043–62.

9 Victor Wilson, *Commerce in Disguise*; Jeppe Mulich, *In a Sea of Empires: Networks and Crossings in the Revolutionary Caribbean* (Cambridge: Cambridge University Press, 2020), 42–55.

10 F. Armytage, *The Free Port System in the British West Indies* (London: Longmans, 1953); R. Grant Kleiser, 'An Empire of Free Ports: British Commercial Imperialism in the 1766 Free Port Act,' *Journal of British Studies* 60, no. 2 (2021): 334–61.

11 Josep M. Delgado, *Dinámicas Imperiales (1650–1796): España, América y Europa En El Cambio Institucional Del Sistema Colonial Español* (Barcelona: Bellatera, 2007).

12 Georges Musset, *Les Ports Francs*; Paul Masson, *Ports Francs d'autrefois et d'aujourd'hui*.

13 Massimo Costantini, *Porto, Navi e Traffici a Venezia* (Venezia: Marsilio, 2004).

14 Louis Dermigny, 'Escales. Échelles et Port Francs'.

15 Corey Tazara, *The Free Port of Livorno*, 15.

16 Corey Tazara, 18.

17 Guillaume Calafat, 'L'indice de La Franchise'.

18 Thomas Kirk, 'Genoa and Livorno'.

19 Philemon-Louis Savary, *Dictionnaire Universel de Commerce...Continué Sur Les Mémoires de l'auteur, et Donné Au Public Par M. Philemon-Louis Savary, Chanoine de l'Église Royale de S. Maur Des Fossez, Son Frère. Nouvelle Édition, Exactement Revue, Corrigée, & Enrichie de Beaucoup d'additions* (Genève: Héritiers Crammer & Frères Philibert, 1742), Vol. II, 1192.

# 12 Lasting and unlasting markets

## From Medieval fairs to free ports

If we consider the room that Savary allocated to free ports in his widely read dictionary, we would be highly surprised or rather disappointed. No more than one page was devoted to the institution before turning all his attention to Marseilles and the privileges the French king had granted to this Mediterranean *entrepôt*. Being a French author, this could seem rather normal. Yet, the question remains as to why such a disregard for an institution which contemporaries treated with so much fervour.

Many scholars who have studied free ports have placed their focus on either of their three mainly attributed features (tax exemptions, diasporic outposts, proper mercantile jurisdictions) without giving much thought to the fact that there was an analogous institution to which Savary provided with much more room: fairs. In full contrast to the space allocated to free ports, the entry fairs were granted more than forty pages. Not only that. Readers were also offered a lengthy and carefully arranged list of fairs held all across Europe.

One might attribute this flaw to the fact that contemporary authors disposed of yet little evidence on one instance and plenty on another. Since fairs dated back to at least the twelfth century, turn-of-the-century writers were in the position to regain easy access to a lot of records. For instance, in 1696, an extremely detailed study was published on the Champagne fairs.[1] Around the mid-eighteenth century, a detailed portable list of fairs along with an introduction was offered to the readers, many of them merchants.[2] As Savary's dictionary was intended to assist merchants in their practical day-to-day trading businesses, there was no reason to gift patrons with unuseful data of little or no interest regarding an almost expiring centuries-old mercantile institution. One more fact. On the cover, readers were reported that this information could be found: "all fairs whether free or the other kind that exist in France or the most famous places elsewhere."

Later, in the mid-century, Turgot wrote the entry fairs for the *Encyclopédie*. His survey was a *laissez-faire*-minded, intendedly devastating yet short and highly convincing inspection. He attacked an atypical form of marketplace that seemed to resist the passage of time. Well-documented research has corroborated that, still in the eighteenth century, fairs were far to be an expiring institution. All the contrary, itinerant and sporadic-held trading meetings

DOI: 10.4324/9780429028199-16

persisted as one of the main institutions that backed commercial structures across Europe.[3] Further, the fourteenth and fifteenth centuries witnessed the explosion of regional fairs that came to replace the former famous international ones. Late Medieval regional fairs are arguably an institutional innovation.[4] Their location and economic functions were a by-product of some of the factors that Turgot mentioned. They were mainly outlets for domestic trade, meeting points between low- and highlands, between husbandry and agricultural zones. They further contributed to the expansion of overland trade routes.

Turgot opposed natural (spontaneous) markets to unnatural (artificial) and induced fairs. We will come back to this very difference in the next chapter. For now, it is enough to say that fairs were seen as trading meetings that took place periodically. In some cases, they referred to markets held in particular cities. In other instances, fairs rather constituted a network of interlinked cities with sequential markets, which made it easier for people to exchange goods and services over the course of the whole year (like in the very much renowned twelfth-century Champagne fairs).

In the nineteenth century, for any reason that would need further research (maybe because of the criticism that fairs received following the French Revolution and the reorganisation of the market space that the event unfolded[5]), free ports were linked to the idea of fairs. This was not a feature proper to the nineteenth century, though. Already in the seventeenth century, Livorno was labelled as a "continuous fair of foreigners."[6] Braudel reported that contemporaries spoke of Amsterdam as a continuous fair.

An essential yet neglected feature of the discussion comes then to the front: lasting versus unlasting markets. Some contemporaries saw free ports as an everlasting fair. Different from their Medieval forerunner (international fairs), the sixteenth-century engineered marketplaces had evolved into being an uninterrupted meeting. In 1814, for instance, in a paper written to support Dunkirk's endangered privileges, reported the free port as a "universal and permanent fair where the whole world comes to seek the supplies of all kinds."[7] Previously in 1802, the advantages of "perpetual fairs" were assessed *vis-à-vis* the disadvantages of periodical markets, which were "subject to a fatal delay," therefore, inciting buyers to postpone their showing up until the expiration's term with the only purpose of "making the law to the seller."[8]

The benefits that resulted from an "unlimited privilege" were self-evident. Free ports were continuous markets in which exchanges could be "repeated without interval." By declaring a universal and everlasting fair, Colbert had reconciled foreign and maritime trade. The minister had dreamed of an enclave where foreigners could purchase commodities shipped from the four corners of the world. A marketplace where any seller was free to sell, buy, and stock merchandise without deadline, with light or no taxes as incentives. Indeed, these enclaves served also to lower transport and travel costs. Free ports, such as Colbert thought of them, were an everlasting fair. And for these continuous fairs to yield any success, unlimited freedom should be granted.

## How do markets emerge?

Two focal yet overlooked aspects deserve more attention: space and time. In other words, scale and duration. These two factors have been downplayed at the instance of free ports' more recurrently studied characteristics. I hold that those market meetings organised periodically underwent a change on matter, evolving from sporadically held meetings to everlasting marketplaces. Free ports were conceived of as perpetual marts. Duration is not the only matter to be taken into consideration, though. Turgot complained that fairs were an artificial unconventional type of marketplace that projected on the space a particular set of unfair privileges. He was putatively among the few to have introduced the spatial issue in the discussion on markets and fairs.[9] For him, market meetings could be projected on the space either as a natural spontaneous encounter or as a distorted and artificially induced meeting.

Turgot's rationale reads as follows.[10] Commerce's natural course should be left free for it to reach its own dimension and extension. For him, the number of sellers on a marketplace would limit prices and impact the number of customers. Therefore, a proportion should exist between the former and the latter.

Let's suppose that for a commodity to cover its trade costs (including the seller's gains), at least 300 units should be sold on the market, which means a market size of roughly 300 families. Let's further suppose that there are three villages each one habited by one hundred families. One can thus deduce that those numbers would be in the position to maintain only one merchant. Consequently, a merchant would settle in the village where the highest number of purchasers could meet at a lower cost. Giving a reduction in costs, purchasers would rather buy from this merchant than from another one living in their own village but selling dearer. Exactly the same principle would apply to other commodities, making that a larger number of commodities sold over same place would lower costs for the benefit of customers. There was a ceiling, though. The number of purchasers would increase the number of sellers and vice versa until the point where those located farther away could not offset their costs through a reduction in prices. "This explains how trading centres or markets came into being," Turgot holds. Distance accounted for the emergence of markets as much as time did, with commodities' durability determining the timing of the meetings and repercuting on distance a seller is able or willing to journey.

In this line, markets radically differed from fairs. The latter, which were seen as a "meeting of nations," projected on the space not cost reductions but privileges: "they are offspring of certain privileges and franchises granted to the community of merchants in a specific time and place whereas trade is overwhelmed with taxes and duties elsewhere." Princes who granted tax exemptions had induced the artificial emergence of fairs all over Europe. The underlying difference between markets and fairs, according to Turgot, lies in the fact that the former resulted from a spontaneous encounter of mutual interests while the latter was the outcome of a wish for privileges. Turgot further provided the reader with a historical explanation of the emergence of fairs. Fiscal reasons had moved feudal lords to lower taxes in the hope to draw a larger number of exchanges under their domains, and with them, to increase their revenues. Once states had regained control, fairs had become one of the best policies to promote trade, cities being granted ceaseless privileges even with the conscious purpose to harm contesters.

In a mid-century publication that offered readers a portable list of French nationwide-held fairs, the anonymous author voiced the lack of a convincing study on the "origin of fairs and markets and the natural causes of their establishment."[11] The author arranged the list of fairs according to provincial limits as this method resulted more useful for his expected readers who barely traded beyond close distances. The author then copied Turgot's encyclopaedic text verbatim. Fairs were defined as "a public place where merchants meet during certain days to sell their merchandise freely." In this sense, a fair was a much bigger market where a larger number of customers and sellers met, all of them attracted by "the franchises and exemptions." These free fairs were visited by foreign merchants or served as marketplaces for commodities shipped from abroad. Guided by his *laissez-faire* approach and impregnated with a rage against antinatural privileges, Turgot was likely to have left unnoticed one of his own ideas: "The natural course of commerce suffices to form this contest and to increase it until a certain extent." Privileges were likely to enhance the extension far beyond the limits this natural course could yield.

## Spacetime and perpetual marketplaces

Savary's dictionary drew a distinction between free fairs and those ones that merely enjoyed partial privileges. It was said that the former enjoyed particular privileges, franchises, and freedoms. Regardless of the vast panoply of existing privileges that a ruler could grant to a city, they could be clustered in five sets. In the first lieu, through the granting of a fair, a ruler committed to offer foreign merchants the security to enter, transit, sojourn, and leave the country as they pleased. This right was also guaranteed to the commodities they carried in or took out. In addition, in accordance with, and following those old customs and freedoms, no taxes were levied. Those free fairs were tax-exempt demarcated places. Furthermore, royal officials were unable to issue debt delays concerning fair transactions. It means, they had no jurisdiction over this place. Finally, merchants enjoyed their proper mercantile jurisdiction.[12]

Among the listed fairs, the dictionary allocated a particular room to the ones held in Lyon and settled on 9 February 1419. The fair had gradually been extended and granted further privileges. At the beginning, the fair lasted only twenty days although forty more days were allowed in 1443. In 1462, a new change was introduced which permitted merchants to meet "four times each one lasting fifty days openable and without interruption." Further, no impositions, charges, or tributes of any kind should be paid. Still more importantly, permission was given for goods to be shipped abroad without being levied any taxes provided that they were properly sealed. For goods to enjoy this franchise, they have to be dispatched one day before the opening of the subsequent fair.[13] Swiss and German merchants enjoyed fifteen more days.

The fifteenth-century emergence of Lyon fairs, which in turn drew on the Medieval Champagne former model, seems at the first glance to have nothing to do with the emergence and design of sixteenth-century free ports. Yet, both institutions were more closely related than has so far been assumed. Gradually, the fair transformed into an international marketplace towards which commodities flew from many parts of Europe and the Levant. Purchasers and sellers came as far as from Turkey, Syria, and Alexandria. A second similarity has been overlooked: commodities could be brought to and shipped from the fair (and from the kingdom) without being charged any imposition.

The fair-system was likely to follow a particular path. It had first emerged as a marketplace for long-distance merchants. Commodities brought from the Levant and traded by Italian merchants were received in exchange for woollen clothes produced in northern Europe. Located in the rural areas of Champagne, the fairs started their decay at the turn of the fourteenth century, at a moment in which fairs took a rather regional horizon. Many reasons had been associated with their decadence. Max Weber held that international fairs had been replaced by urban trading networks.[14] Regional fairs have been said to be the backbone of the pre-modern economy. They are said to be an institutional innovation. Here, however, we are more interested in international fairs. By the time Livorno emerged as a free port, international fairs had already created continental-wide network circuits. Some of them like the Lyon fair had gradually specialised in finance and money exchanges.[15]

It is agreed upon that fair-oriented trade based on overland routes flourished and helped lowering transaction costs. An effective enforcement of contracts is assumed to be on the grounds of the emergence of that rapid commercial expansion. Milgrom, North, and Weingast addressed the underpinning reasons for this boom.[16] For these scholars, the geographical extension of trade is closely related to the willingness and capacity of merchants to costless renegade contracts or repudiate agreements. A lack of continuous information on potential partners' behaviour made persistent trade difficult. Precisely, law-merchant courts that operated in the international fairs contributed in reducing those costs. Not through their capacity to enforce the law but thanks to a reputation mechanism in which the state was absentee or too weak or unable to enforce contracts. Merchants attended the international trading meetings halfway north and south Europe because courts assured contract enforcement.

The impacts and effects of private-order contract enforcement mechanisms versus public ones have abundantly been discussed in both economic theory and economic history.[17] The arguments the above scholars advanced suffered from several shortcomings. On the one hand, even if one takes for granted the effectiveness and low costs of the merchant-courts enforcing institution, these explanations would be unlikely to ascertain why the fairs emerged in a specific location. A reduction in transaction costs is likely to have a bigger impact on economic growth than the reduction in production costs. Yet, transport costs could impose restrictions on the distance that merchants were able or willingly to journey.[18] On the other hand, the private-order mechanism held as responsible for the rise and success of Medieval international marketplaces barely fit with, or match historical records.[19]

Compared to institutions, location has been attributed a lesser impact in explaining the fairs' ascendency (even in the case of those towns located along important and historical overland routes).[20] It is very likely that the rise of the Champagne fairs owed much to the granting of "generalised" provisions (the term was coined by Edwards and Ogilvie). In this line of research, rulers would have granted to any fellow of a mercantile community (irrespectively of their nation) the same guarantees on their property rights and lives. In full contrast to what North and his co-authors affirmed, historical evidence shows that rulers carried many efforts to ensure the lives of those coming in and leaving the fairs, even on a scale that surpassed local fairs' geographic effulgence. Moreover, in full contrast to what North and his co-authors uphold, contract enforcement was framed within a princely-justice system in which overlapping jurisdictional contest would have made justice more efficient. Security and contract enforcement appear among the services rulers provided with, not to mention other services such as "infrastructure, loan guarantees, and constraints on local merchant's privileges."[21] In those times, rulers could avail themselves of different stimuli: generalised guarantees or particular privileges. Precisely, the fairs' success resulted from the implementation of generalised guarantees. This explanation, which draws deeply on historical records, sheds light on the fairs' ascendancy and decay. In this interpretation, nonetheless, transport costs seem to play no role in explaining geographical locations.

Let's suppose that competition among rulers for capturing a larger share of revenues (this is the agreed-upon reason why rulers would have attempted to introduce specific measures) compelled them to offer the same kind of generalised guarantees. The question remains as to how merchants would choose a location. Still, as the Lyon fair and the Genois investors show, the location could apparently be changed with no much cost. It seems that, as Turgot ascertained, tax privileges could repercuted in time and space attracting a larger number of shoppers.

## Ab introitu iudicum and ius stepulae

For artificial marketplaces (fairs) to be created, two mechanisms could be put at play. In this sense, Huvelin's interpretation of the evolution of fairs and markets throughout the Medieval times remains of utmost interest. In his nineteenth-century law dissertation, he mentioned two rights upon which markets and fairs had continually been shaped and reshaped over centuries. On the one hand, *ab introitu iudicum*, and on the other hand, *ius stepulae*. According to his legal interpretation, fairs and markets owed their origins to a particular historical process through which kings would have devolved jurisdiction upon local lords. The concession of this jurisdiction would have happened in a gradual manner.

At the turn of the tenth century, a privilege was gradually introduced allowing lords to levy impositions on customers and sellers who gathered within their jurisdictions. At that moment, market meetings were commonly held in the monasteries' surroundings. It was only later that local lords were allowed to claim the monopoly on saying justice at the markets under their respective jurisdictions. So, they were now responsible for keeping peace. Huvelin maintained that the granting of such specific privileges would have been led by a desire for economic improvement and not only guided by fiscal concerns.[22] Peace was, therefore, a prealable condition for markets to emerge. At the dawn of time, markets would have grown out of *malli:* frequent meetings during which justice was said.[23] *Ab introitu iudicum* played an essential role in the consolidation of those markets. Right holders could, for instance, exclude royal judges from saying justice on the conceded jurisdiction, or rather, "the royal judges had no control other than the one right holders granted to them." This in turn remembers the above point on "fair-wardens."

The second right, which worked in favour of cities, was the one called the "step" (*ius stapulae*). Merchants transiting through cities located along commercial routes could be legally stopped and compelled to sell their goods on the city market. Drawing on sixteenth- and seventeenth-century jurists, Huvelin discussed the different variants these rights took, being more or less stricter: *ius stapulae minus plenum* and *ius emporii*.[24] Cities that enacted the former right compelled transit merchants to seal and weigh goods before continuing their journey to their final destination. A tax could be levied although merchants were left free not to sell their goods. The latter was the strictest of all regulations a city could put into effect. Merchants were obliged not only to sell their merchandise on the city market, but also, a veto was imposed on others than the city's inhabitants to transact with transiting merchants. These two rights, as we will see, played an essential role in the creation of free ports. It is, in the transformation of fairs from unlasting to everlasting marketplaces. Changes could be on matter or manner.

## Notes

1 P. Huvelin, *Essai Historique Sur Le Droit Des Marchés et Des Foires*, 244.
2 Anonymous, *Foires et Marchés Du Royaume, Ouvrage Contenant: 1. Un État Des Foires Les plus Fameuses de La France & Des Pays étrangers. 2. Une Indication Par Ordre Alphabétique de Toutes Les Foires & Marchés Francs, Qui Se Tiennent Dans Tous Le Royaume, & Rangée Par Ordre Des Provinces.*
3 Dominique Margairaz, *Foires et Marchés.*

4 Setephan Epstein, 'Regional Fairs, Institutional Innovation'.
5 Dominique Margairaz, *Foires et Marchés.*
6 Corey Tazara, *The Free Port of Livorno*, 13.
7 Anonymous, *Mémoire Sur La Nécessité Du Rétablissement de La Franchise Du Port et de La Ville de Dunkerque* (Dunkerque: Typographie de Vanderest, 1814).
8 M. Battur, ed., 'Mémoire de La Chambre de Commerce de Dunkerque, Sur Les Ports Francs (1802)', in *Questions Des Entrepòts et Ports Francs Contenant Onze Lettres Publiées Dans Le Journal Le Commerce de Dunkerque et Du Nord* (Paris: Librairie Encyclopédique de Roret, 1845), Vol. II, 3–15.
9 Dominique Margairaz, 'La Formation du Réseau des Foires et des Marches: Stratégies, Pratiques et Idéologies', *Annales. Economies, Sociétés*, Civilisations 41, no. 6 (1986): 1215–42.
10 Gustave Schelle, *Oeuvres de Turgot*, Vol. I, 507–13.
11 Anonymous, *Foires et Marchés Du Royaume.*
12 Philemon-Louis Savary, *Dictionnaire Universel de Commerce*, Vol. II, 454–55.
13 Philemon-Louis Savary, Vol. II, 464.
14 Setephan Epstein, 'Regional Fairs, Institutional Innovation'.
15 Marc Brésard, *Les Foires de Lyon Aux XVe et XVIe Siècles* (Paris: Auguste Picard éditeur, 1914); Domenico Gioffrè, *Gênes et Les Foires de Change de Lyon à Besançon* (Paris: Sevpen, 1960); Luciano Pezzolo and Giuseppe Tattara, '"Una Fiera Senza Luogo": Was Bisenzone an International Capital Market in Sixteenth-Century Italy', *Journal of Economic History* 68, no. 4 (2008): 1098–1122.
16 Paul R. Milgrom, Douglass North, and Barry R. Weingast, 'The Role of Institutions'.
17 Avner Greif, 'Coercion and Exchange: How Did Markets Evolve', in *Institutions, Innovation and Industrialization: Essays on Economic History and Development* (Princeton, NJ: Princeton University Press, 2015), 71–96; Avner Greif, *Institutions and the Path to the Modern Economy: Lessons from the Medieval Trade* (Cambridge: Cambridge University Press, 2006).
18 John H. Munro, 'The "New Institutional Economics"'.
19 Jeremy Edwards and Sheilagh Ogilvie, 'What Lessons for Economic Development'.
20 Robert-Henri Bautier, 'Les Foires de Champagne'.
21 Jeremy Edwards and Sheilagh Ogilvie, 'What Lessons for Economic Development'.
22 P. Huvelin, *Essai Historique Sur Le Droit Des Marchés et Des Foires*, 169.
23 P. Huvelin, 146.
24 P. Huvelin, 208–9.

# 13 Institutional diversity

## Free ports, the navigation act, and the drawback system

### "An entrepôt for the general wants"

In his book *Les intérêts de la France*, Goudar recommended a set of policies that sought to expand the French navy without imposing a burden to the Exchequer. He asserted that it was possible to increase the fleet in size in a non-artificial way. Prospective measures should essentially target carrying trade, which would increase national cargo. According to Goudar, it was well known that the apparent success of a national navy hinged on the capacity of a state to promote the transport of national goods and staples, but above all, to attract the carrying of foreign trade. This was the maxim that should guide the design of future policies. It found support in the fact that rich countries were those ones that transported foreign products. Consequently, he recommended the establishment of what he called *entrepôts*.

Goudar showed no support for the settlement of free ports although the institution was not even mentioned in his book. Yet, he spoke of free ports indirectly. According to him, both English and Dutch governments had discovered a successful strategy to steadily and perpetually increase their respective navies. Holland had been remodelled into an "*entrepôt* for all the wants of the different nations." Therefore, both luxury commodities and essentials were brought to their ports from all over the world just to be reshipped. Holland's rise to commercial dominance was grounded on its capacity to intermingle wholesale and retail trade. Distance and time explained the advantages that both countries had been profiting from for a long time. Climate and distance imposed severe constraints on customers for them to purchase those commodities in the original markets. Dutch merchants had found a manner to be "always" in the condition to supply customers directly at their own marketplaces. Foreign exports produced cargo twice for the Dutch mercantile navy: from the original markets to the Dutch magazines, and later, from Holland to the markets where those goods were finally consumed. Besides, their magazines stocked commodities from all over the world ready to be shipped anytime.

Those nations that aspired to control transport services should first become an *entrepôt*. For this purpose to be achieved, and always drawing on the example

DOI: 10.4324/9780429028199-17

of countries that already led the contest, governments should drawback the duties of those goods imported to be re-exported. Further, bounties should be disbursed. Conversely, no port in particular should be granted any privilege. In other words, according to Goudar, no free port should be declared. Goudar envisaged that all ports in France be transformed into *entrepôts*. This policy was grounded on the merchants' own interests. Merchants should be left free for them to carry their goods wherever they wanted.[1]

Two decades earlier, Richard Cantillon had written his famous *Essai sur la nature du commerce*. His book was only published just a year before Goudar's but the manuscript had already circulated widely.[2] The book was translated into English in 1759, and two decades later, into Spanish. A Catholic Irish and banker, Cantillon had witnessed and profited from Law's speculative bubble.[3] The events surrounding the writing of his manuscript as well as Cantillon's own interests made that, commonly, monetary theory be granted far more attention. His ideas on commerce are quite striking, though. Written in the context of the booming public debates on commercial policies held in England at the turn of the eighteenth century, the book reverberated some of those ideas. Further, Cantillon recommended different commercial policies. The conclusions Cantillon and Goudar reached are radically different.

Cantillon's model of free ports resulted from his assumption that "everything in the world is purchased by labour."[4] In line with his value theory, each "thing" had an intrinsic value that was proportionate to the value of land, labour, risk, and time necessary to produce it "into use and form."[5] According to him, England's foreign trade's decay resulted from the nocive impact of an ill-designed tax system consisting in "unequal taxes, or heavy duties on our imports, our Monopolies and Prohibitions all which enhance the price of Labour beyond its natural proportion to that of other countries." The only means to repair this damage was to open the British ports and attract to them "the product of the whole world." This means making Britain the "depositary of nations," emulating the Dutch model.[6]

Both practice and theory showed that taxes and tariffs should be used to encourage labour and industry since they were the actual means through which riches were produced. So, artificially stimulating those means meant expanding the nation's wealth. Cantillon recognised the bounties' benefits and foresaw disadvantages in the extraction of duties and excises. Premiums and bounties should essentially perform two goals. On the one hand, to increase a nation's made-in. On the other hand, to lower the price of imported raw materials. A contradiction might arise in this regard. Some were led to believe that paid bounties on grain exportations negatively impacted England's manufacturing exports. It was believed that by underselling grain, importers help reducing the costs of the neighbours' wages. According to Cantillon, those who raised such a criticism should be aware that policies implemented in 1689 had sought not to make the price fall on international markets but to promote England's exports and to increase the tonnage its navy could carry. Drawing from the customs house's data, Cantillon estimated that 200,000 pounds in subsidies paid to the farmers produced sevenfold gains.

Duties and excises served totally different purposes. They negatively impacted prices by creating a "fictitious" and "unnatural" value. Whenever the government taxed the "necessaries of life," it inhibited its subjects from "going to a market upon an equality with our neighbours." In a word, taxes, customs, and excises artificially increment the value of all imports. While Cantillon drew on Davenant for the negative impacts of taxes, he also agreed with De witt with the assumption that navigation, trade, fisheries and manufactures, as the four pillars of a state, "should not be weakened or encumbered by taxes and customs." Even leaving all English ports free, there would be no unbalance. Imports would essentially be made up of those raw materials needed to produce manufactures that, once processed, increased their value tenfold. In those countries where ports were left free, merchants and traders filled the warehouses "in cheap times, with the goods and merchandise of all nations in order to export them to foreign markets."[7]

Cantillon reassured his readers that England should implement policies already successfully tested in Holland. Thanks to a set of low duties, the whole country had become a magazine, or rather, a "collection of all the products of the world." Something different happened in England due to the regulations in practice. Taxes partially incremented capital invested in the transformation of raw materials. It was not to be expected that the drawback of such impositions could have any positive effect: "we cannot by this favour be upon a par with our neighbours, as the office's fees, with the interest of the first advance of these duties is a dead loss to the first importer." In so doing, Cantillon assessed the impact of the drawback system from a capital perspective. From this viewpoint (echoed again at the turn of the nineteenth century), the institution appears destitute of all its apparent strengths "we ourselves furnish foreigners with the means of rivalling us in trade; and yearly, as they improve we decline."[8]

Both Goudar and Cantillon lived in the same years and experienced the same economic downturns proper to the 1730s. Nonetheless, their advice on economic matters for France and England was quite different. In spite of the fact that both authors built on the Dutch case, their conclusions led in different directions. On the one hand, Goudar upheld that the success of the Dutch nation was a consequence of the cheap transport services it was able to offer. To achieve this goal, France should imitate the English system implementing the 1651 Navigation act. In order to increase its navy, however, the country should first become a magazine. Cantillon agreed with the idea of creating a global magazine, however, his analysis focused not on transport services but on production. For him, taxes created an artificial value that prevented a country from underselling its products. Exactly the same legislation that Goudar prized lost its benefits when it was appraised from the perspective of capital. The English system is described as less effective.

## The navigation act: translation and dissension

Goudar began the third volume of his *Les intérêts de la France* introducing a translation of the 1661 Navigation act. In his account, the vile state of the French marine should be attributed not to a domestic decline, but above all, to the progress that the English navy had achieved in the last years as a result of wise regulations. Cromwell was to be considered as the "greatest politician in the universe." His regulations "ultimately tilted the balance of maritime power in favour of England" as one could agree that the creation of a powerful national fleet was the only sure means for expanding both domestic and foreign trade. Consequently, any nation which aspired to accomplish mercantile ascendancy should avoid falling into the dependence on foreign transport services. In Goudar's eyes, this was far to be only a matter of international competition. Paid freights caused the outflow of large sums of bullion that ultimately benefited contestants. Imposing at least three-quarters of the national crew had further strengthened England's navy. Given the high demand that Asian and colonial commodities had already yielded in its domestic market, forbidding their transport onboard foreign vessels had further increased its national mercantile fleet. Equally, imposing high duty on fish fished and transported by foreign vessels had favourably impacted the building shipping industry.

The foreseen effects of the passed legislation were realised sooner than expected. Soon after, other European fleets had seen their decline. Any author who dared to doubt that the Navigation act accounted for such a success could compare the English navy's size prior and after 1660. Drawing on Child's book, Goudar posited that under Charles I, England had only three vessels each with a capacity of 300 tonnes. This was the same number of vessels each London merchant owned at the turn of the eighteenth century. Due to the Navigation act, England had converted itself into the "natural carrier" of the whole world, rising to the centre of the world marine.[9]

Goudar was not alone in France to admit that the English maritime legislation should be emulated yet agreement was far to prevail. The idea was echoed by Gournay and some of the fellows of his circle, but apparently, not by all of them.[10] Neither Forbonnais nor Butel-Dumont thought those policies actually matched France's political and geographical situations. The explanations both authors advanced are worth mentioning.

As fellows of Goudar's network both authors actively participated in the translation of British books.[11] Four years after the publication of Les *intérêts de la France mal entendus*, Georges Marie Butel-Dumont published himself a translation of the Navigation act.[12] Nonetheless, already in his free and heavily revised translation of Cary's *Discourse on Trade* that first appeared in 1755,[13] he expressed his understanding of the English regulations. He voiced how hard it was to track down both the economic and social foundations of rules enacted in England, not alone its innovation. Butel admitted that the English Parliament strongly consecrated to trade matters, and recognised that regulations unceasingly varied in accordance with changing situations. New regulations recalled old ones therefore forming a confusedly intertwined chain.[14]

In his *Essai sur l'état du commerce* d'*Angleterre*, Butel-Dumont offered a highly peculiar reading on the impacts of the Navigation act. Taking distance from Goudar, Butel-Dumont believed that original as the regulations were, and perfectly suited for England's geographical conditions as they seemed, their benefits derived from a set of policies that dated back to Henry VIII (1509–47). The foundations of the Navigation act were oldest than commonly accepted. In fact, the years that followed Henry VIII's reign had seen a suspension of the legislation, however, a re-enactment followed soon after. During the Commonwealth, the regulations had remained practically unenforceable and England's cargo had continued to be transported on Dutch vessels. Very similar laws had finally passed again in 1660. Butel-Dumont highlighted that "although most of the dispositions had been derogated soon after," agreement existed that "given the circumstance of the time in which they had been set up" they "had been one of the best designed and wise bills the Parliament had ever passed, being the source of the maritime strength that made of England one of the main powers of Europe."[15] The trendsetting legislation had provoked the increase in the number of ships, ultimately beating the Dutch powerful navy.

Thanks to this set of regulations, England could undersell both staples and manufactures abroad and could bring up the prices of foreign commodities in the domestic market. The system was inapplicable in continental countries, though. For large terrestrial continental countries like France, those policies were unfit. A strong and globally-respectable navy was not a sure source of strength for nations surrounded by enemies. In those countries, a different set of policies should be enforced. Butel-Dumont thought that it was much recommendable to refrain foreigners from colonial trade and cabotage but at the same time to leave the ports open to free competition.[16]

Outside France, authors recognised the implausibility of implementing England's dispositions. First published in 1724 and translated into both English and French in the 1750s (the 1753 French translation being made by Forbonnais himself), *Theórica y Práctica del comercio* offered readers a translation of the Navigation act.[17] Uztáriz told his readers that the utmost diligence had been made to obtain "books or accounts" in which he could find the tariff and the rules endorsed by the English government. Further, he had procured books from London in a try to obtain this information yet neither the language nor the content had been of any help. "They contain only acts of parliament made upon a variety of occasions, and though they included some provisions in favour of commerce, it is not in that extent and so particularly as they should be." The form and content of the information made it quite hard for him to deduce the main rules that guided English rulers in matters of navigation. At least not with the same precision that French examples taught. In the absence of clear data, he had resorted to "some fragments and loose papers."[18] Uztáriz briefly pointed out the reductions on duties that the government had issued in the first years of the 1720s. Before offering a translation of the Navigation act, he confined himself to inform that the legislation showed the principles that England applied regardless of treaties or war and peace times.

While Uztáriz drew from the English parliamentary printed discussions, the intellectual exchanges held in France in the 1750s were filtered by the ideas that Child had addressed in Chapter 4 of this *Discourse of Trade.* Published in the last decade of the seventeenth century, Gournay himself (along with Butel-Dumont's help) had translated the book although the extensively commented translation made by Gournay remained unpublished. Butel-Dumont, in turn, translated and published the Navigation act in 1760, years after Goudar. This set of interpretations of the Navigation act shows how invention, emulation, and dissension worked on the ground.

Child, the apparent main source of the 1750s French generation, had confidence that in relation to trade, power, profit, and shipping, the regulation was "one of the choice and most prudent acts that ever was made in England."[19] Without these laws, England would not own half of its trade and would not employ half of its seafarers. At the time Child wrote his book, criticism had aroused in England spreading the idea that even without the favours a similar legislation, Holland had ascended to the domain over the seas. Child explained Dutch commercial power through a specific set of reasons "great stocks, low interest, multitude of merchants, and shipping." There was, nonetheless, a particular advantage that clearly explained Dutch success. The *causa causam* of Holland's rise had been its low interest rates. No nation could compete with Dutch merchants under the same conditions whose markets run at 6 per cent interest rate.[20] For Child, the Navigation act was intended to get to grips with this advantage.

Child's monocausal interpretation (*causa causam*) split into varying branches once the debate reached other countries and was totally detached from the strict English–Dutch contest into which it was born. A year earlier to the launching of Goudar's book, Forbonnais had published two books in which he discussed some points regarding the Navigation act. In his *Éléments du Commerce*, he disagreed with those who, following Child's footsteps, believed that the size of the mercantile navy could be held as a good index of a country's balance of commerce. Anyone could agree upon that a country that showed no care for its navy ultimately abandoned the improvements of its agriculture and industry at the mercy of "navigator states." This could, indeed, put the country into a circle of dangerous dependence.

Sharing Goudar's views, Forbonnais also agreed with Butel-Dumont that such set of policies were unfit for France. Forbonnais' rationale was, however, more theoretically grounded in a sense. Two maxims should guide a country that sought to improve its navy. On the one hand, trying not to promote a foreign country's shipping industry at the expense of the national one. On the other hand, discouraging the introduction of foreign goods and staples on board foreign vessels. Those maxims were well-suited for England yet badly-suited for emulation "not all circumstances are suitable to apply the principles in the same way."[21] Or as Child said "that which is fit for one nation to do in relation to its trade, is not fit for all"[22] Those laws went not without shortcomings. Had every country decided to apply the same model, England would have seen many benefits unrealised. Local circumstances, however, left countries with no possibility to enact a likely set of measures.

There was, according to Forbonnais, a different path to achieve the same goals. The best legislation a country could implement in order to escape from the dependence of any foreign navy was to set the conditions for the "greatest possible concurrence."[23] That concurrence should involve both seafarers and merchants. The emergence of a large concurrence hinged on the number of ports a nation opened up to foreigners. A caveat to this maxim should be considered: free ports. A country could declare free ports seeking not to be deprived of the benefits left by the re-exportation of foreign goods forbidden in its domestic market. Yet, Forbonnais anticipated that this led to nocive results. In an attempt to avoid the enactment of privileges that merely restricted the emergence of free competition, he recommended that the best policy to follow was to grant the category of *entrepôt* to any port and avoid awarding privileges to only one or a few of them.[24]

In his translation of the English journal the *British Merchant*, which was extensively prefaced and annotated with explanatory footnotes, Forbonnais offered still more details.[25] Forbonnais recognised that the Navigation act should be held as the main source of England's maritime power; however, his understanding of the rules differed from other authors like Goudar. Instead of focusing on transport, Forbonnais did on the balance of trade. In England, manufactures were allowed to be exported duty-free, and in some cases, bounties were paid in order to promote their fabrication. Those bounties encouraged exports so as to convince national producers that a demand existed abroad. As regards re-exports, the Navigation act had transformed the island into a kind of free port that only acted "in favour of its nationals." The system operated only in favour of nationals because taxes were drawn back according to the flag under which the commodities were re-exported. Besides, the system fostered the introduction of goods later reshipped out. For all the advantages of the regulation, it seems that, unlike free ports, the drawback system was less effective as paid duties held back merchant's capital for a while. Forbonnais argued that free ports could increase re-exports. Free ports' benefits should, therefore, be considered not into the analysis of domestic but foreign and colonial trade.

## Institutional diversity matters

Many agreed that the Navigation act had thrown the English navy. As the above instances illustrate, it remains clear that in spite of the particular interest shown in translating the English legislation, misunderstanding was rampant as to the origins and actual impacts of the regulations and their appropriateness for countries other than England. Translators seem to have had little concern for the regulations' underpinning causes or the groups of interests that had lobbied for the bill.

Child appraised both issues carefully. He noticed that strict bans on the carrying of goods from and into England had been enacted in an attempt to outcompete countries in which the interest rates were lower "if interest of money were with us reduced to the same rate it is with them, it would be in a short time render us rich and considerable in trade.[26]" Furthermore, Child replied to the complaints raised by different groups of interests. Contradiction arose in different sectors struck by the new legislation. On the one hand, interloper merchants could feel in the very short-run the impact of the measure since freights would suddenly increase. They, of course, would prefer Dutch transport services. On the other hand, colonial planters would refuse to be compelled to give up on the "best markets."

As regards the Navigation act, indetermination still remains regarding either the authorship of the legislation or the involved groups of interests. Disagreement also exists on the primary causes and actual consequences of the bill. Regardless of the cliques (interlopers or joint-stock companies) favoured with the enactment of the new trading rules, it is worth highlighting, for the sake of this chapter, that the public and legislative debates were accompanied by a debate on free ports.[27]

The complementarity or discrepancy between the Navigation act and free ports has deserved rather little attention. Few argued for the need to supplement the embargo-like legislation with a declaration on free ports. Supporters challenged that both institutions were not "contradictory in nature."[28] Debates held by the committee appointed to deal with free ports' usefulness were published in a pamphlet written by Worsley. In 1650, discussions were held on whether or not to declare London a free port. Due to conflicting interests and dissension among the members of the Council of trade, the petition received no endorsement. What seems much more clear is that those who backed the model drew on the "Amsterdam phenomenon," and believed that the city or the island should be transformed into the emporium of the universe.

Free ports and the Navigation act were seemed as complementary institutions. The idea first developed during the Commonwealth and remained unchanged for the decades to come. England's first experiment with free ports turned into a fiasco, though. England had its own failing experiments. Some of them remain as yet less studied. Tangier and Bombay passed to English dominion as part of the dowry of Catherine de Braganza. The Mediterranean city was soon to be declared a free port. Claims were also made coming from the East India company to transform Bombay into a free port. Livorno was referred to as a successful model worth emulating.[29] Tangier's charter granted the city particular privileges that were far beyond the levy of slight duties and customs, which had been implemented in an attempt to syphon Mediterranean trade into the African corner. In accordance with the regulation, the city was granted a merchant court. In an anonymous 1674 description of the city, the author recounted this mercantile body as one of the three main privileges the charter had granted to the city. The court was made up by a lawyer and four merchants who should expeditiously and inexpensively solve mercantile conflicts. This was a one-instance court not found anywhere else in the empire. Not even London, whose merchants had offered huge sums to the king, had been granted such a privilege. The institution resembled the ones existing in France and Italy. The city remained open for any foreign merchant to settle, granting anyone liberty of cult. The anonymous author also called to mind that Tangier was the only port upon British sovereignty where any religion could be freely practiced.[30]

Decades later, and in the context of the war of the Spanish succession and the 1713 Treaty of Utrecht, Joshua Gee wrote his book on *Trade and Navigation*. A wealthy merchant, industrialist, and advisor of the Board of Trade, Gee is said to have been a Whig. Settling him apart from most of his contemporaneous was the fact that Gee envisioned French policies as worth emulating.[31] Chapter 23 of his renowned book *Trade and Navigation* discussed the likely benefits that England could obtain from declaring free ports.[32] He argued that trade "will not remain long in any place where it meets with coldness and indifference." Along with other pamphleteers and scholars in England, he acknowledged that the best way to encourage trade was to complement the Navigation act system with the declaration of free ports. In the mindset of his time, he endorsed the idea that the institution should be understood in a twofold manner: in general and in particular. In general: free ports' advantages were far beyond doubt. In particular: no port in England should be declared free.

On the other hand, Gee offered a particular definition of free ports that somehow differed from Forbonnais'. For him, free ports should not be defined in a narrow sense by the liberty of importing and exporting goods free from duty. Instead, free ports' main feature was the particular jurisdiction granted to merchants for them to run their own court. Assurances on both justice and property drew a large number of merchants to those free ports. Merchant courts' positive impact was a topic already discussed by Child who highlighted their existence across Holland as a proof of their usefulness. Seventeenth-century pamphleteers endorsed the creation of these merchant courts.

Gee opposed the settlement of free ports homeland but suggested the transformation of Gibraltar and Port-Mahon into free ports. Both ports enjoyed a perfect location at the "very mouth" of the Mediterranean sea. They were perfectly located to store unsold goods shipped from Spain and Portugal, avoiding English merchants to carry them faraway to Livorno because of the "high duties" levied in the Iberian countries. He foresaw that the establishment of those free ports would remove a good part of the trade from the Tuscan port, which was "the only free port of note" in the Mediterranean. Nonetheless, Gee was yet unconvinced as those who recommended: "all the ports of England made free, all our custom houses demolished, and all the products and manufactures of the world brought in free of all duty, that we may send them out again." Some were misled into believing that this was the maxim that ruled in Holland, the Hansa towns, Hambourg, and Livorno, being the very cause that propelled their capacity to furnish other nations with foreign commodities.

Dutch merchants were somehow misled although their system matched their mercantile interests. In contrast to a widely held but false belief, in Holland, duties were levied on imports and customs houses did exist. Therefore, the difference was minor in comparison with the regulations enforced in England. The main contrast lay on their duties being extremely small, resulting from the fact that a large share of the imports were reshipped inland through a huge network of rivers the country was endowed with. Specific impositions were levied on goods destined to the domestic market, as high or higher than the ones levied in English customs houses. So, Gee concluded that "nor is our management in this affair different from that of the Dutch, as to the matter but only in the manner."[33] England's model imposed high duties on luxury goods but drawback duties on re-exports.

The idea of setting free ports in England had profusely been discussed in the mid-seventeenth century, and had been put into practice rather unsuccessfully. Few of those who espoused the cause of free ports found inspiration in the Dutch model. In his broadly cited pamphlet on *Free ports*,[34] Worsley sought to move public opinion and convinced his countrymen that England should build a "mart" in the same way the Hollanders had done.[35] As the Dutch experiment had already evidenced, England could gain a lot. The institution would increase England's maritime and overland power. Donver was a good instance, which was a kind of free port and which had transformed into a vital port in the channel.

Free ports made trade expeditious, and furthermore, helped lowering the prices of foreign commodities. They redirected trade for "every man will bring in, when he knows he may (if he finds no market here) freely carried it out again." Governments benefited from the measure as much as merchants did. Not only free ports contributed in preventing famines but also increased the amount of bullion brought in as well as the share of taxes gathered. The fiscal aspect should also be considered with great precaution. For one reason. Free ports were a way for rulers to indirectly tax foreigners' consumption in the same way that impositions were levied on domestic demand. Law import-duties offered to the government "some millions of good yearly." Those who refused the institution's benefits just contravene the achievement of a "universal intercourse of traffic as is desired."

## From imperium to emporium

Holland captured the imagination of many in seventeenth-century England. In the country, the Dutch were recurrently cited as a source of evidence.[36]

This was a time in which Englishmen and England's institutions were "going Dutch."[37] This was also a time in which England caught up with Holland and the rest of Europe.[38] On the island, some wish to emulate Holland, others, instead, planned a political union. In particular, three aspects of the Dutch economy and prosperity robbed the attention of English observers: the herring fisheries, low interest rates, and their command in the transport of foreign products.[39] The country was frequently featured as a "Universal Emporium." Many set their sights on transforming either England or London into a universal mart.[40]

Allegedly, the first to have endorsed and reverberated the idea with great success was Henry Robinson in his 1641 pamphlet.[41] A London merchant and pamphleteer, Robinson had been the source of inspiration for Temple's *Observations upon the United Provinces,* and also for Worsley's *Free Ports.*[42] In the same vein, some of the Child's suggestions had already been echoed by Robinson. In total, Robinson stated fourteenth proposals. Ten of the fifteen policies advanced by Child to overcome Dutch competition came from Robinson.[43] Mid-seventeenth-century English pamphleteers were the source of the policies that Child advocated, and that later, Gournay and his circle discussed as Child's own.

One of Robinson's policies precisely reads "By free exporting of foreign commodities with little or no custom, which will make England the emporium of all other countries." This implies transforming England into the "Emporium or Warehouse from whence other nations may be furnished." For that purpose, foreign commodities should be exported free of duties and the paid duties reimbursed once re-exported. The general rule to follow was to furnish nations cheaper than they could purchase those goods from other countries "for this is the main engine wherewith some people advance themselves and hinder others."

The idea reverberated once and again over the whole century. Universal emporium or emporium was a watchword used to some extent in pamphlets throughout the century, yet curiously, in most of those pamphlets, the word is mentioned no more than once. The emporium was gradually linked with the idea of building a magazine or mart where all sorts of goods could be found ready for being shipped worldwide. In the latter part of the century, Petty asked what "spot of the *Earth's-Globe* were fittest for a general and universal *Emporium,* whereby all the People thereof may best enjoy one another's Labours and Commodities."[44]

Some dreamed of England as that "great Emporium and Exchange of the world."[45] England's geographical location and the Dutch experience both phenomena nurtured such a utopic conception of the marketplace. For some, it was England's destiny, given the location in which nature had placed it, to realise that much coveted magazine. The unimpaired location was a reiterated feature attributed to many places and not only to the British island. As we will see, Lisbon's free port was partially built on the rationale that the port was marvellously located midway the Mediterranean and the Atlantic. Those in England who highlighted the island's perfect location not only propose the emulation of the Dutch model. For them, Venice's policies were worth implementing as well. A writer regretted the fact that English rulers had not "exemplified the policy of the wise Venetians to encourage and promote our trade and commerce." Had the kings followed those same measures, England would have profited from "being posted by nature on the Emporium of the world."[46]

Merchants and travellers alike resounded this daydream magazine where global commodities would be stored to fulfil the desires of customers worldwide. In *The Delights of Holland*, a traveller found a source of amazement on the fact that an "inconsiderable place" had become "the most celebrated Emporium of the Universe" and that this nation could compete "with the greatest cities in the world." Its navy made Holland the nation that "now drives the greatest part of the commerce which was formerly carried on by those ancient and renowned cities."[47]

It was not only in England that this idea found echo. Uztáriz, who minutiously reviewed tariff measures implemented by the most powerful European nations, asserted that Holland was a free port where it was possible "to receive and deposit vast quantities of goods and fruits collected from all the four quarters of the world." He also stated that most of those commodities and staples were "distributed all over the world, Hollanders themselves being the carriers of a share, the other share being sold to foreigners in their own country." Had the Hollanders imposed a 10–15 per cent imposition on imports, they would not be able to outcompete their neighbours. Trade had boomed because they levied "so a small a duty upon imports and exports" some of which pass totally duty-free. Yet, those regulations should not be considered as a pattern for other states "whose nature, situation, and circumstances are not the same." The author remembered that "it is only that of Genoa, a small barren country which bears some resemblance to it in miniature." On the other hand, the capacity of the Hollanders to keep their magazines well supplied hinged on the cheap freights they provided with. Cheap freights resulted from many reasons among which the universal pattern of trade they had established. For many countries, it was more convenient to purchase those commodities from Holland than to "import (them) from the fountainhead."[48] Uztáriz listed each one of the commodities and staples stored in Dutch magazines as well as market destinations. He probably drew this information from Huet, who, in the first decades of the eighteenth century, wrote widely read histories of trade. Not surprisingly, Uztáriz was the translator into Spanish of Huet's *Le grand trésor historique*.

Published in 1713, the book instructed readers on Holland's commercial success from a twofold historical and political approach.[49] The author announced that he had lived in the country and prayed his readers not to take his oeuvre as mere speculations deduced from a "man of letters" but as the mind of expert Dutch merchants who "one should always take as the true oracles of commerce." His Dutch experience had taught him all he knew on commerce-related topics. With them, he learned, for instance, that commerce was "one of the main branches of politics." Owing to this Dutch experience, he had taken commercial matters more seriously, and had set to study trade conducted not only by the Dutch but also by the English, Portuguese, and other nations. Observations gathered by many travellers had further improved his knowledge. Perhaps not surprisingly, his historical narrative is set with the Medieval fairs.

His account goes that the counts of Flanders had contributed to improve trade by the settling of free fairs around 960 "drawing all the neighbours in crowds." People came to purchase merchandise that they afterwards carried out in great quantities owing to their being totally free of duties. After reviewing the process that led to the sixteenth century, Huet admitted that Antwerp had become a universal magazine "contest of all the main nations that traded there transformed the city into the most famous magazine of all Europe, perhaps of all the Universe."[50] For him, "Antwerp was in that time what in the current time Amsterdam is." It remains to be studied whether Antwerp played any role in the imagination of the Commonwealth. For monarchists, Antwerp was a case in point that proved that when it was well regulated, trade could flourish either in a republic or in a monarchy.

All these references clearly show that outside Holland, writers saw the whole country or their harbours as free ports. Interestingly, the model was never implemented in the country before the eighteenth century. In the 1740s onward, proposals were debated and discussions held on the need to create a free port. Many referred to the English model as the reason why the institution should be implemented. At least three measures were in order meant to redress Holland's position in international trading affairs. Of the three, Jacques Accarias de Serionne inclined himself for what he called a "limited free port." Of utmost interest for understanding this refashioning of the institution is the fact that, as Acarias himself brought to mind, in 1740, the prince had advanced such an idea. At that time, the colleges had discussed the project with care but no approval had been granted.

Even though Accarias de Serionne endorsed the idea that free ports could get Holland out of the commercial crisis the country was undergoing, he showed himself disdain for the manner in which the institution had been modelled in the 1740s. The so-called limited free port somehow combined the idea of free ports and the English drawback system.[51] Goods were, therefore, catalogued into two sets. On the one hand, those which could be imported and re-exported duty-free. On the other hand, goods which must be taxed at their entrance but whose duties were refunded once a demonstration of their re-exportation handled or a similar value of goods manufactured in the country exported. The measures were intended to protect the national industry and avoid possible fiscal losses. However, as the author proved, neither goal was reached by framing the free port into these lines.

## Notes

1 Ange Goudar, *Les Intérêts de La France Mal Entendus, Dans Les Branches de l'agriculture, de La Population, Des Finances, Du Commerce, de La Marine, & de l'industrie. Par Un Citoyen*, 3 vols. (Amsterdam: Chez Jacques Coeur , à la corne d'abondance, 1756), Vol. III, 150–55.
2 Antoin E. Murphy, *Richard Cantillon: Entrepreneur and Economist* (Oxford: Clarendon Press, 1986), 248.
3 Arnaud Orain, *La Politique Du Merveilleux. Une Autre Histoire Du Système de Law (1695–1795)* (Paris: Fayard, 2018).
4 Philip Cantilllon, *The Analysis of Trade, Commerce, Coin, Bullion, Banks, and Foreign Exchanges Wherein the True Principles of This Useful Knowledge Are Fully but Briefly Laid down and Explained, to Give a Clear Idea of Their Happy Consequences to Society When Well Regulated Taken Chiefly from a Manuscript of a Very Ingenious Gentleman Deceased and Adapted to the Present Situation of Our Trade and Commerce* (London: Printed for the author, 1759), IV.
5 Philip Cantillon, 34.
6 Philip Cantillon, 134–35.
7 Philip Cantillon, 141, 158–59, 142.
8 Philip Cantilllon, 159, 162.
9 Ange Goudar, *Les Intérêts de La France Mal Entendus*, Vol. III, 9.
10 Loïc Charles, Frédéric Lefebvre, and Christine Théré, *Le Cercle de Vincent de Gournay: Savoirs Économiques et Pratiques Administratives En France Au Milieu Du XVIII* (Paris: Institut National d'Études Démographiques, 2011).
11 Sophus Reinert, *Translating Empire: Emulation and the Origins of Political Economy* (Cambridge, MA: Harvard University Press, 2011); Sophus Reinert, 'The Empire of Emulation: A Quantitative Analysis of Economic Translations in the European World, 1500–1849', in *The Political Economy of Empire in the Early Modern World*, eds. Sophus Reinert and Pernille Roge (New York: Palgrave Macmillan, 2013), 105–30.
12 Georges-Marie Butel-Dumont, *Acte Du Parlement d'Angleterre, Connu Sous Le Nom d'acte de Navigation, Passé En 1660. Traduit Littéralement de l'anglois, Avec Des Notes* (Amsterdam: Charles Antoine Jombert, 1760).
13 Georges-Marie Butel-Dumont, *Essai Sur l'état Du Commerce d'Angleterre*, 2 vols. (London: Nyon, 1755).
14 Georges-Marie Butel-Dumont, Vol. I, 8.
15 Georges-Marie Butel-Dumont, Vol. II, 108.
16 Georges-Marie Butel-Dumont, Vol. II, 111.
17 Gerónimo de Uztáriz, *Theórica y Práctica de Comercio y de Marina: En Diferentes Discursos y Calificados Exemplares Que, Con Específicas Providencias, Se Procuran Adaptar a La Monarquía Española, Para Su Pronta Restauración, Beneficio Universal y Mayor Fortaleza Contra Los Émulos de La Real Corona, Mediante La Soberana Protección Del Rey Nuestro Señor Don Phelipe V* (Madrid: Imprenta Antonio Sanz, 1757).
18 Gerónimo de Uztáriz, *The Theory and Practice of Commerce and Maritime Affairs. Written Originally in Spanish, by Don Geronymo de Uztariz*, Translated from the Original by John Kippax (Dublin: George Faulkner, 1752), 88.
19 Josiah Child, *A New Discourse of Trade* (London: T. Sowle, 1698), 112.
20 Josiah Child, 114.
21 François Véron Duverger de Forbonnais, *Eléments Du Commerce* (Leyden, 1754), Vol. I, 356.
22 Josiah Child, *A New Discourse of Trade*, 113.
23 François Véron Duverger de Forbonnais, *Eléments Du Commerce*, Vol. I, 357.
24 François Véron Duverger de Forbonnais, Vol. I, 360.

25 François Véron Duverger de Forbonnais, *Le Négociant Anglais, Ou Traduction Libre Du Livre Intitulé The British Merchant, Contenant Divers Mémoires Sur Le Commerce de l'Angleterre Avec La France, Le Portugal et l'Espagne* (Amsterdam: François Changuion, 1755).
26 Josiah Child, *A New Discourse of Trade*, 8.
27 Ivan Roots, 'Cromwell's Ordinances: The Early Legislation of the Protectorate', in *The Interregnum: The Quest for Settlement, 1646–1660*, ed. G. E. Aylmer (London: Mcmillan, 1972), 143–64.
28 J. E. Farnell, 'The Navigation Act of 1651, the First Dutch War, and the London Merchant Community', *Economic History Review* 16, no. 2 (1961): 439–54, 446.
29 Tristan Stein, 'Tangier in the Restoration Empire'.
30 Chantal de la Véronne, ed., *Tanger Sous l'occupation Anglaise d'après Une Description Anonyme de 1674* (Paris: Librairie orientaliste Paul Geuthner, 1972), 15–16.
31 Sophus Reinert, *Translating Empire*, 145.
32 Joshua Gee, *The Trade and Navigation of Great Britain* (London: A. Bettesworth and C. Hitch, 1738).
33 Joshua Gee, 165.
34 Benjamin Worsley, *Free Ports, and the Nature of Them Stated* (London: William Du-Gard, 1651).
35 Thomas Leng, *Benjamin Worsley (1618–1677): Trade, Interest, and the Spirit in Revolutionary England* (London: Royal Historical Society, 2008); Thomas Leng, 'Commercial Conflict and Regulation in the Discourse of Trade in Seventeenth-Century England', *Historical Journal* 48, no. 4 (2005): 933–54.
36 J. Appleby, *Economic Thought and Ideology in Seventeenth-Century England* (Princeton, NJ: Princeton University Press, 1978), 73.
37 Steve Pincus, *1688: The First Modern Revolution* (New Haven, CT: Yale University Press, 2009), 49–69.
38 Stephan Epstein, *Freedom and Growth*.
39 J. Appleby, *Economic Thought and Ideology*, 74.
40 Richard Drayton, *Nature's Government: Science, Imperial Britain and the Improvement of the World* (New Haven, CT: Yale University Press, 2000), 56.
41 Henry Robinson, *Englands Safety in Trades Increase* (London: E. P. for Nicholas Bourne at the South Entrance of the Royal Exchange, 1641).
42 William Temple, *Observations upon the United Provinces of the Netherlands by Sir William Temple* (London: A. Maxwell for Sa. Gellibrand, 1673).
43 William Letwin, *The Origins of Scientific Economics: English Economic Thought 1660–1776* (London: Methuen & co, 1963), 15.
44 William Petty, *An Essay Concerning the Multiplication of Mankind: Together with Another Essay in Political Arithmetick, Concerning the Growth of the City of London: With the Measures, Periods, Causes, and Consequences Thereof, 1682* (London: Robert Clavel and Henry Mortlok, 1698).
45 John Nalson, *The Present Interest of England, or, A Confutation of the Whiggish Conspirators Anti-Monyan Principle Shewing from Reason and Experience the Ways to Make the Government Safe, the King Great, the People Happy, Money Plentifull, and Trade Flourish* (London: Thomas Dring, 1683).
46 Anonymous, *The Proposal for Raising the Price of Tin &c* (s.l.: s.n., 1700).
47 William Mountague, *The Delights of Holland: Or, A Three Months Travel about That and the Other Provinces With Observations and Reflections on Their Trade, Wealth, Strength, Beauty, Policy, &c. Together with a Catalogue of the Rarities in the Anatomical School at Leyden* (London: John Stuorton, near Serjeant's-Inn Gate, in Chancery Lane; and A. Bosvile, at the Dial over-against St. Dunstan's Church, in Fleet-Street, 1696), 119.
48 Gerónimo de Uztáriz, *The Theory and Practice*, 102, 105.

49 Pierre Daniel Huet, *Le Grand Trésor Historique et Politique Du Florissant Commerce Des Hollandais, Dans Tous Les États et Empires Du Monde. Quelle Est Leur Manière de Le Faire, Son Origine, Leur Grand Progrés,Leur Possessions & Gouvernements Dans Les Indes. Comment Ils Se Sont Rendus Maîtres de Tout Le Commerce de l'Europe* (Haye: Henry Frik, 1713).
50 Pierre Daniel Huet, 14.
51 Jacques Accarias de Serionne, *Le Commerce de La Hollande Ou Tableau Du Commerce Des Hollandais Dans Les Quatre Parties Du Monde* (Amsterdam: Changuion Libraire, 1768), Vol. II, 248.

# 14 A Mediterranean silk road

## Venice, Genoa, and Piedmont

### Venice and Genoa

English policymakers should find a source of inspiration in the economic policies that the "wise" Venetians had already enacted in order to promote trade. This was one of the advices made by a seventeenth-century English pamphleteer. Indeed, emulating Venice in a time in which the *Serenissima* was apparently going through a stagnating commercial situation may sound like a rather bizarre strategy. Venice had enjoyed an *entrepôt* condition for a long time. The city's rise to eternal glory precisely resulted from its staple condition. The port had long been a continental-wide redistribution centre for eastern luxuries and spices and a re-export centre for northern European clothes. Venice, like Amsterdam much later, had risen out of nothing (at the turn of the ninth century, people fleeing terror had found refuge in a set of islands located faraway mainland where only salt could be exploited) to become the centre of the known world. The *Serenissima* had gradually enlarged its domain both mainland and all across the Adriatic golf, transforming it in its *mare clausum*.[1]

At the turn of the seventeenth century, when the impacts of the Portuguese new route to Asia were already felt, the city was threatened by both the commercial presence of northern newcomers and the emergence of Livorno and its new free port model. From the 1570s onwards, English ships navigated more and more frequently in the Adriatic waters, and as they gradually advanced over, staples produced in the Ionian islands began to be carried out directly to England on English vessels. Currants were a particular object of envy, much of the production being destined to English markets. Threatened by the English competition, the *Serenissima* replied with a new tariff known as *Nuova imposta*, which was issued in 1580. The tariff's main goal was to discourage the carrying out of currants on foreign ships and to syphon out northern imports to the rialto channel. A new imposition of ten *ducats* was to be levied on every thousand weight of currants that foreigners exported on foreign ships out of the Ionian island "for every place in the West beyond the Strait of Gibraltar." In turn, English goods introduced into the island such as kerseys, woollen cloth, and wool were also charged otherwise persecuted as

DOI: 10.4324/9780429028199-18

smuggling.[2] Banning the export of "colonial" commodities on foreign ships and claiming the right to distribute imports, both goals somehow resembled the ones that the Navigation act sought to fulfil much later. The question remains as to whether we should look for the origins of the Navigation act not merely in the lobby English stock companies and adventurer merchants made and whether or not the new policies were partially rooted in the lessons that English merchants had learned in the Adriatic waters.

Nuisance came not only from newcomers but also from new models. By drawing foreign merchants into its walls and by redirecting Mediterranean trade through the levy of slight duties and customs, Livorno rose to challenge the old maritime and naval Mediterranean powers at the turn of the seventeenth century. Further, Venice witnessed how the transformation of Ancone into a free port began to challenge its commercial dominance inside its own narrow sea.[3] Yet, Venice, as Naples later, chose not to play the game of free ports. Or to be more accurate, the play was played just for a few years. As the quote of Genovesi recalls, sometimes there is no choice but to do what others do.

In 1661, a proposal was forwarded to the *Cinque Savii* containing new policies that sought the transformation of the rialto city into a "free port." Regardless of the terms employed to define the new policies, the implemented model somehow deviated from the one that had previously been settled in Livorno. Different from the Tuscan port or in full contrast to Ancone whose policies Venice sought to contest, tariff reforms tackled only commodities introduced into the city. The economic advisers of the committee of *Cinque Savii* found a little strange the advice of discharging any exported commodity of duties and customs. The words were highly vague "in removing all the duty of entry from the sea in declaring this free port" "and in decreeing that merchants might have free entrance from any imposition." Fiscal concerns were raised, as the policies removed the 6 per cent duty imposed on goods coming from Levant and the taxes known as the "*ponente*."[4] Doubts were cast on the plausibility that staples extracted from Adriatic ports could be introduced free of taxes. Curiously, no change was introduced regarding export duties, foreign merchants being compelled to pay 10 per cent.

Those measures were enforced for only two decades, and then finally lifted. This was precisely the moment in which Genoa began to gradually redesign its warehouse policies. The model would rebound far beyond the Tyrrhenian sea. Overland routes began to be integrated into the free port's overseas horizons.

Discussions and the following short-lasting enactment of a free port in Venice almost coincide with the implementation in Genoa of a set of new regulations on transit trade. The Genoese model was a highly flexible one; from the very beginning, the institution's regulations were thought as temporal and subject to revision every ten years. In that sense, the regulations settled at the turn of the century were not properly the outcome of any top-bottom policy but a spontaneous outcome from a periodically held revision. The changes introduced in the free port of Genoa had unexpected consequences for both the goals and the specific policies later enacted in Turin, which, as we will see, were in turn recalled when the Lisbon project was under study in the 1780s.

Contest with Livorno played an essential role in the discussions held in the Ligurian city. But on this occasion, overland and not merely overseas stakes were at contest. In 1696, reforms were enacted with the intent to reinforce Genoa's transit trade thereby limiting the aspirations of other Ligurian ports. Other changes were implemented which tackled the manner in which duties were levied: taxes were now estimated according to the weight's bales and according to the nature of the commodities and its value. This meant a considerable reduction in taxes. Further, restrictions on Livorno's transit trade were lifted. In particular and the utmost interest for this chapter were the privileges granted to raw silk whose duties were revisited. Assessment reports later submitted by the customs house were daunting but apparently misled. Partially due to this reason, the new revision set in 1710 lifted the recently enacted regulations and a decision was made on going back once again to the previous 1692 ones.

In 1736, a new Neapolitan board of trade was consulted about the best strategies the kingdom should follow *vis-à-vis* Venice's lately implemented changes on tariffs. At the beginning, news coming from the city made believed that a new free port was about to be established. Yet, papers received later changed the minds of the board's members. Many reasons led the board to believe that tariff reforms did not necessarily imply the establishment of a free port. A free port properly speaking, the members of the government body upheld, was one in which ships were allowed to call at the port's harbour without any regard for their flag and without being levied any customs or duties whatsoever. It was true that in Venice tariff policies had lowered both import and export taxes for vessels calling at from or leaving the port for any other Adriatic or Levant port. For merchants to benefit from those reductions, nonetheless, goods must be transported on ships flying the Venetian flag. In the same fashion, vessels of any flag coming from western ports also enjoyed particular reductions. Governments, indeed, had the right to enact this kind of reforms to promote trade in accordance with the *ius gentium*. Arguments were addressed on whether or not to transform Pesca and Brindisi into free ports as the more suitable measure to face the new conditions that had unfolded following the creation of a free port in Trieste and tariff reductions in Venice. Ultimately, the board refrained from suggesting any of these policies.[5]

In the 1730s, new regulations were put into practice also in Genoa, few of them concerning overland transit trade.[6] The main idea was to transform the Ligurian coast into a transit zone for the supply of the Duchy of Milan now under the Habsburg domain. Specific itineraries were stipulated over which commodities could be extracted to neighbouring countries. Goods transported out of Liguria over non-authorised routes were considered as smuggling. These policies allowed ports located on the Riviere the opportunity to introduce commodities destined to Piedmont or Lombardy.

From the 1680s, petitions have repetitively been forwarded to the city coming from Ligurian ports that asked for the extension of free-port privileges to other ports like Savona. Any attempt had been blocked, however. Consultations had also been held on whether or not to transform La Spezia into a free port. Among many advantages, nonetheless, petitioners recalled in particular the overland trade route. A report forwarded to Genoa in 1723 estimated the tariff effects on trade conducted from Starzana when compared with similar commercial operations made from Massa at the other side of the Tuscan border. High taxes increased the prices of commodities introduced inland from the former, therefore, improving the opportunities of Toscan contests. Later, complaints coming from the western side of the Riviere procured to include Savona among those ports which could enjoy free-port privileges. One of the articles of the 1751 new regulations allowed commodities unloaded in Savone to be shipped out to the Piedmont or Montferrand. A year after, a lowering of duties was determined for those commodities that were transported inland over previously determined itineraries. These spontaneous policies, gradually implemented, transformed the Ligurian riviera into a transit duty-free zone that somewhat resembled Holland and its liquid routes. Those rules lasted for a century.

In this overland trade, silk was at stake. At the turn of the century, the English envoy in Turin already communicated back to London how many English merchants could profit from the establishment of a free port at Savona.[7] According to consulted London-based manufacturers, roughly 500 bales of Piedmont silk were in demand, the bulk of the raw material being transported overland north, and finally, shipped from Holland to England. Merchants also argued for the plausibility of deviating that trade via Ville-Franche given the lack of good roads and the high costs. "An easy passage of fifteen miles only by land will bring from the sea to the Po all our commodities, which by water carriage and with the stream will supply almost all commerce from other places." In exchange for an assortment of varying goods, English merchants could receive, among other staples, raw silks "the cheapest and best anywhere." The projected plan was to convert Piedmont into another Portugal.

Nice was said to be geographically very well emplaced. The port of the city was the only maritime gate for the highlands. Silk of the best qualities and prices found their way out through the port. Already in the sixteenth century, Charles-Emmanuel I had emulated some of the measures implemented in Livorno transforming VilleFranche into a free port. Policies had been enacted in a gradual manner between 1612 and 1627. The privileged geographical situation was reinforced with monopolistic laws granted to the city. Gradually, in the first decades of the eighteenth century, the free-port status was transformed into a duty-free zone that, upon the Genoese model, sought mainly to transform the Nice strip into a transit zone for the supply of those markets located beyond the Duchy of Savoy. After long discussions held over the 1730s among those who backed the privileges and those who contradicted them, a new set of regulations were finally issued in 1749.[8]

## Notes

1 Guillaume Calafat, *Une Mer Jalousée*.
2 Maria Fusaro, *Political Economies of Empire in the Early Modern Mediterranean: The Decline of Venice and the Rise of England, 1450–1700* (Cambridge: Cambridge University Press, 2015), 55.
3 Alberto Caracciolo, 'Il Dibattito Sui "Porti Franchi"'.
4 Archivio di Stato Venezia, *Cinque savi alla mercanzia-Seconda serie*, Pezzo 137, memoria mercantile n. 238 Porto Franco. According to Constantini, the ponente duty was a 15–16 *ad valorem* duty for foreigners and 6–10 for Venetians.
5 Società Napoletana di Storia Patria, XX, D. 30. Archivio Stato di Napoli, *Tribunali antichi*, stanza 235, 1728.
6 Giulio Giacchero, *Origini e Sviluppi Del Portofranco*, 155–80; Antonio Iodice, 'Il Porto Franco', 184–90.
7 Franco Venturi, 'Il Piemonte Dei Primi Decenni Del Settecento Nelle Relazioni Del Diplomatici Inglesi', *Bollettino Storico-Bibliografico Subalpino* 54 (1956): 227–71.
8 Françoise Hildesheimer, 'Entre La Méditerranée et Les Alpes: Nice et Son Port Franc Au XVIIIe Siècle', *Provence Historique* 27 (1977): 197–212.

# 15 Tyre and Carthage

## Failed projects and new glocal fairs

### Lisbon: failed projects

A free port was established in Lisbon on 13 May 1796.[1] It is very likely that its creation followed some suggestions conveyed from Turin a decade earlier, which, as we have already seen, endorsed a set of regulations enacted in Genoa decades earlier. This was far from being the first occasion in which a diplomat recommended the implementation of a free port in Portugal. Similar proposals had been made since at least the seventeenth century. At least twice, suggestions had been advanced on the benefits of the Mediterranean institution. It could therefore be said that in regard to Lisbon's free port, the idea had deep roots and had already circulated among Portuguese diplomatic circles from the former years of the century.[2]

What seems certain is that the process that led to the establishment of a free port barely involved any petitions coming from the community of local national or foreign merchants. It is hard to find records that show merchants as an interested party in the nasty process that ended up with the creation of a short-lived, and apparently, scandalous free port. The voice of some members of the local mercantile community was heard a couple of times after petitions were made by the board of trade.[3] By the same token, no records have been unearthed that make one to think that the free port could have been established following the initiative of the local municipal corporate bodies. For all these reasons, it is safe to assume that the enactment of a free port was mainly the result of diplomatic guidance, more in particular, suggestions reported from Turin in the 1780s.

Proposals for the establishment of a free port were discussed at the board of trade at least twice: first in 1782 and then in 1795. It is hard to assert the reasons why such a trading policy called the court's attention precisely in those years. Suggestions conveyed from Turin in the 1780s would explain why the king ordered the board of trade to confer about the benefits and disadvantages of implementing a likely institution.[4] However, it is much harder to accurately determine the reasons why, again a decade later, the institution came back as a mighty way of promoting trade. Probably, fiscal reasons inclined the officials to take profit from the institution.

DOI: 10.4324/9780429028199-19

According to Ratton (a French Lisbon-based merchant), the idea of creating a free port in Lisbon could be attributed to the ambassador in Turin,[5] Rodrigo de Souza Coutinho.[6] In one of his papers regarding tariffs, Souza Coutinho backed the simultaneous implementation of the drawback system along with the establishment of a free port. Both institutions should serve to free the carrier trade from any duties. This was also an opportunity for the royal exchequer to benefit from revenues levied on storage. Still more importantly, revenues could be levied on goods transported from Portugal to Spain overland. Fundamentally, Souza Coutinho envisaged the idea of transplanting Liguria's and Piedmont's models to the Iberian transit trade. In the same manner that had been authorised in Genoa decades earlier, in Portugal, goods could be allowed to transit in order to be ultimately reshipped to Spain. Spain could thus become Portugal's Piedmont.[7] Further, and not less importantly, a Portuguese free port could come to supplant Gibraltar.

One of Souza Coutinhos's pieces of advice precisely focused on Gibraltar. One of the free ports he projected for Portugal should be located somewhere across the southern cost. After the American independence, his narrative went on, English capital had been reinvested back in European commercial circuits via Gibraltar. Therefore, English merchants had transformed the strait into a "great *entrepôt*." For Portugal to compete with Britain, free ports should be created in the Algarve. Souza Coutinho also projected a free port for Lisbon, which should become the *enteprôt* of all the trade carried in the Mediterranean and the North Atlantic.

In conclusion, when the project was seriously examined for the first time, officials reflected on the possibility to build a new customs house along with new warehouses. The projected free port was understood as an *entrepôt.* Members of the board of trade suggested the building of new warehouses in the outskirts of Lisbon. Some, in contrast, showed opposition to this plan due to the fact that it implied the running of a parallel customs office, with the many disadvantages this practice might provoke. The causes why the proposal regained no support remain largely unknown. Several years later, the board of trade discussed the issue once again.

## Emulating the English model

On the second occasion in which the project was under discussion, some members of the mercantile board demurred against the model suggested ten years earlier. They argued that a free port was of no necessity. Opposition to the institution was grounded on the existence of a set of fiscal policies already at work, which, for the members of the board, accomplished the same alleged benefits. Those measures had already been enacted in order to promote Indo-Portuguese trade and cut duties on re-exports to merely 4 per cent *ad valorem.* Some members of the board were even persuaded on the advantages of extending the same tariff to non-nationals who used Lisbon as a transhipment port. Furthermore, they suggested that those slight duties should be levied on goods shipped to either Asian Portuguese colonies or any other foreign port in Asia. Two merchants, however, showed their dissent, and instead, embraced the old plan, it is, the building of new warehouses.[8]

Actually, there was much misunderstanding on free port's functions and advantages when compared with the drawback system. Both institutions were said to serve the same purposes. There is little doubt that those who opposed the building of new warehouses backed their arguments on a paper written by the Lisbon-based merchant Joaquim Rebelo.[9] It is very likely that Rebelo wrote the paper for advising the members of the board of trade. Apparently, the paper did not go to print and circulated only in manuscript form.[10]

Rebelo raised many objections on free ports. His paper began by listing cities in which free ports had been declared along with countries in which the institution was rather unfamiliar. According to his account, there were free ports both in Italy and France. In contraposition, Holland had implemented a wiser system of slight tariffs. In the Adriatic Sea, Ostend had been transformed into a free port. In the Baltic Sea, Hamburg profited from similar features. Although duties were levied and rigorously paid in Sweden, re-exported goods paid merely 1 per cent. It seemed that the system had never been discussed or implemented in Spain. A case apart was the Basque country, a zone which enjoyed particular privileges than in nothing resembled free ports. In England, anticipating the many issues free ports caused, a totally different system had been enacted. Incentives were granted through allowances, bounties, premiums, and particularly, the drawback of duties.

Different from Souza Coutinho, for whom both the free port and the drawback system complemented each other, Rebelo showed a penchant for the British model. He was of the mind that the previously enhanced tax cuts had positively impacted overseas trade, and in consequence, free ports were not needed at all. Tax reductions granted to Lisbon merchants could be of advantage to non-nationals interested in re-exporting goods to and from the Indian Ocean. Reductions should be levied at the customs house in charge of overseeing colonial trade known as the *Casa da Índia*. Experience demonstrated that many merchants had already benefited from those wise regulations.

While there is no doubt that cuts or refunds evidently promoted colonial trade, free ports could harm national commerce and the mercantile navy alike. Those who voiced Lisbon's exceptional geographical location halfway the North Atlantic and the Mediterranean should be aware of the fact that Portugal could hardly compete with England and the Baltic countries. There was unlikeliness that a free port could help strengthen the Portuguese mercantile fleet. Goods carried from the Mediterranean ports could be hardly undersold at northern markets. All things considered, staples transported from the northern to the Mediterranean markets could meet demand; however, those gains came at the cost of enriching other nations and at the expense of Portuguese capital and the national fleet. A free port was a trap, there was an opportunity for foreign merchants to seize at the same time the Lisbon market and the carrying trade. In the same line that Genovesi and Broggia, Rebelo showed a penchant for national trade and industry.

On the one hand, Rebelo's plan sought to promote national merchants through the promotion of the shipbuilding and manufacturing sectors. Those goals could be achieved through the enactment of a few policies. To begin with, national manufactures should be granted slight, or when possible, being totally freed from any taxes. In addition, for the shipbuilding industry to flourish, timber should be imported duty-free. Cargo transported on brand new ships should be totally exempted in order to enlarge the national fleet. Finally, the introduction of commodities on foreign ships should be discouraged. He argued that scarcity and abundance determined the value of things, so allowing the free entrance of colonial goods would negatively impact prices. Still worse, warehousing allowances for Asian manufactures would totally ravage Indio-Portuguese trade, ultimately leading to the destruction of national capital invested in oceanic ventures. As a consequence, both domestic and colonial markets would be lost to foreigners.

The so-called "old model" prevailed and a free port was established following the discussions held at the board of trade. Iberian trade was a crucial stake. Transforming Spain into a Piedmont was an idea that had apparently found a great force. The new free port should serve to stimulate terrestrial trade. In the discussions held later, many complaints were raised regarding the disorderly manner in which goods were introduced into Portugal in order to be reshipped to the border. It was said that he official in charge of the management of the free port had formulated a statute which granted him discretionary power decision over the store and reship permissions. Sooner than later, privileges were granted for the introduction of commodities supposedly destined to Spain but actually sold in Portugal. Two years later, regulations were modified in order to prevent disorders in the terrestrial trade. Drawing again on the Genoese model, a 4 per cent transit tax was enforced. In Liguria, the transit tax varied according to distance.

Records related to the management of Lisbon free port are really scarce. This should be one of the reasons why the institution has passed completely unnoticed. Moreover, its short-living operations could partially be explained why records are so difficult to find: the free port functioned just for less than a decade for, in 1806, orders were issued for its closure. The institution is seen as a failure either for contemporaries or for authors who at the time of the 1820s Liberal Revolution argued again in favour of free ports. The scattered evidence leads one to think that failure was the consequence of interconnected phenomena, which, unfortunately, were simply appraised as smuggling. The issue was much more complex, though. The failure and ultimately shutdown of Lisbon free port was closely related to global and colonial trade issues. It tells precisely a history of winners and losers of globalisation and liberalisation of trade.

## Taxes for interwave global circuits

Indo-Portuguese trade underwent a deep reorganisation in the 1760s.[11] In order to favour merchants, the crown promoted a free navigation beyond the Cape of Good Hope. So, in full contrast to the British and Dutch company monopolies, in Portugal, merchants were totally free to outfit commercial ventures destined to Indo-Portuguese overseas ports. Later, merchants started demanding privileges for importing and re-exporting goods paying only slight taxes. The administration of Goa customs house suffered a radical transformation at this moment as well. Transhipment taxes were reduced from 32 per cent to just 4 per cent. Textiles shipped to Lisbon and imported from foreign possessions would pay 50 per cent rate *ad valorem*. According to a new 1783 tariff, Asian manufactures sold in Portugal should pay 29 per cent while re-exported goods pay only 24 per cent. Goods shipped to the Atlantic overseas colonies paid 17 per cent in Lisbon but were levied no taxes at the final port of destination.

In 1795, new changes were introduced in order to promote re-exports to and from Asia imposing a 4 per cent tariff. The same applied to Asian goods transported on Portuguese ships and re-exported to European markets. This is precisely the measure to which Rebelo had drawn attention to. Similar privileges had been granted at least from 1778.[12] In 1783, the board of trade analysed a proposal regarding drawbacks on goods introduced at Goa's customs house. The board endorsed still more liberal measures and suggested that transhipment benefits should include goods introduced from any port in Asia and not only from Portuguese ones.[13]

Merchants, in particular those investing in the slave trade, rapidly saw the chances the free port offered for introducing goods into Brazilian and African markets. It is worth bearing in mind that the slave trade hinged on an adequate supply of Asian-manufactured textiles.[14] For those merchants, attempting to illegally introduce commodities to the free port could turn into a juicy business. They could save up to 18 per cent in taxes. The board of trade even heard some petitions in this regard. In 1797, Manuel de Souza Freire and company asked the board of trade a particular privilege: permission for selling in Angola commodities reshipped from the free port. This was outlawed as the board upheld.[15] The board of trade denied one more instance. José Caetano Monteiro asked authorisation for purchasing two ships in Asia and bringing them westward to Lisbon with goods intended for the free port. Denial followed his petition. The merchant thus once again petitioned before the king. He argued that foreign merchants had no issues in importing goods from Asia and storing them in the free port's warehouse. National merchants were being denied privileges that foreign ones were granted at the detriment of national trade. One member of the board of trade recommended approval upon the condition that taxes were paid on the Asian-manufactured goods and imported ships in order to avoid any harm caused to merchants who were compelled to outfit the venture from Lisbon. The deputy went even further: if frauds were suspected, it would be much better to order the closure of the free port.

Officials of the customs house also raised concerns about the free port's misuses. In 1799, the overseer of the customs house complained before the king on this particular matter: goods introduced from London were stored in the free port and legally transferred into the customs house in order to be finally introduced for the domestic or imperial markets. This illegal operation had a twofold impact. On the one hand, merchants who invested their capital in Asian trade were outcompeted. On the other hand, these illegal actions damaged the national industry. Some estimates were advanced: 1,000 bales of Asian textiles worth 200,000,000 *reis* in Asia doubled their value once in Lisbon. Instead of purchasing commodities in London for a fletched price of 400,000,000 *reis*, the sum could be transferred to Asia where merchants could purchase the same quantity of goods and advance money for next-year orders. He held that this was at the advantage of the exchequer, the navy, and national commerce alike. When purchased in London, on the contrary, only the exchequer could obtain small gains.[16] This official was not the only one to complain about the free port's misuses.

## "Everybody is complaining"

In 1801, Francisco Gomes Loureiro, Portuguese consul at the Malabar Coast, convened advice on some reforms to be implemented in Portuguese colonies' customs house. In his report, he spoke out that the free port had been transformed into a kind of "auction house" in which Asian commodities could be purchased cheaply and easily. In particular, textiles auctioned there were reshipped to Brazil and Africa. In 1800, an order was issued forbidding such illegal auctions.[17] The consul's complaints were but the tip of the iceberg of a series of discontents that the free port had provoked. The Spanish consul in Lisbon also reported his dissatisfaction with the endless permissions free port's authorities granted. He was not the only one to speak out. In the words of a Lisbon official: "everyone is complaining." Portuguese merchants groused that goods supposedly shipped to the border were actually sold in Portugal. Spaniards, in turn, feared the damages the introductions caused. As the same official stated: in this regard "everyone is right."

Besides, 2,000 weavers raised their voices against the evils that the free port had provoked. No one could find a job. The fabrics were ruined. Portuguese-made or painted textiles found no demand. The domestic market had completely been lost to smuggling commodities, which were illegally reshipped to imperial markets. According to the petition, one João Correa de Paiva was one of the partners of those merchants who reshipped smuggling textiles to Brazil and Africa. He imported goods from England in order to reship them to Brazil. He had fit out at least four ships with cargo intended for Bahia and Rio de Janeiro. He had exceeded any line. Upon his request, the customs house's stamp had been faked so he could easily reship the goods without any fear. Complainers found several reasons why the free port should be finally closed down. Fiscal reasons and the continuous outflow of bullion were listed among the main concerns. Not to mention that it was seemingly unfair that "twenty vassals enriched at the cost of two thousand who perished of hunger while it was actually their work which truly enriched the State."

Weavers and craftsmen were not alone in their despair. Merchants who traded to Asia and Brazil argued against the free port. Lisbon fabric owners observed the losses the free port had caused to their businesses, which could be estimated at 28,000,000 or 30,000,000 *cruzados*. They further estimated that the wares supposedly intended for foreign ports but actually shipped to Brazil reached roughly 8,000,000 *cruzados*. The free port was finally closed down in 1806.

## Glocal fairs

Once again, in the 1820s, Spain was referred to in a series of discussions concerning the re-establishment of a free port in Lisbon. As we have already seen, in the 1790s, the Lisbon free port had been designed as an opportunity for transship overland trade. Yet, in the 1820s, debates conducted on the institution's benefits and disadvantages were closely associated with the 1817 enactment of free ports issued in Spain. Spain, in fact, had been a country in which free ports had seemingly found no support throughout the eighteenth century, the first free ports having been established late in the 1810s. This time there was, nevertheless, a different intellectual and political background in which the discussions took place. Liberal times compelled authors to redesign the free port's main features and to sell them otherwise. New assessments of the institution followed closely the exchange of views provoked by Sismondi's book and his intellectual battle against Herrenschwand. The former advocated the relevance of free ports.[18] The latter denied any of the free port's claimed benefits.[19]

In 1822, a merchant commission was asked to suggest a set of economic policies for the promotion of Portuguese languishing trade and navigation. The commission recalled the benefits of free ports and suggested that one was established, the main reason being that anywhere free ports had been established trade had flourished. Genoa, the Hanseatic cities, and Gibraltar, all these cities offered telling instances that showed how beneficial free ports were.

Lisbon could be transformed into a global warehouse in accordance with its excellent and incomparable geographical location. The city could even channel Hamburg's traffic, it was believed. England's warehouses would be empty. Not to mention Gibraltar whose free port could not stand Lisbon competition. The envisaged port would result instrumental in promoting not only maritime but also terrestrial trade. Once again, transit trade was mentioned as one of the main attributes of the port. As happened in France, Holland, and Hamburg whose merchants devoted themselves to reship goods to Flanders and Switzerland, Spain could be supplied from Portugal at the benefice of Portuguese merchants.[20]

In particular, attention was paid to transit trade, which was alleged should be left free from any duty. This fact clearly proves that as late as 1820s, Souza Coutinho's suggestions still echoed in public opinion. The suggestions also showed that, at this moment, free ports were still conceived of as warehouses intended for the storage and reshipping of goods. However, at the same time, the free ports began to change their face. While the members of the commission kept in mind the old *entrepôt* model, some authors began to envision them as "glocal fairs." Their proposals were framed within particular intellectual discussions and implemented economic policies. On the one hand, Sismondi versus Herrenschwand debate, and on the other hand, the establishment of free ports in Spain.

## A new Braganca for the Jews

A public debate had anteceded the discussions held by the 1822 commission. Previously in 1818, a journal published a series of articles on the reasons why a free port should be established. According to the editor of the *O investigador Portuguez*, his inspiration came from the Spanish 1817 act which created four free ports in Spain. Readers were warned that the decree had immediately been revoked, nonetheless, the revocation could not serve as an excuse for Portuguese officials not to survey the matter.[21]

The editor argued for the need to establish one or more free ports in Portugal. In his view, Portugal could see its trade necessarily impacted by the establishment of free ports in Spain, their creation compelling the country to act the same way. This somehow remembers the arguments held by Genovesi. Luíz da Cunha's 1730 plan was brought to mind by the editor who notified his readers that a free port had already been created several years earlier, after advice conveyed by Souza Coutinho. Mismanagement and smuggling were assumed to have been the main reasons why it had ultimately been closed down. In Portugal, the author went on, precedence was always given to functionaries over institutions, so, instead of punishing the officials for their misbehaviour, the free port had finally been closed down. Nonetheless, that experience seemed not to be a reason why not to settle in a free port. Conversely, it had taught the government how to prevent prospective abuses.

In full opposition to Cunha's and Souza Coutinho's, the editor's plan was not to create an *entrepôt* but a truly "free market." In this line of thinking, the new free port should be placed in a location far away from Lisbon. France's example was really telling in this regard. In France, free ports were located in ports like Breast, Dunkirk, Ostend, Toulon, and Marseilles. Spain had placed its recently-created four free ports in Santander, Corunna, and Alicante. Instead of paying attention to the harbours' capacity, in Portugal, local conveniences and interests received more care. All in all, Aveiro was the best-suited port for the new experiment.[22]

Furthermore, the new model radically diverted from the failed one. Entrance should be allowed for any goods no matter their port of origin. Taxes should be lowered to merely 0.5 per cent *ad valorem*. The free port's management should be sheltered from any government intervention. Here we find one of the main changes. As this was a mercantile institution, merchants and not officials should be in charge of its administration. In his attempt to redesign the institution, the editor looked for inspiration in an old-centuries Spanish institution. A merchant guild would manage the free port. Therefore, a *Consulado* (merchant guild or chamber of commerce) should be established. Portugal had witnessed the creation of a short-living merchant guild in 1592 so the model was not unknown. More changes were proposed. The port should be administered upon the same form of a joint-stock company. Not only nationals but also foreign merchants could invest their capital. The editor anticipated that it would be hard to find the adequate number of merchants interested in investing their capital. To solve the issue, one more regulation should be implemented. Emulating policies enacted in Livorno in 1593,[23] the free port should be sold as an opportunity for foreign merchants to change their residence. This measure should in particular seek the coming back of descendants of Portuguese Jews.

## A new Cape of Good Hope and national well-being

As the 1822 merchant commission recalled, there were several measures that could contribute to promoting trade: a faster and efficient mercantile justice; the building of a competitive mercantile fleet; an efficient bureaucracy. Yet, according to an anonymous author, all those measures were perfectly suited for those nations which had at least a languishing trade. This was, however, not Portugal's situation at the turn of the nineteenth century. Portuguese merchants had been unable to maintain a quasi-monopolistic trade in some regions of Africa and Asia. Further, Brazil's independence had worsened things off. The colonial market in South America, to which both manufactures from Asia and enslaved Africans were shipped, had been completely lost to foreign competition. In conclusion, Portugal was compelled to reset its commercial relations.

A free port could turn into a new Cape of Good Hope for Portugal. A privileged geographical position would transform the city into a store for merchants coming from all over the world. A crossroad midway the new and ancient worlds.

The author held that by freeing trade, Portugal could regain what mercantilist privileges had caused the nation to lose. Making trade absolutely free could be achieved through the establishment of a global fair where people coming from the four corners of the world could meet with no restrictions. A "glocal fair" supplied with all kinds of commodities. European merchants could come over to purchase those global goods in exchange for their manufactures. The fair's success would lie in its three main features: (i) it would make transactions easier as a high offer of different goods could be found in the marketplace; (ii) a high demand and supply would favourably impact prices therefore benefiting both sellers and customers worldwide, but above all, national ones; (iii) no distances lowered transport costs.

Lisbon could be metamorphosed into the greatest magazine on earth.[24] For some authors, free ports (such as they were now conceived of in Portugal) had radically mutated their form. At least in two ways. On the one hand, the free port was no longer seen merely as a lighted-taxed warehouse where commodities could be introduced and re-exported tax-exempt. The free port was now visualised as a 'glocal fair'. Sketching out free ports as a utopian global fair was in part a logical implication of linking a centuries-long mercantile institution with a new set of assumptions. The perception of the institution had altered in one more sense. In the eighteenth century, as it had happened since its refashion in the sixteenth century, free ports had essentially been coined as privileges.[25] This feature was, nonetheless, untenable after Smith's *Wealth of Nations*, and more in particular, after the French Revolution and what it had meant for French free ports like Marseilles and Dunkirk.[26]

Those who supported free ports were now compelled to offer a different set of arguments that could demonstrate their potential to create public well-being. The anonymous author desperately sought for arguments that proved how free ports benefited all citizens and not merely a group of merchants. Free ports not only promoted trade and enriched merchants but also positively impacted different economic sectors: "free ports protect agriculture, leads the industry, and raises commerce."[27] Let's focus on his arguments.

Firstly, agriculture could profit from free ports. Plenty of ships at the harbour along with an increasing number of worldwide customers would assure a high demand for national staples. Not to mention that merchants and crews would spend money in the city and fit out their ships before setting sail. A fair would further assure far-flung markets for Portuguese staples. Commodities should be exempted from any tax. In this sense, there was a seemingly golden rule for the promotion of agriculture: "a government must abstain from a bit in order to gain a lot." Taxing agricultural exports led to a loss of competitiveness, and ultimately, to a decrease in national production. No exports meant no revenues. Conversely, a government that promoted the exportation of national agricultural output obtained larger benefits in charging increasing imports. This, in turn, contributed to strengthening the mercantile fleet.

Some might argue that a free introduction of agricultural imports could negatively impact national production. The author recognised that there was no way in which fully opposing interests could be finally reconciled. There was no doubt that consumers would immediately realise the benefits of a free port while farmers would on the contrary raise their voices. Anyone could get a benefice, though. A free port came to reassure consumers on their famine fears since stocks were always ready to enter the market whenever needed. Smuggling or fiscal frauds should not be feared as warehouses could be controlled in an orderly manner. This could in turn prevent the farmers' complains since commodities would enter into the domestic market only after having paid the due taxes.[28]

Secondly, the national industry could profit from free ports. He cited at least three advantages in this regard. To begin with, free ports averted contraband by supplying the market with foreign commodities of all sorts. Plenty of goods and a high number of customers assured good prices for nationals. Moreover, foreign monopolies of any sort could completely be avoided, benefiting the national industry. Finally, foreign manufactures could contribute to improving national arts and fabrics. Manufacturers and craftsmen would have at hand a sustained and vast array of patterns that they could imitate in order to provide the domestic market with fashionable goods.

Free ports strengthened a nascent industry and at the same time incremented the existing one. The author mentioned at least six advantages. (i) tariffs could be easily adjusted in order to promote manufactures and to prevent contraband; (ii) domestic consumption would increase and new markets would be found for national handicrafts; (iii) raw materials would be imported cheaper and without investing national capital; (iv) artists and manufacturers would get inspiration from foreign fashions creating new patterns; (v) the introduction of new technologies and machines would help saving labour force while improving workers' skills; (vi) foreign manufacturers and artists would move to the port in order to benefit from the five above advantages.[29]

The old idea of warehouses along with a tax-exempt deposit system was replaced by a new conception according to which free ports were coined as a "free cleared fair." For the author, "the fair of the free port is to become the world's fair." It had as its main target the global market. Yet, as this fair took place at the borders of a domestic one, its management should take into account simultaneously the interests of both international and domestic trades.

## Carthage and Tyre: a global fair

The above is exactly the same image that Antonio Maximinio Dulac shared.[30] In his paper, which got published only two years later, he conveyed the idea of transforming Lisbon into a free market, one which would immediately become the centre of the commercial world.[31] In some ways, however, Dulac's notion of free ports differed from the one advanced in the *Reflexões a favor do estabelecimento*. The latter displayed a logical and empirical approach in order to deduce and demonstrate the institution's advantages. The former instead backed his arguments basically on historical evidence. Chapter 3, for instance, is completely devoted to giving the reader a historical and comparative summary on the "main commercial emporiums" both ancient and modern. He sought to highlight how, over the centuries, several cities had availed themselves from their geographical location. In this regard, for instance, he had thoroughly read Sismondi's book on the history of Italian cities. Dulac not only supported his analysis of historical data, he also drew on Sismondi's *Richesse Commercial*, who had devoted a full chapter of his book to free ports.

Historical evidence proved that a liberal system had made Tuscany recover its standing in a globalised commercial world that had become extremely competitive. Livorno was a proof of slight duties' benefits. Further, a moderate tax system had converted Holland into a "country-*entrepôt*." Drawing on the comte Chaptal's book, Dulac maintained that Dutch merchants had become brokers who connected producers and consumers worldwide. Yet, Chaptal also held that when own-produced manufactures were considered, Dutch people would also rank at the top of the commercial nations. This latter conclusion led Ducal to assert that a warehouse system hardly fit Portugal's needs and that the institution required to be totally refashioned. Under the current Portuguese situation, national production could barely offer enough cargo to enlarge the national mercantile fleet. For these reasons, conceded privileges should be of a large breath. Only these "sacrifices" would attract trade.[32]

Free ports, as they had been conceived of centuries before, totally unfit Portugal's conditions. This was Dulac's departure point. The main feature attached was the deposit system. According to him, exactly the same definition of a free port had been reproduced for every author that dealt with the issue in such a manner that it seemed they had copied verbatim from each other. After having carefully revised the cases of Ancona and Livorno, Dulac chose Genoa as the model that better fit Portugal's needs. Further, he came up with the idea that *ad valorem* taxes prejudiced warehouse's users. For this reason, only weight should be considered, imposing a 1 per cent tax.[33] Lower taxes would attract a share of the traffic: seafarers would alter their itineraries in the North Atlantic and the Mediterranean giving preference to Lisbon.

Portugal's commercial conditions had radically been altered. Brazil's independence had compelled the country to look for new trading relations. Dulac was certain that the establishment of a free port could completely refashion the metropole's and colony's old-centuries ties. Historical evidence proved that this had happened once and again. A free port would bring well-being for Portuguese and Brazilian nationals alike. The stronger their "social interests" the larger the benefits for both nations: such as had happened to Carthage and Tyre. A free port in Lisbon could offer Brazilian ships the same kind of mutual protection that held together the Hanseatic cities.[34] Lisbon would become a Brazilian port, one located at Europe's door, "at the centre of the commercial world, Lisbon could stand for Brazilian commodities what Carthage did for Phoenician goods."[35]

## Notes

1 António Delgado da Silva, ed., *Coleção Da Legislação Portuguesa Desde a Última Compilação Das Ordenes, Redigida Pelo Desembargador António Delgado Da Silva. Legislação de 179–1801* (Lisboa: Typographia Maigrense, 1828), 279–80.

2 Luís da Cunha, *Instruções Políticas (1733)* (Lisboa: Comissão Nacional dos Descobrimentos portugueses, 2001).

3 On Lisbon Board of Trade see, Jorge Pedreira, *Os Homens de Negócio Da Praça de Lisboa de Pombal Ao Vintismo (1755–1822): Diferenciação, Reprodução e Identificação*

*de Um Grupo Social* (Lisboa: Universidade nova de Lisboa, 1995); Nuno Luís Madureira, *Mercado e Privilégios. A Indústria Portuguesa Entre 1750 e 1834* (Lisboa: Editorial Estampa, 1997).

4 Rodrigo de Souza Coutinho, *Textos Políticos, Económicos e Financeiros 1783–1811* (Lisboa: Banco de Portugal, 1993), Vol. I, 5–27.

5 Jacome Ratton, *Recordações de Jacome Ratton Sobre Ocorrências Do Seu Tempo Em Portugal Durante o Lapso de Sessenta e Três Anos e Mais Alias de Maio 1747 a Setembro de 1810 Que Residiu Em Lisboa Acompanhadas de Algumas Subsequentes Reflexões Suas* (London: H. Bryer, 1813), 106–12.

6 André Mansuy-Diniz Silva, *Portrait d'un Homme d'État: D. Rodrigo de Souza Coutinho, Conte de Linhares, 1755–1812* (Paris: Centre Culturel Calouste Gulbenkian, 2006); José Luís Cardoso, *O Pensamento Econômico Em Portugal Nos Finais Do Século XVIII, 1780–1808* (Lisboa: Editorial Estampa, 1989); José Luís Cardoso and Alexandre Mendes da Cunha, 'Enlightened Reforms and Economic Discourse in the Portuguese-Brazilian Empire (1750–1808)', *History of Political Economy* 44, no. 4 (2012): 619–41.

7 Rodrigo de Souza Coutinho, *Textos Políticos*, Vol. I, 76.

8 Arquivo Nacional Torre do Tombo, *Junta do Comércio*, Livro 129, f. 143r–145v.

9 Manuel Joaquim Rebelo, *Economia Política Feita Em 1795 Por M. J. R.* (Lisboa: Banco de Portugal, 1992).

10 ANTT, *Secretaria de Estado*, mç. 357, cx. 218 dc. 8.

11 José Roberto Amaral Lapa, *A Bahia e a Carreira Da Índia* (São Paulo: Companhia editorial Nacional, 1968); Ernestina Carreira, *Globalising Goa (1660–1820). Change and Exchange in a Former Capital of Empire* (Goa: Publishing Goa 1556, 2014); Celsa Pinto, *A Commercial Resurgence, 1770–1830* (Tellicherry: Irish, 2002).

12 Arquivo Histórico Ultramarino, *Códice 962*, f. 6r-v., 7r-8r., 10r-v.

13 ANTT, *Junta do Comércio*, Livro 121, f. 125r-v.

14 Pedro Machado, *An Ocean of Trade: South Asian Merchants, Africa and the Indian Ocean, ca. 1750–1850* (Cambridge: Cambridge University Press, 2014), 125–34; Richard Roberts, 'West Africa and the Pondicherry Textile Industry', *Indian Economic and Social History Review* 31, no. 2 (1994): 117–45; Giorgio Riello and Prasannan Parthasarathi, eds., *The Spinning World: A Global History of Cotton Textiles, 1200–1850* (Oxford: Oxford University Press, 2011); Giorgio Riello and Roy Tirthankar, eds., *How India Clothed the World: The World of South Asian Textiles, 1500–1850* (Leiden: Brill, 2009).

15 ANTT, *Junta do Comércio*, Livro 130, f. 134r-v.

16 ANTT, *Junta do Comércio*, Livro 130, f. 26r-27r.

17 ANTT, *Junta do Comércio*, Livro 130, f. 92r-94v.

18 J. C. L. Sismondi, *De La Richesse Commerciale, Ou Principes d'économie Politique Appliqués à La Législation Du Commerce* (Genève: J. Paschoud, 1803).

19 Jean Herrenschwand, *De l'économie Politique Moderne Discours Fondamental Sur La Population* (Paris: Maradan librairie, L'an III).

20 *Memória Dos Trabalhos Da Commissão Para Melhoramento Do Comércio Nesta Cidade de Lisboa Creada Por Determinação Das Cortes Geraes, Extraordinarias, e Constituintes Da Nação Portuguesa de 28 de Agosto de 1821. Composta de 24 Membros Eleitos Por Todos Os Negociantes Da Mesma Praça* (Lisboa: Typographia rollandiana, 1822), 14, 98–99.

21 *O Investigador Portuguez Em Inglaterra Ou Journal Litterario Politico* (London: H. Bryer, 1811), July 1818, 107.

22 *O Investigador Portuguez*, August 1818, 324–27.

23 Guillaume Calafat, "L'indice de La Franchise."

24 Anonymous, *Reflexões a Favor Do Estabelecimento de Um Porto Franco Em Lisboa Que a Seus Compatriotas Tem a Honra de Oferecer **** (Lisboa: Typografia de Deziderio Marques Leão Largo do Calharis 12, 1825).
25 Guillaume Garnier, 'Introduction: L'économie Du Privilège, Réflexions Sur Les Privilèges En Europe Occidentale (XVIe–XIXe Siècles)', in *Die Ökonomie Des Privilegs, Westeuropa 16.-19. Jahrhundert*, ed. Guillaume Garnier (Frankfurt: Vittorio Klostermann, 2016), 1–30; Hilton Root, *The Fountain of Privilege. Political Foundations of Markets in Old Regime France and England* (Berkeley: University of California Press, 1994); Jeff Horn, *Economic Development in Early Modern France. The Privilege of Liberty, 1650–1820.*
26 Anonymous, *Mémoire Sur La Nécessité Du Rétablissement de La Franchise Du Port et de La Ville de Dunkerque.*
27 Anonymous, *Reflexões a Favor Do Estabelecimento de Um Porto Franco*, 50, 57.
28 Anonymous, 33–34.
29 Anonymous, 46–47.
30 Antonio Maximino Dulac, *Exame Crítico, Comparativo Do Estado Actual de Portugal Considerado Na Penúria Dos Seus Productos e Urgência de Suprimentos, Com Observações Demostrativas Dos Recursos Que Lhe Oferece a Vantagem Da Sua Situação Geographica* (Lisboa: N.p., 1827).
31 Antonio Maximino Dulac, VIII.
32 Antonio Maximino Dulac, 77.
33 Antonio Maximino Dulac, 62,85.
34 Antonio Maximino Dulac, 109–10.
35 Antonio Maximino Dulac, 99.

# "Maximus totius orbis emporium"

This book tells an alternative history of global commerce. It places the marketplace and not the market at the core of the account, and further, challenges prevalent approaches that overstate theoretical justifications for free trade, expected moralising benefits of *doux commerce*, and intellectual origins of jealousy of trade. Instead, the book discloses a persisting yet obliterated figure that, like a spectre, has chased many over centuries: the plausibility of building a global marketplace. In ancient times, the idea was celebrated upon the Strabonian figure of the *Maximus totius orbis emporium*. In early modern times, the figure was revived in the form of a universal magazine. More recently, we call it Amazon.

The book revolves around three main actors: a travelling intellectual (Pierre Poivre), a propagandist economist (Ange Goudar), and a global institution (free port). Taking distance from most histories of economic thinking, the book focuses on two nowadays forgotten writers who, nonetheless, were held in high regard in the eighteenth century: Pierre Poivre and Ange Goudar. Instead of devoting the attention to first-rank authors as it is common, the book is concerned with a couple of low-rank ones: workers of the "republic of economists." Besides, the deep history of an institution is added to the account.

This book grasps this perennial anxiety for "a universal intercourse of traffic as is desired" from the perspective of a global history of knowledge on the ground. It differs in a twofold manner from the history of economic thinking, and additionally, sheds light on the emergence of political economy at the very moment in which, for the first time, economics was given the shape of science. On the one hand, knowledge production is studied here from the existential ground upon which it emerges and takes form, it is, the set of experiences in which it was anchored. On the other hand, and in a line that separates it from mainstream approaches, it places its attention on institutions and institutional innovation and not merely on theoretical thinking or abstract reasoning. In so doing, it reconciles theory and practices, and further, argues for the need to appraise the institutional foundations of knowledge production along with the intellectual foundations of institutional evolution.

DOI: 10.4324/9780429028199-20

This is an interdisciplinary account that attempts to bridge different fields and overcome pervasive overspecialisation.

The first part has put the focus on "the granary of the universe." The wish for a universal magazine made it necessary to establish a "garden" in which plants brought from all over the world could be cultivated. In the 1740s, Pierre Poivre travelled across Asia in search of the coveted seeds. This experience offered him the opportunity to gather data that he later reshaped into the form of a travel account. This particular platform for knowledge building knew a wide use in the century, economists being among its most popular users. Poivre's *Voyages d'un philosophe* reached a huge echo and was widely read and discussed. The reception conditions of his travel account reveals an "empirical turn" that took shape in the mid-century; an intellectual contest that opposed economists to other circles of the enlightened republic of letters. Compelled to demonstrate their assumptions, the economists disclosed a global history of landed property. Along with China, the Incas, and the ancient cities (particularly Sparta), different societies contributed to shaping a debate on the validity of abstract principles drawn from natural law.

The second part has unveiled disputes over and concerns with the emergence of a "universal magazine of workforce." Ange Goudar was held by his contemporaneous as a famous economic author although he remains unknown nowadays. Author of a vast oeuvre, his *Intérêts de la France mal entendus* was widely read beyond France. A tireless traveller, his being an outsider allowed him the opportunity to write with total freedom, no author being spared criticism. He gained his life writing on economic matters, a field in which he was impressively learned. His vast oeuvre reminds us that economists were also workers in the republic of letters, that most of them had to gain their life somehow, and that the knowledge they produced was not a mere outcome of abstract reasoning. This is not to say that knowledge hinged on the life of an author or that one can find in his experienced world a coherence to his oeuvre. Goudar's oeuvre, like his travelling experience, encompassed an analysis of South Europe as a whole. Besides France, his attention was devoted to Portugal and Naples. His was an attempt to explain the South's pervasive backwardness, but also, an attempt to explain from a non-institutional perspective (as was common at the time) the rise of England. Moreover, a careful reading of his books sheds light on the philosophical foundations of economic theory, an overlooked matter. "Cartesian economics," as I call it, took the form of maxims upon which Goudar (among many others included Quesnay with his *Maxims on Government*) reflected on topics such as delocalisation, deurbanisation, and luxe. The intensification of commercial exchanges, Goudar held, put countries in a hard situation: the dependence of the basic goods. Depending on others to be fed or to be clothed was a high-risk policymakers should carefully be concerned with. Global histories of commerce, which for the most part focus on free trade, overrated this risk that was at the very core of Goudar's analysis.

Finally, the third part has analysed attempts made to build "a universal magazine" and the institutional impacts such utopia generated. Free ports were an everlasting institution. They are the forerunners of our current free trade zones. They are told to be a novelty first designed in the last quarter of the sixteenth century. Since then, they reached a global spread, having mushroomed in the Mediterranean, the Baltic, and the Caribbean. I approach free ports within the debate that I call innovation in persistence. The question being: Why do some institutions (and ideas) successfully propagate while others just remain in the shadows? Indeed, there is no answer to such a big question. I approach free ports from this perspective. This is not an account of why, how, and where free ports were established locally. In contrast, I tell a deep history that pays attention to the different shapes the same institution took over time. I uphold that Medieval fairs evolved from seasonal-held meetings to become everlasting marketplaces. In so doing, I unveil the two underlying precepts upon which markets were configured spatially over and over: *ab introitu iudicum* and *ius stepulae*. Along with the intellectual foundations of institutional innovation, institutional diversity's impact is taken into consideration. In both England and Holland, opposition to free ports was spread, and in consequence, different institutions were designed with similar goals in mind. The Navigation act, for instance, was told to achieve free port's same purposes. Free port's spread over the eighteenth century shows different waves in which the institution was enacted once and again in order to propel trade and its changes on matter and form over time.

# Bibliography


Acemoglu Daron, Cantoni Davide, Johnson Simon, and Robinson James A. 'The Consequences of Radical Reform: The French Revolution'. *American Economic Review* 101, no. 7 (2011): 3286–307.

Acemoglu Daron, Egorov Georgy, and Sonin Konstantin. 'Institutional Change and Institutional Persistence'. *Becker Friedman Institute-Political Economics Initiative Working Papers* 127 (2020).

Acemoglu Daron, and Robinson James. *Why Nations Fail? The Origins of Power, Prosperity and Poverty*. New York: Crown Publishers, 2012.

———. *The Narrow Corridor: States, Societies, and the Fate of Liberty*. New York: Penguin Press, 2019.

Acemoglu Daren, and Johnson Simon. 'Unbundling Institutions'. *Journal of Political Economy* 113, no. 5 (2005): 949–95.

Acemoglu Daren, Johnson Simon, and Robinson James. 'The Colonial Origins of Comparative Development: An Empirical Investigation'. *American Economic Review* 9, no. 5 (2001): 1369–401.

Ademollo Alessandro. *Un Avventuriere Francese in Italia Nella Seconda Metà Del Settecento*. Bergamo: Fr. Cattaneo editori, 1891.

Allen Robert. *The British Industrial Revolution in Global Perspective*. Cambridge: Cambridge University Press, 2009.

———. 'The High Wage Economy and the Industrial Revolution: A Restatement'. *Economic History Review* 68, no. 1 (2015): 1–22.

Amodio Paolo. *Il Disincanto Della Ragione e l'assolutezza Del Bonheur. Studio Sull'Abate Galiani*. Naples: Alfredo Guida, 1997.

Aoki Masahiko. *Toward a Comparative Institutional Analysis*. Boston: MIT, 2001.

Appleby Joyce. *Economic Thought and Ideology in Seventeenth-Century England*. Princeton, NJ: Princeton University Press, 1978.

Arendt Hannah. *The Human Condition*. Chicago, IL: Chicago University Press, 2018.

Armytage Frances. *The Free Port System in the British West Indies*. London: Longmans, 1953.

Aston T. H., and Philpin C. H. E., eds. *The Brenner Debate: Agrarian Class Structure and Economic Development in Pre-Industrial Europe*. Cambridge: Cambridge University Press, 1985.

Barbour Richmond. *The Third Voyage Journals: Writing and Performance in the London East India Company, 1607–10*. New York: Palgrave Macmillan, 2009.

Barreto José. 'O Discurso Político Falsamente Atribuído Ao Marquês de Pombal'. *Revista de História Das Ideias* 4, no. 1 (1982): 385–422.

Bautier Robert-Henri. 'Les Foires de Champagne. Recherches Sur Une Évolution Historique'. In *La Foire*, 97–148. Bruxelles: Editions de la librairie encyclopédique, 1953.

Bazzoni Augusto, ed. *Lettere Ferdinando Galiani al Marchese Bernardo Tanucci*. Florence: Gio. Pietro Vieusseux, 1880.

Bernardi Bruno. 'L'idée d'équilibre Européen Dans Le Jus Gentium Des Modernes: Esquisse d'histoire Conceptuelle'. In *Penser l'Europe Au XVIIIe Siècle: Commerce, Civilisation, Empire*, edited by Antoine Lilti and Céline Spector, 19–46. Oxford: Voltaire Foundation, 2014.

Blaufarb Rafe. *The Great Demarcation: The French Revolution and the Invention of Modern Property*. Oxford: Oxford University Press, 2016.

Bleichmar Daniela. *Visible Empire: Botanical Expeditions and Visual Culture in the Hispanic Enlightenment*. Chicago, IL: Chicago University Press, 2012.

Bloch Marc. *La Société Féodale*. Paris: Albin Michel, 1968.

Bourdieu Pierre. *L'ontologie Politique de Martin Heidegger*. Paris: Les éditions de minuit, 1988.

———. *Esquisse d'une Théorie de La Pratique (Précédé de Trois Études d'ethnologie Kabyle*. Paris: Seuil, 2000.

Braudel Fernand. *Civilisation Matérielle, Économie et Capitalisme (XVe–XVIIIe Siècle)*. Paris: Armand Colin, 1979.

Brésard Marc. *Les Foires de Lyon Aux XVe et XVIe Siècles*. Paris: Auguste Picard éditeur, 1914.

Brixius Dorit Maria Nicola. 'French Empire on the Ground: Plants, Peoples, and Knowledge in the Services of Eighteenth-Century Isle of France'. European University Institute, 2017.

Bruni Luigino, and Porta Pier Luigi. 'Economia Civile and Pubblica Felicità in the Italian Enlightenment'. *History of Political Economy* 35, no. Supplement 1 (2003): 361–85.

Brunner Otto. *Land Und Herrschaft: Grundfragen Der Territorialen Verfassungsgeschichte*. Darmstadt: Wissenschaftliche Buchgesellschaft, 1984.

Buckle Stephen. *Natural Law and the Theory of Property: Grotius to Hume*. Oxford: Clarendon Press, 2002.

Burke Peter. *A Social History of Knowledge: From Gutenberg to Diderot*. Cambridge: Polity Press, 2000.

Burt Ronald S. *Neighbor Networks: Competitive Advantage Local and Personal*. New York: Oxford University Press, 2010.

———. *What Is the History of Knowledge?* Cambridge: Polity Press, 2016.

Calafat Guillaume. 'L'indice de La Franchise: Politique Économique, Concurrence de Ports Francs et Condition Des Juifs En Méditerranée à l'époque Moderne'. *Revue Historique* 686, no. 2 (2018): 275–320.

———. *Une Mer Jalousée. Contribution à l'histoire de La Souveraineté (Méditerranée, XVIIe Siècle)*. Paris: Seuil, 2019.

Caracciolo Alberto. 'Il Dibattito Sui "Porti Franchi" Nel Settecento: Genesi Della Franchigia Di Ancona'. *Rivista Storica Italiana* 75, no. 3 (1963): 538–58.

Cardoso José Luís. *O Pensamento Econômico Em Portugal Nos Finais Do Século XVIII, 1780–1808*. Lisboa: Editorial Estampa, 1989.

Cardoso José Luís, and Cunha Alexandre Mendes da. 'Enlightened Reforms and Economic Discourse in the Portuguese-Brazilian Empire (1750–1808)'. *History of Political Economy* 44, no. 4 (2012): 619–41.

Carreira Ernestina. *Globalising Goa (1660–1820). Change and Exchange in a Former Capital of Empire*. Goa: Publishing Goa 1556, 2014.

Cedrini Mario, and Fontana Magda. 'Just Another Niche in the Wall? How Specialization Is Changing the Face of Mainstream Economics'. *Cambridge Journal of Economics* 42, no. 2 (2018): 427–51.

Certeau Michel de. *The Practice of Everyday Life*. Berkeley: University of California Press, 2011.

Charles Loïc. 'The Visual History of the Tableau Économique'. *European Journal of the History of Economics* 10, no. 4 (2010): 527–50.

Charles Loïc, Lefebvre Frédéric, and Théré Christine. *Le Cercle de Vincent de Gournay: Savoirs Économiques et Pratiques Administratives En France Au Milieu Du XVIII*. Paris: Institut National d'Études Démographiques, 2011.

Charles Loïc, and Théré Christine. 'Jeux de Mots, Narrative and Economic Writing: The Rhetoric of Anti-Physiocracy in French Economic Periodicals (1764–1769)'. *European Journal History of Economic Thought* 22, no. 3 (2015): 359–82.

Chartier Roger. 'La Académie de Lyon Au XVIIIe Siècle: Étude de Sociologie Culturelle'. In *Nouvelles Études Lyonnaises*, edited by Roger Chartier, L. Desgraves, and J.-M Dureau-Lapeyssonie, 133–250. Paris: Librairie Droz, 1969.

———. *Culture Écrite et Société: L'ordre Des Livres XIVe–XVIIIe*. Paris: Albin Michel, 1996.

———. *Inscrire et Effacer. Culture Écrite et Littérature. XIe-XVIIIe*. Paris: Seuil/Gallimard, 2006.

Cheney Paul. *Revolutionary Commerce: Globalization and the French Monarchy*. Cambridge, MA: Harvard University Press, 2010.

Citton Yves. *Portrait de l'économiste En Physiocrate: Critique Littéraire de l'économie Politique*. Paris: Harmattan, 2000.

Clément Alain. 'Nicolas Baudeau, an Anti-Physiocrat? Éphémérides Du Citoyen Prior to "Conversion" (1765–1766)'. *European Journal of the History of Economic Thought* 22, no. 3 (2015): 534–63.

Confine Michael. 'Les Enquêtes Économiques de La "Société Libre d'économie de Saint-Petersbourg" (1765–1820)'. *Revue Historique* 227, no. 1 (1962): 155–80.

Congost Rosa. 'Property Rights and Historical Analysis: What Rights? What History?' *Past and Present* 181 (2003): 73–106.

Costa Leonor Freire, Maria Manuela Rocha, and Rita Martins de Sousa. *O Ouro Do Brasil. Lisboa*. Lisboa: Imprensa Nacional, 2013.

Costantini Massimo. *Porto, Navi e Traffici a Venezia*. Venezia: Marsilio, 2004.

Darnton Robert. 'The High Enlightenment and the Low-Life of Literature in Pre-Revolutionary France'. *Past and Present* 51 (1971): 81–115.

———. *The Business of Enlightenment: A Publishing History of the Encyclopédie*. Cambridge, MA: Belknap Press of Harvard University, 1979.

———. *The Great Cat Massacre: And Other Episodes in French Cultural History*. New York: Basic Books, 1984.

———. *The Forbidden Best-Sellers of Pre-Revolutionary France*. New York: W. W. Norton, 1995.

De la Véronne Chantal, ed. *Tanger Sous l'occupation Anglaise d'après Une Description Anonyme de 1674*. Paris: Librairie orientaliste Paul Geuthner, 1972.

Delgado Josep M. *Dinámicas Imperiales (1650–1796): España, América y Europa En El Cambio Institucional Del Sistema Colonial Español*. Barcelona: Bellatera, 2007.

Demsetz Harold. 'Toward a Theory of Property Rights'. *American Economic Review* 57, no. 2 (1967): 347–59.

Denis-Delacour Christopher. 'Entre Normes et Pratiques. Les Étrangers Des Trafics Maritimes Romains (1742–1797)'. Aix-Marseille/Istituto Italiano di Scienze Umane, 2012.

Dermigny Louis. 'Escales. Échelles et Port Francs Au Moyen Âge et Aux Temps Modernes'. In *Les Grandes Escales. Période* Contemporaine et Synthèse Génèrales, 3:213–644. Bruxelles: Éditions de la librairie encyclopédique, 1974.

Dickey Laurence. 'Doux-Commerce and Humanitarian Values. Free Trade, Sociability and Universal Benevolence in Eighteenth-Century Thinking'. *Grotiana (New Series)* 22/23, no. 2 (2001): 271–318.

Dioguardi Gianfranco. *Un Avventuriero Nella Napoli Del Settecento.* Palermo: Sellerio editore, 1983.

Drayton Richard. *Nature's Government: Science, Imperial Britain and the Improvement of the World.* New Haven, CT: Yale University Press, 2000.

Easterby-Smith Sarah. *Cultivating Commerce: Culture of Botany in Britain and France, 1760–1815.* Cambridge: Cambridge University Press, 2018.

Edwards Jeremy, and Ogilvie Sheilagh. 'Contract Enforcement, Institutions, and Social Capital: The Maghribi Traders Reappraised'. *Economic History Review* 65, no. 2 (2012): 421–44.

———. 'What Lessons for Economic Development Can We Draw from the Champagne Fairs?' *Explorations in Economic History* 49, no. 2 (2012): 131–48.

*Epistolario Bernardo Tanucci.* Vol. 20. Naples: Società Napoletana de Storia Patria, 2000.

Epstein Stephan. 'Regional Fairs, Institutional Innovation, and Economic Growth in Late Medieval Europe'. *Economic History Review* 47, no. 3 (1994): 459–82.

———. *Freedom and Growth: The Rise of States and Markets in Europe, 1300–1750.* London: Routledge, 2000.

Farnell J. E. 'The Navigation Act of 1651, the First Dutch War, and the London Merchant Community'. *Economic History Review* 16, no. 2 (1961): 439–54.

Ferrier F. L. A. *Essai Sur Les Ports Francs.* Bayonne, Bordeaux, and Paris: Messidor an II.

Findlay Ronald and O'Rourke Kevin H. *Power and Plenty: Trade, War, and the World Economy in the Second Millennium.* Princeton, NJ: Princeton University Press, 2007.

Flynn Dennis O. and Giraldez Arturo. 'Born with a "Silver Spoon": The Origin of World Trade'. *Journal of World History* 6, no. 2 (1995): 201–22.

Foucault Michel. *L'archéologie Du Savoir.* Paris: Gallimard, 1969.

———. *L'herméneutique Du Sujet. Cours Au Collège de France (1981–1982).* Paris: Seuil/Gallimard, 2001.

———. *Sécurité, Territoire et Population. Cours Au Collège de France (1977–78).* Paris: Gallimard/Seuil (Collection Hautes Études), 2004.

Frank Andre Gunder. *ReOrient: Global Economy in the Asian Age.* Los Angeles: University of California Press, 1998.

Fraser Terjanian Anoush. *Commerce and Its Discontents in Eighteenth-Century French Political Thought.* Cambridge: Cambridge University Press, 2016.

Fusaro Maria. *Political Economies of Empire in the Early Modern Mediterranean: The Decline of Venice and the Rise of England, 1450–1700.* Cambridge: Cambridge University Press, 2015.

Garnier Guillaume. *État, Économie, Territoire En Allemagne. L'espace Dans Le Caméralisme et l'économie Politique*, 1740–1820. Paris: EHESS, 2006.

———. 'Introduction: L'économie Du Privilège, Réflexions Sur Les Privilèges En Europe Occidentale (XVIe–XIXe Siècles)'. In *Die Ökonomie Des Privileges, Westeuropa 16.-19. Jahrhundert*, edited by Guillaume Garnier, 1–30. Frankfurt: Vittorio Klostermann, 2016.

Geertz Clifford. 'The Bazaar Economy: Information and Search in Peasant Marketing'. *American Economic Review* 68, no. 2 (1978): 28–32.

Getzler Joshua. 'Theories of Property and Economic Development'. *Journal of Interdisciplinary History* 26, no. 4 (1996): 639–69.

Gioffrè Domenico. *Gênes et Les Foires de Change de Lyon à Besançon*. Paris: Sevpen, 1960.

Goldberg Jessica. 'Choosing and Enforcing Business Relationships in the Eleventh-Century Mediterranean: Reassessing the Magrhibi Traders'. *Past and Present* 216, no. 3 (2012): 3–40.

Good Ann. 'The Construction of an Authoritative Text: Peter Kolb's Description of the Khoikhoi at the Cape of Good Hope in the Eighteenth Century'. *Journal of Early Modern History* 10, no. 1–2 (2006): 61–94.

Gottmann Felicia. *Global Trade, Smuggling, and the Making of Economic Liberalism: Asian Textiles in France 1680–1760*. London and New York: Palgrave Macmillan, 2016.

Goutte Pierre Henri, and Klotz Gérard. 'Turgot: A Critic of Physiocracy? An Analysis of the Debates in Éphémérides Du Citoyen and in Correspondence with Dupont'. *European Journal History of Economic Thought* 22, no. 3 (2015): 500–33.

Grafe Regina, and Gelderblom Oscar. 'The Rise and Fall of the Merchant Guilds: Re-Thinking the Comparative Study of Commercial Institutions in Pre-Modern Europe'. *Journal of Interdisciplinary History* 40, no. 4 (2010): 477–511.

Greif Avner. *Institutions and the Path to the Modern Economy: Lessons from the Medieval Trade*. Cambridge: Cambridge University Press, 2006.

———. 'Coercion and Exchange: How Did Markets Evolve'. In *Institutions, Innovation and Industrialization: Essays on Economic History and Development*, edited by Avner Greif, Lynne Kiesling and John Nye, 71–96. Princeton, NJ: Princeton University Press, 2015.

Grove Richard Hug. *Green Imperialism: Colonial Expansion, Tropical Island Edens and the Origins of Environmentalism, 1600–1860*. Cambridge: Cambridge University Press, 1995.

Harris Ron. *Going the Distance: Eurasian Trade and the Rise of the Business Corporation, 1400–1700*. Princeton, NJ: Princeton University Press, 2020.

Hartog François. *Le Miroir d'Hérodote: Essai Sur La Représentation de l'autre*. Paris: Gallimard, 1980.

Hauc Jean-Claude. *Ange Goudar: Un Aventurier Des Lumières*. Paris: Honoré Champion, 2004.

Hayek F. A. *Law, Legislation and Liberty*. New York: Routledge, 1982.

Heidegger Martin. *Being and Time*. New York: State University of New York Press, 2010.

Hirschman Albert O. *The Passions and the Interests: Political Arguments for Capitalism before Its Triumph*. Princeton, NJ: Princeton University Press, 2013.

Hodgson Geoffrey M. 'Much of the "Economics of Property Rights" Devalues Property and Legal Rights'. *Journal of Institutional Economics* 11, no. 4 (2015): 683–709.

Hont Istvan. 'The Early Enlightenment Debate on Commerce and Luxury'. In *The Cambridge History of Eighteenth-Century Political Thought*, edited by Mark Goldie and Robert Wokler, 379–418. Cambridge: Cambridge University Press, 2006.

———. *Jealousy of Trade: International Competition and the Nation-State in Historical Perspective*. Cambridge, MA: Harvard University Press, 2010.

Hont Istvan, and Ignatieff Michael, eds. *Wealth and Virtue: The Shaping of Political Economy in the Scottish Enlightenment*. Cambridge: Cambridge University Press, 1983.

Horn Jeff. *Economic Development in Early Modern France. The Privilege of Liberty, 1650–1820*. Cambridge: Cambridge University Press, 2015.

Hufton Olwen. 'Social Conflict and the Grain Supply in Eighteenth-Century France'. *Journal of Interdisciplinary History* 14, no. 2 (1983): 303–31.

Hume David. *Political Essays*. Cambridge: Cambridge University Press, 1994.

Huvelin P. *Essai Historique Sur Le Droit Des Marchés et Des Foires*. Paris: Arthur Rousseau, 1897.

Iodice Antonio. 'Il Porto Franco, Diffusione Di Un Modello Economico: Politiche, Attori, Ideologie, Mito. Due Realtà a Confronto: Genova e Marsiglia (1590–1817)'. Aix-Marseille, 2017.

Kammerling Smith David. 'Structuring Politics in Early Eighteenth-Century France: The Political Innovations of the French Council of Commerce'. *Journal of Modern History* 74, no. 3 (2002): 490–537.

Kaplan Steven L. *Raisonner Sur Les Blés. Essais Sur Les Lumières Économiques*. Paris: Fayard, 2017.

Khazeni Arash. 'Indo-Persian Travel Writing at the Ends of the Mughal World'. *Past and Present* 243, no. 1 (2019): 141–74.

Kirk Thomas. 'Genoa and Livorno: Sixteenth and Seventeenth-Century Commercial Rivalry as a Stimulus to Policy Development'. *History* 86, no. 281 (2001): 3–17.

Kochan Jeff. *Science as Social Existence. Heidegger and the Sociology of Scientific Knowledge*. Cambridge: Open Book Publishers, 2017.

Kopsidis Michael, and Bromley Daniel W. 'The French Revolution and German Industrialization: Dubious Models and Doubtful Causality'. *Journal of Institutional Economics* 12, no. 1 (2016): 161–90.

Kula Witold. *Théorie Économique Du Système Féodal*. Paris: Mouton, 1970.

Kumar Dharma. 'Private Property in Asia? The Case of Medieval South India'. *Comparative Studies in Society and History* 27, no. 2 (1985): 340–66.

Labrousse C. E. *Esquisse Du Mouvement Des Prix et Des Revenus En France Au XVIIIe Siècle*. Paris: Librairie Dalloz, 1933.

Landes David. *The Wealth and Poverty of Nations Why Some Are So Rich and Some So Poor*. New York: W. W. Norton Company, 1999.

Lapa José Roberto Amaral. *A Bahia e a Carreira Da Índia*. São Paulo: Companhia editorial Nacional, 1968.

La Porta Rafael, Lopez-de-Silanes Florencio, Shleifer Andrei, and Vishny Robert W. 'Law and Finance'. *Journal of Political Economy* 106, no. 6 (1998): 1113–55.

Larrère Catherine. 'L'arithmétique Des Physiocrates: La Mesure de l'évidence'. *Histoire et Mesure* 7, no. 1–2 (1992): 5–24.

———. *L'invention de l'économie Au XVIIIe Siècle. Du Droit à La Physiocratie*. Paris: Presses Universitaire de France, 1992.

———. *Actualité de Montesquieu*. Paris: Sciences Po, 1999.

———. 'Montesquieu et Le "Doux Commerce": Un Paradigme Du Libéralisme'. *Cahiers d'histoire. Revue d'histoire Critique* 123 (2014): 21–38.

Leckey Column. *Patrons of Enlightenment: The Free Economic Society in Eighteenth-Century Russia.* Newark: University of Delaware Press, 2011.

Leng Thomas. 'Commercial Conflict and Regulation in the Discourse of Trade in Seventeenth-Century England'. *Historical Journal* 48, no. 4 (2005): 933–54.

———. *Benjamin Worsley (1618–1677): Trade, Interest, and the Spirit in Revolutionary England.* London: Royal Historical Society, 2008.

Letwin William. *The Origins of Scientific Economics: English Economic Thought 1660–1776.* London: Methuen & co, 1963.

Libecap Gary D. 'Property Rights in Economic History: Implications for Research'. *Explorations in Economic History* 23 (1986): 227–52.

Lilti Antoine. *Le Monde Des Salons: Sociabilité et Mondanité à Paris Au XVIIIe Siècle.* Paris: Fayard, 2013.

Livingstone David N. *Putting Science in Its Place: Geographies of Scientific Knowledge.* Chicago, IL: Chicago University Press, 2003.

Maas Harro, and Morgan Mary S. 'Observation and Observing in Economics'. *History of Political Economy* 44, no. Annual supplement (2012): 1–24.

Machado Pedro. *An Ocean of Trade: South Asian Merchants, Africa and the Indian Ocean, ca. 1750–1850.* Cambridge: Cambridge University Press, 2014.

Madureira Nuno Luís. *Mercado e Privilégios. A Indústria Portuguesa Entre 1750 e 1834.* Lisboa: Editorial Estampa, 1997.

Malherbe Michel. 'Hume's Reception in France'. In *The Reception of David Hume in Europe*, edited by Peter Jones, 43–97. London: Thoemmes Continuum, 2005.

Malpas Jeff. *Heidegger's Topology: Being, Place, and World.* Cambridge: MIT, 2006.

Mannheim Karl. *Ideology and Utopia.* New York: Routledge, 1998.

Margairaz Dominique. 'La Formation Du Réseau Des Foires et Fes Marchés: Stratégies, Pratiques et Idéologies'. *Annales. Economies, Sociétés, Civilisations* 41, no. 6 (1986): 1215–42.

———. *Foires et Marchés Dans La France Préindustrielle.* Paris: EHESS, 1988.

———. 'Institutions et Espaces de Marché: De l'abstrait Au Concret'. In *Genèse Des Marchés*, edited by Françoise Bayard, Patrick Fridenson, and Albert Rigaudière, 49–65. Paris: Institut de la gestion publique et du développement économique/ Comité pour l'histoire économique et financière de la France, 2015.

Martínez Ruíz José Ignacio. 'De Tánger a Gibraltar: El Estrecho En La Praxis Comercial e Imperial Británica (1661–1776)'. *Hispanica* 65–3, no. 221 (2005): 1043–62.

Masson Paul. *Ports Francs d'autrefois et d'aujourd'hui.* Paris: Hachette, 1904.

Maxwell Kenneth. *Pombal, Paradox of the Enlightenment.* Cambridge: Cambridge University Press, 1995.

Mazoyer Louis. 'Explotation Forestière et Conflits Sociaux En France- Comté, à La Fin de l'Ancien Régime'. *Annales d'histoire Économique et Sociale* 16 (1932): 339–58.

Mazzucato Mariana. *The Entrepreneurial State: Debunking Public vs. Private Sector Myths.* London: Penguin Press, 2018.

McCloskey Deirdre. *Bourgeois Dignity: Why Economics Can't Explain the Modern World.* Chicago, IL: Chicago University Press, 2010.

Meijling Jespers. 'La Lenta Diffusione Di Un Modello: Il Porto Franco Da Livorno a Marstrand Nel Settecento'. *Nuovi Studi Livornesi* 17, no. 2010 (2010): 95–120.

Meyssonnier Simone. *La Balance et l'horloge. La Genèse de La Pensée Libérale En France Au XVIIIe Siècle.* Paris: Éditions de la passion, 1989.

Milgrom Paul R., North Douglass, and Weingast Barry R. 'The Role of Institutions in the Revival of Trade: The Law Merchant, Private Judges, and the Champagne Fairs'. *Economics and Politics* 2, no. 1 (1990): 1–23.

Miller Judith A. *Mastering the Market: The State and the Grain Trade in Northern France, 1700–1860.* Cambridge: Cambridge University Press, 1998.

Minard Philipe. *La Fortune Du Colbertisme: État et Industrie Dans La France Des Lumières.* Paris: Fayard, 2014.

Mokyr Joel. *The Gifts of Athena: Historical Origins of the Knowledge Economy.* Princeton, NJ: Princeton University Press, 2004.

———. 'The Intellectual Origins of Modern Economic Growth'. *Journal of Economic History* 65, no. 2 (2005): 285–351.

———. *The Enlightened Economy: An Economic History of Britain 1700–1850.* Princeton, NJ: Princeton University Press, 2012.

Montesquieu. *The Spirit of the Laws.* Cambridge: Cambridge University Press, 1989.

Mulich Jeppe. *In a Sea of Empires: Networks and Crossings in the Revolutionary Caribbean.* Cambridge: Cambridge University Press, 2020.

Müller-Wille Staffan. 'Nature as a Marketplace: The Political Economy of Linnaean Botany'. *History of Political Economy* 35, no. Annual Supplement (2003): 154–72.

Mulsow Martin. *Prekäres Wissen. Eine Andere Ideengeschichte Der Frühen Neuzeit.* Berlin: Suhrkamp, 2012.

Munro John H. 'The "New Institutional Economics" and the Changing Fortunes of Fairs in Medieval and Early Modern Europe: The Textiles Trades, Warfare, and Transaction Costs'. *Vierteljahrschrift Für Sozial-Und Wirtschaftsgeschichte* 88, no. 1 (2000): 1–47.

Murphy Antoin E. *Richard Cantillon: Entrepreneur and Economist.* Oxford: Clarendon Press, 1986.

———. 'Nicolas Du Tot and John Law'. In *Economic Development and Social Change: Historical Roots and Modern Perspectives*, edited by George Stathakis and Gianni Vaggi, 171–89. New York: Routledge, 2006.

Musacchio Aldo, and Turner John D. 'Does the Law and Finance Hypothesis Pass the Test of History?' *Business History* 55, no. 4 (2013): 524–42.

Musset Georges. *Les Ports Francs. Étude Historique.* Paris: Ernest Leroux éditeur, 1904.

North Douglass. *The Rise of the West World: A New Economic History.* London: Cambridge University Press, 1973.

———. *Institutions, Institutional Change and Economic Performance.* Cambridge: Cambridge University Press, 1991.

———. *Understanding the Process of Economic Change.* Princeton, NJ: Princeton University Press, 2010.

North Douglas, and Weingast Robert. 'Constitutions and Commitment: The Evolution of Institutional Governing Public Choice in Seventeenth-Century England'. *Journal of Economic History* 49, no. 4 (1989): 803–32.

Noya Virgilio. *O Ouro Brasileiro e o Comércio Anglo-Português.* São Paulo: Companhia editora Nacional, 1979.

Oncken Auguste, ed. *Oeuvres Économiques et Philosophiques de F. Quesnay Fondateur Du Système Physiocratique Accompagnées Des Éloges et d'autres Travaux Biographiques Sur Quesnay Par Différents Auteurs.* Paris: Jules Peelman & cia, 1888.

Orain Arnaud. 'Figures of Mockery. The Cultural Disqualification of Physiocracy (1760–1790)'. *European Journal History of Economic Thought* 22, no. 3 (2015): 383–419.

———. *La Politique Du Merveilleux. Une Autre Histoire Du Système de Law (1695–1795).* Paris: Fayard, 2018.

Osterhammel Jürgen. *Unfabling the East: The Enlightenment's Encounter with Asia.* Princeton, NJ: Princeton University Press, 2018.

Palma Nuno. 'Money and Modernization in Early Modern England'. *Financial History Review* 25, no. 3 (2018): 231–61.

———. 'Reconstruction of Money Supply over the Long Run: The Case of England, 1270–1870'. *Economic History Review* 71, no. 2 (2018): 373–92.

Pandolfi Jean. 'Beccaria Traduit par Morellet'. *Dix-Huitième Siècle* 9 (1977): 291–316.

Pauly Michel. 'Vom Regionalen Messesystem Zum Internationalen Netz von Messestädten'. In *Netzwerke Im Europäischen Handel Des Mittelalters: Herausgegeben Vom Konstanzer Arbeitskreis Für Mittelalterliche Geschichte,* edited by Hans J. Gilomen and Gerhard Fouquet, 49–100. Ostfildern: Jan Thornecke Verlag, 2010.

Pedreira Jorge. 'Os Homens de Negócio Da Praça de Lisboa de Pombal Ao Vintismo (1755–1822): Diferenciação, Reprodução e Identificação de Um Grupo Social'. Universidade nova de Lisboa, 1995.

Pénigaud Théophile. 'The Political Opposition of Rousseau to Physiocracy: Government, Interest, Citizenship'. *European Journal History of Economic Thought* 22, no. 3 (2015): 473–99.

Perna Maria Luisa. 'L'edizione Delle Lezioni Di Commercio Di Antonio Genovesi'. In *Genovesi Economista,* edited by Bruno Jossa, Rosario Palatano, and Eugenio Zagari, 59–66. Naples: Istituto Italiano per gli studi filosofici, 2007.

Perrot Jean-Claude. 'La Comptabilité Des Entreprises Agricoles Dans l'économie Physiocratique'. *Annales. Économies, Sociétés, Civilisations* 33, no. 3 (1978): 559–79.

———. *Une Histoire Intellectuelle de l'économie Politique.* Paris: EHESS, 1992.

Pezzolo Luciano, and Tattara Giuseppe. '"Una Fiera Senza Luogo": Was Bisenzone an International Capital Market in Sixteenth-Century Italy'. *Journal of Economic History* 68, no. 4 (2008): 1098–122.

Pii Eluggero. *Antonio Genovesi: Dalla Politica Economica Alla 'Politica Civile'.* Florence: Leo S. Olschki, 1984.

Piketty Thomas. *Capital et Idéologie.* Paris: Seuil, 2019.

Pinto Celsa. *A Commercial Resurgence, 1770–1830.* Tellicherry: Irish, 2002.

Platania Marco. 'Montesquieu Und Der "Doux Commerce": Wie Der Handel Gesellschaft Und Politik Verwandelt'. In *Der Moderne Staat Und 'Le Doux Commerce': Politik, Ökonomie Und Internationale Beziehungen Im Politischen Denken Der Aufklärung,* edited by Olaf Asbach, 69–90. Baden-Baden: Nomos, 2014.

Pocock J. G. A. *Virtue, Commerce, and History: Essays on Political Thought and History. Chiefly in the Eighteenth Century.* Cambridge: Cambridge University Press, 1985.

Polanyi Karl. *The Great Transformation: The Political and Economic Origins of Our Time.* Boston, MA: Beacon Press, 2001.

Polanyi Karl, Arensberg Conrad M., and Pearson Harry W., eds. *Trade and Market in the Early Empires: Economies in History and Theory.* Glencoe: Falcon's Wing Press, 1957.

Pomeranz Kenneth. *The Great Divergence. China, Europe, and the Making of the Modern World.* Princeton, NJ: Princeton University Press, 2009.

Pratt Mary Louise. *Imperial Eyes: Travel Writing and Transculturation.* London and New York: Routledge, 1992.

Proudhon Pierre-Joseph. *What Is Property? Or an Inquiry into the Principle of Right and of Government.* Cambridge: Cambridge University Press, 1994.

Provost Audrey. 'Le Luxe Publié Au Dix-Huitième Siècle: Questions de Formes'. *L'atelier Du Centre de Recherches Historiques* 8 (2011).

Raj Kapil. *Relocating Modern Science. Circulation and the Construction of Knowledge in South Asia and Europe, 1650–1900.* New York: Palgrave Macmillan, 2007.

Rausing Lisbet. 'Underwriting the Oeconomy: Linnaeus on Nature and Mind'. *History of Political Economy* 35, no. Annual Supplement (2003): 173–203.

Reinert Sophus. 'The Sultan's Republic: Jealousy of Trade and Oriental Despotism in Paolo Mattia Doria'. In *Enlightenment Reform in Southern Europe and Its Atlantic Colonies, c. 1750–1830*, edited by Gabriel Paquette, 253–70. Farnham: Ashgate, 2009.

———. *Translating Empire: Emulation and the Origins of Political Economy.* Cambridge, MA: Harvard University Press, 2011.

———. 'The Empire of Emulation: A Quantitative Analysis of Economic Translations in the European World, 1500–1849'. In *The Political Economy of Empire in the Early Modern World*, edited by Sophus Reinert and Pernille Roge, 105–30. New York: Palgrave Macmillan, 2013.

———. *The Academy of Fisticuffs: Political Economy and Commercial Society in Enlightenment Italy.* Cambridge, MA: Harvard University Press, 2019.

Reinert Sophus, and Fredona Robert. 'Political Economy and the Medici'. *Business History Review* 94, no. 1 (2020): 125–77.

Richard Roberts. 'West Africa and the Pondicherry Textile Industry'. *Indian Economic and Social History Review* 31, no. 2 (1994): 117–45.

Riello Giorgio, and Parthasarathi Prasannan, eds. *The Spinning World: A Global History of Cotton Textiles, 1200–1850.* Oxford: Oxford University Press, 2011.

Riello Giorgio, and Tirthankar Roy, eds. *How India Clothed the World: The World of South Asian Textiles, 1500–1850.* Leiden: Brill, 2009.

Riley James C. *The Seven Years War and the Old Regime in France: The Economic and Financial Toll.* Princeton, NJ: Princeton University Press, 1986.

Riskin Jessica. *Science in the Age of Sensibility: The Sentimental Empiricists of the French Enlightenment.* Chicago, IL: Chicago University Press, 2002.

Rives Jean. 'Dîme et Défrichement En Gascogne et Query Au XVIIIe Siècle'. *Annales Du Midi: Revue Archéologique, Historique et Philologique de La France Méridionale* 92, no. 146 (1980): 57–66.

Robertson John. 'The Enlightenment above National Context: Political Economy in the Eighteenth-Century Scotland and Naples'. *Historical Journal* 40, no. 3 (1997): 667–97.

———. *The Case for the Enlightenment: Scotland and Naples, 1680–1760.* Cambridge: Cambridge University Press, 2005.

Roche Daniel. *Humeurs Vagabondes. De La Circulation Des Hommes et de l'utilité Des Voyages.* Paris: Fayard, 2003.

Root Hiltont. *The Fountain of Privilege. Political Foundations of Markets in Old Regime France and England.* Berkeley: University of California Press, 1994.

Roots Ivan. 'Cromwell's Ordinances: The Early Legislation of the Protectorate'. In *The Interregnum: The Quest for Settlement, 1646–1660*, edited by G. E. Aylmer, 143–64. London: McMillan, 1972.

Rosenthal Jean-Laurent. 'The Political Economy of Absolutism Reconsidered'. In *Analytic Narratives*, edited by Robert H. Bates, 63–108. Princeton, NJ: Princeton University Press, 1998.

Rosenthal Jean-Laurent, and Wong Bing. *Before and Beyond Divergence: The Politics of Economic Change in China and Europe.* Cambridge, MA: Harvard University Press, 2009.

Rothschild Emma. 'Global Commerce and the Question of Sovereignty in the Eighteenth-Century Provinces'. *Modern Intellectual History* 1, no. 1 (2004): 3–25.

Rubiés Joan-Pau. *Travel and Ethnology in the Renaissance: South India through European Eyes, 1250–1625*. Cambridge: Cambridge University Press, 2004.

Rubin Jarced. *Rulers, Religion, and Riches: Why the West Got Rich and the Middle East Did Not*. Cambridge: Cambridge University Press, 2017.

Ruzé Françoise. 'L'Utopie Spartiate'. *Kentron. Revue Pluridisciplinaire Du Monde Antique* 26 (2010): 17–48.

Saether Arild. *Natural Law and the Origin of Political Economy: Samuel Pufendorf and the History of Economics*. New York: Routledge, 2017.

Schaeper Thomas J. *The French Council of Commerce 1700–1715: A Study of Mercantilism after Colbert*. Columbus: Ohio State University Press, 1983.

Schelle Gustave, ed. *Oeuvres de Turgot. Et Documents Le Concernant*. 5 vols. Paris: Institut Coppet, 2018.

Secord James A. 'Knowledge in Transit'. *Isis* 95, no. 4 (2004): 654–72.

Sepppel Marten, and Tribe Keith, eds. *Cameralism in Practice: State Administration and Economy in Early Modern Europe*. Cambridge: Boydell & Brewer, 2018.

Shovlin John. *The Political Economy of Virtue: Luxury, Patriotism, and the Origins of the French Revolution*. Ithaca, NY and London: Cornell University Press, 2006.

———. *Trading with the Enemy: Britain, France, and the 18th-Century Quest for a Peaceful World Order*. New Haven, CT: Yale University Press, 2021.

Silva André Mansuy-Diniz. *Portrait d'un Homme d'État: D. Rodrigo de Souza Coutinho, Conte de Linhares, 1755–1812*. Paris: Centre Culturel Calouste Gulbenkian, 2006.

Skornicki Arnault. 'Liberté, Propriété, Sûreté. Retour Sur Une Devise Physiocratique'. *Corpus, Revue de Philosophie* 66 (2004): 17–36.

———. *L'économiste, La Cour et La Patrie. L'économie Politique Dans La France Des Lumières*. Paris: CNRS Éditions, 2011.

Small Albion W. *The Cameralists: The Pioneers of German Social Polity*. Chicago, IL: University of Chicago Press, 1909.

Spary E. C. *Utopia's Garden: French Natural History from Old Regime to Revolution*. Chicago, IL: Chicago University Press, 2000.

Spector Céline. 'Commerce'. In *A Montesquieu Dictionary*, n.d. http://dictionnaire-montesquieu.ens-lyon.fr/en/home/.

———. *Montesquieu: Pouvoirs, Richesses et Sociétés*. Paris: Presses Universitaires de France, 2004.

Stapelbroek Koen. *Love, Self-Deceit, and Money. Commerce and Morality in the Early Modern Neapolitan Enlightenment*. Toronto: University of Toronto Press, 2008.

Steve Pincus. 'Neither Machiavellian Moment nor Possessive Individualism: Commercial Society and the Defenders of the English Commonwealth'. *American Historical Review* 103, no. 3 (1998): 708–36.

———. *1688: The First Modern Revolution*. New Haven, CT: Yale University Press, 2009.

Subrahmanyam Sanjay. *Three Ways to Be Allien: Travails and Encounters in the Early Modern World*. Waltham, MA: Brandeis University Press, 2011.

Tarde Gabriel. *The Laws of Imitation*. New York: Henry Holt and Company, 1903.

Taylor George H., ed. *Lectures on Ideology and Utopia. Paul Ricoeur*. New York: Columbia University Press, 1986.

Tazara Corey. 'Managing Free Trade in Early Modern Europe: Institutions, Information, and the Free Port of Livorno'. *Journal of Modern History* 86, no. 3 (2014): 493–529.

———. *The Free Port of Livorno and the Transformation of the Mediterranean World*. Oxford: Oxford University Press, 2017.

Théré Christine, and Charles Loïc. 'The Writing Workshop of François Quesnay and the Making of Physiocracy'. *History of Political Economy* 40, no. 1 (2008): 1–42.

Vaghi Massimiliano. *La France et L'Inde. Commerce et Politique Impériale Au XVIIIe Siècle*. Fano: Éditions Mimésis, 2016.

Vardi Liana. *The Physiocrats and the World of the Enlightenment*. Cambridge: Cambridge University Press, 2012.

Velde François R. 'The Life and Times of Nicolas Dutot'. *Journal of the History of Economic Thought* 34, no. 1 (2012): 67–107.

Venturi Franco. *Settecento Riformatore. De Muratori a Beccaria*. Torino: Giulio Einaudi, 1969.

———. *Utopia e Riforma Nell'illuminismo*. Torino: Einaudi, 1970.

———. *Settecento Riformatore*. 2 vols. Torino: Einaudi (edizione speciale per il Giornale), 1998.

Wahnbaeck Till. *Luxury and Public Happiness: Political Economy in the Italian Enlightenment*. Oxford: Clarendon Press, 2004.

Walraevens Benoît. 'Jealousy of Trade in Hume and Smith'. *History of Economic Ideas* 25, no. 2 (2017): 11–36.

Weingast Barry R. 'Exposing the Neoclassical Fallacy: Mccloskey on Ideas and the Great Enrichment'. *Scandinavian Economic History Review* 64, no. 3 (2016): 189–201.

Werner Michel, and Zimmermann Bénédicte. 'Penser l'histoire Croisée: Entre Empirie et Réflexivité'. *Annales. Histoire, Sciences Sociales* 58, no. 1 (2003): 7–36.

Weulersse Georges. *Le Mouvement Physiocratique En France (1756–1770)*. 2 vols. Paris: Félix Alcan éditeur, 1910.

Wise M. Norton. 'Making Visible'. *Isis* 97, no. 1 (2006): 75–82.

Zagari Eugenio. 'Il Metodo, Il Progetto e Il Contributo Analitico Di Antonio Genovesi'. *Studi Economici* 92 (2007): 5–32.

## Archives

Archivio di Stato de Venezia
Archivio di Stato di Napoli
Archivio di Stato di Salerno
Arquivo Histórico Ultramarino
Arquivo Nacional Torre do Tombo
Bibliothèque National de France
Chambre de Commerce de Marseille
Società Napoletana de Storia Patria

## Seventeenth- and eighteenth-century books

Abbé de Mably. *Doutes Proposés Aux Philosophes Économistes Sur l'ordre Naturel et Essentiel Des Sociétés Politiques*. Haye: Chez Nyon quai des augustins, Veuve Durand, rue S. Jacques, 1768.

Anonymous. *The Proposal for Raising the Price of Tin &c.* s.l.: s.n., 1700.

———. *Observations Sur La Liberté Du Commerce Des Grains*. Amsterdam: Chez Michel Lambert libraire-imprimeur rue de la Comédie, 1759.

———. *Mémoire Sur Les Défrichements*. Paris: Chez la veuve D'houry Imp. Lib. de Magr. le duc d'Orléans, rue de la vieille Bouclerie, 1760.

———. *Foires et Marchés Du Royaume, Ouvrage Contenant: 1. Un État Des Foires Les plus Fameuses de La France & Des Pays étrangers. 2. Une Indication Par Ordre Alphabétique de Toutes Les Foires & Marchés Francs, Qui Se Tiennent Dans Tous Le Royaume, & Rangée Par Ordre Des Provinces.* Genève: Chez la Veuve Duchesne, libraire rue St. Jacques au Temple du goût, 1765.

———. *Lettres à Un Ami Sur Les Avantages de La Liberté Du Commerce Des Grains et Le Danger Des Prohibitions.* Amsterdam: Chez Desaint, libraire, rue du Foin, 1768.

———. *Résultats de La Liberté et de l'immunité Du Commerce Des Grains, de La Farine et Du Pain.* Amsterdam: Chez Desaint, libraire, rue du S. Jacques, 1768.

———. *Cio Che è Utile Farsi Per Lo Bene Del Regno Di Napoli Neli Anno 1797.*

———. *Mémoire Sur La Nécessité Du Rétablissement de La Franchise Du Port et de La Ville de Dunkerque.* Dunkerque: Typographie de Vanderest, 1814.

———. *Reflexões a Favor Do Estabelecimento de Um Porto Franco Em Lisboa Que a Seus Compatriotas Tem a Honra de Oferecer ***.* Lisboa: Typografia de Deziderio Marques Leão Largo do Calharis 12, 1825.

Auffray M. 'Considérations sur les Manufactures Dans Les Villes Maritimes et Commerçantes'. *Journal de L'agriculture, du Commerce, et des Finances* Juillet (1768): 130–81.

Battur M., ed. 'Mémoire de La Chambre de Commerce de Dunkerque, Sur Les Ports Francs (1802)'. In *Questions Des* Entrepòts et Ports Francs *Contenant Onze Lettres Publiées Dans Le Journal Le Commerce de Dunkerque et Du Nord*, 3–15. Paris: Librairie Encyclopédique de Roret, 1845.

Boesnier de l'Orme M. *De l'esprit Du Gouvernement Économique.* Paris: Chez Debure, freres, libraires quai des Augustin près la rue Pavée, 1775.

Boulainvilliers M. de. *Etat de La France, Contenant XIV. Lettres Sur Les Anciens Parlements de France Avec l'histoire de Ce Royaume Despuis Le Commencement de La Monarchie Jusqu'a Charles VIII. On y a Joint Des Mémoires Présentés à M. Le Duc d'Orléans.* Londres: Chez W. Roberts; & se vend chez J. Brindley in New Bond-street, où on trouve les deux premiers volumes, 1728.

Brissot J. P. *Testament Politique de l'Angleterre.* Philadelphie: s.n., 1780.

Butel-Dumont G. M. *Essai Sur l'état Du Commerce d'Angleterre.* 2 vols. London: Nyon, 1755.

———. *Acte Du Parlement d'Angleterre, Connu Sous Le Nom d'acte de Navigation, Passé En 1660. Traduit Littéralement de l'anglois, Avec Des Notes.* Amsterdam: Charles Antoine Jombert, 1760.

Cantilllon Philip. *The Analysis of Trade, Commerce, Coin, Bullion, Banks, and Foreign Exchanges Wherein the True Principles of This Useful Knowledge Are Fully but Briefly Laid down and Explained, to Give a Clear Idea of Their Happy Consequences to Society When Well Regulated Taken Chiefly from a Manuscript of a Very Ingenious Gentleman Deceased and Adapted to the Present Situation of Our Trade and Commerce.* London: Printed for the author, 1759.

Child Josiah. *A New Discourse of Trade.* London: T. Sowle, 1698.

*Correspondance Littéraire, Philosophique et Critique de Grimm et Diderot, Depuis 1753 Jusqu'en 1790. Nouvelle Édition, Revue et Mise Dans Un Meilleur Ordre, Avec Des Notes et Des Éclaircissements, et Ou Se Trouvent Rétablies Pour La Première Fois Les Phrases Supprimées Par La Censure Impériale.* Paris: Chez Furne, librairie quai des augustins, n. 37 et Landrage, même quai, 19, 1829.

Cour Mathon de la. *Dissertation Sur Les Causes et Les Degrés de La Décadence Des Loix de Lycurgue. Par Quelles Causes et Par Quels Degrés Les Loix de Lycurgue Se Sont*

*Altérées Chez Les Lacédémoniens Jusqu'à Ce Qu'elles Ayent Été Anéanties*. Lyon: Chez Durand libraire rue Saint-Jacques, 1767.
Coutinho Rodrigo de Souza. *Textos Políticos, Económicos e Financeiros 1783–1811*. Lisboa: Banco de Portugal, 1993.
Cunha Luís da. *Instruções Políticas (1733)*. Lisboa: Comissão Nacional dos descobrimentos portugueses, 2001.
D'Holbach Paul Henri Dietrich. *La Politique Naturelle ou Discours Sur Les Vrai Principes Du Gouvernement*. Londres, 1773.
Dulac Antonio Maximino. *Exame Crítico, Comparativo Do Estado Actual de Portugal Considerado Na Penúria Dos Seus Productos e Urgência de Suprimentos, Com Observações Demostrativas Dos Recursos Que Lhe Oferece a Vantagem Da Sua Situação Geographica*. Lisboa: s.n., 1827.
Du Pont de Nemours Pierre. *De l'origine et Des Progrès d'une Science Nouvelle*. Londres: Chez Desaint, libraire, rue du Foin, 1778.
Dutot Nicolas. *Réflexions Politiques Sur Les Finances, et Le Commerce Où l'on Examine Quelles Ont Été Sur Les Revenues, Les Denrées, Le Change Étranger, et Conséquemment Sur Notre Commerce, Les Influences Des Augmentations & Des Diminutions Des Valeurs Numéraires Des Monnoyes*. 2 vols. Haye: Chez les frères V. Aillant & Nicolas Prevost, 1738.
Éphémérides Du Citoyen, Ou Bibliothèque Raisonnée Des Sciences Morales et Politiques. Paris: Chez Nicolas Augustin Delalain, 1767.
Forbonnais François Véron de. *Eléments du Commerce*. 2 vols. Leyden, 1754.
———. *Le Négociant Anglais, Ou Traduction Libre Du Livre Intitulé The British Merchant, Contenant Divers Mémoires Sur Le Commerce de l'Angleterre Avec La France, Le Portugal et l'Espagne*. Amsterdam: François Changuion, 1755.
———. *Principes et Observations Oeconomiques*. 2 vols. Amsterdam: Chez Marc Michel Rey, 1767.
Galiani Ferdinando. *Dialogues Sur Le Commerce Des Bleds*. Londres: s.n., 1770.
Genovesi Antonio. *Lezioni Di Commercio o Sia d'economia Civile*. Bassano: Spese Remondini, 1769.
Goudar Ange. *A General History of the Late Revolution of Genoa*. London: Printed for the Author, 1752.
———. *Questions Sur Le Commerce Des François Au Levant*. Marseille: Chez Carapatria, Libraire près de la loge, 1755.
———. *Les Intérêts de La France Mal Entendus, Dans Les Branches de l'agriculture, de La Population, Des Finances, Du Commerce, de La Marine, & de l'industrie. Par Un Citoyen*. 3 vols. Amsterdam: Chez Jacques Coeur, à la corne d'abondance, 1756.
———. *Relation historique Du Tremblement de Terre à Lisbonne Le Premier Novembre 1755. Avec Un Détail Contenant La Perte En Hommes, Eglises, Convents, Palais, Maisons, Diamands, Meubles, Marchandises, &c.Precédée d'un Discours Politique Sur Les Avantages Que Le Portugal Pourrait Retirer de Son Malheur. Dans Lesquels l'auteur Développe Les Moyens Que l'Angleterre Avait Mis Jusques-Là En Usage Pour Ruiner Cette Monarchie*. Haye: Chez Philanthrope, à la vérité, 1756.
———. *Profecía Política, Verificada En Lo Que Está Sucediendo a Los Portugueses Por Su Ciega Afición a Los Ingleses: Hecha Luego Después Del Terremoto Del Año de Mil Setecientos Cincuenta y Cinco*. Madrid: Imprenta de la Gaceta, 1762.
———. *Lettres d'un Allemand à l'auteur de l'espien Chinois*. Geneve: Au depens de l'auteur, 1764.

———. *L'espien Chinois, Ou l'envoyé Secret de La Cour de Pekin, Pour Examiner l'état Présent de l'Europe. Traduit Du Chinois.* 6 vols. Cologne, 1765.

———. *The Chinese Spy; or, Emissary from the Court of Pekin Commissioned to Examine into the Present State of Europe.* Translated from the Chinese. London: M. A. McGuire, 1765.

———. *Staatsfehler Der Mehresten Höfe Im Französischen Gemählde. Eine Uebersetzung von Johann Albrecht Philippi.* Berlin und Leipzig: Rüdigerischen Buchhandlung, 1766.

———. *Naples Ce Qu'il Faut Faire Pour Rendre Ce Royaume Florissant.* Amsterdam: s.n., 1771.

———. *Los Intereses de La Francia Mal Entendidos: Destierro de Errores Comunes En La Agricultura, Industria, Comercio, Población y Navegación: Plan de Sistema Económico. Traducción Del Francés Por D. Domingo de Marcoleta.* Madrid: Oficina de Blas Román, 1772.

Gourcy François Antoine Étienne de. *Histoire Philosophique de Lacédémone, et Des Loix de Lycurgue, Où l'on Recherche Par Quelles Causes & Par Quels Degrés Ces Loix Se Sont Altérées, Jusqu'à Ce Qu'elles Ayent Été Anéanties; & Se Précipita Ver Sa Ruine, Par Les Mêmes Causes & Les Mêmes Degrés.* Nancy & se trouve à Paris: Chez Delalain, Libraire, rue Saint Jacques/Chez Valade, Libraire, rue de Parcheminerie, maison de M. Grangé, 1768.

Herbert Claude Jacques. *Observations Sur La Liberté Du Commerce Des Grains.* Amsterdam: Michel Lambert, 1759.

Herrenschwand Jean. *De l'économie Politique Moderne Discours Fondamental Sur La Population.* Paris: Maradan librairie, L'an III.

Huet Pierre Daniel. *Le Grand Trésor Historique et Politique Du Florissant Commerce Des Hollandais, Dans Tous Les États et Empires Du Monde. Quelle Est Leur Manière de Le Faire, Son Origine, Leur Grand Progrés, Leur Possessions & Gouvernements Dans Les Indes. Comment Ils Se Sont Rendus Maîtres de Tout Le Commerce de l'Europe.* Haye: Henry Frik, 1713.

Law John. *Money and Trade Considered: With a Proposal for Supplying the Nation with Money.* Glasgow: Printed and Sold by R. & A. Foulis, 1750.

Melon Jean-François. *Essai Politique Sur Le Commerce. Nouvelle Édition. Cette Édition Est Augmentée de Sept Chapitres, & Les Lacunes Des Éditions Précédentes y Son Remplies.* s.l.: s.n., 1736.

———. *A Political Essay upon Commerce.* Written in French by Monsieur M. Translated, with Some Annotations, and Remarks by David Bindon. Dublin: Printed for Philip Crampton, 1738.

*Memoria Dos Trabalhos Da Commissão Para Melhoramento Do Comércio Nesta Cidade de Lisboa Creada Por Determinação Das Cortes Geraes, Extraordinarias, e Constituintes Da Nação Portuguesa de 28 de Agosto de 1821. Composta de 24 Membros Eleitos Por Todos Os Negociantes Da Mesma Praça.* Lisboa: Typographia rollandiana, 1822.

Mirabeau Honoré-Gabriel Riqueti. *Essais Sur Le Despotisme. Seconde Édition Augmentée et Corrigée Par l'éditeur de Cet Ouvrage.* Londres, s.n., 1776.

Mountague William. *The Delights of Holland: Or, A Three Months Travel about That and the Other Provinces With Observations and Reflections on Their Trade, Wealth, Strength, Beauty, Policy, &c. Together with a Catalogue of the Rarities in the Anatomical School at Leyden.* London: John Stuorton, near Serjeant's-Inn Gate, in Chancery Lane; and A. Bosvile, at the Dial over-against St. Dunstan's Church, in Fleet-Street, 1696.

Muratori Lodovico Antonio. *Della Pubblica Felicità, Oggetto de Buoni Principi*. Luca: s.n., 1749.

Nalson John. *The Present Interest of England, or, A Confutation of the Whiggish Conspirators Anti-Monyan Principle Shewing from Reason and Experience the Ways to Make the Government Safe, the King Great, the People Happy, Money Plentiful, and Trade Flourish*. London: Thomas Dring, 1683.

*New Discoveries Concerning the World, and Its Inhabitants. In Two Parts. Part I Containing a Circumstantial Account of All the Islands in the South-Sea, That Have Been Lately Discovered or Explored; the Situation, Climate, and the Soil of Each; Their Natural Productions, Including Many Species of Animals and Vegetables Hitherto Unknown; the Persons, Dresses, Extraordinary Manners and Customs, Manufactures, Buildings, Government, and Religion of the Various Inhabitants, Their Domestic Utensils, and Weapons of War, Their Ingenuity, Mental Endowments, Skill in Navigation, and Other Arts and Sciences. Comprehending All the Discoveries Made in the Several Voyages of Commodore (Now Admiral) Byron, Captains Wallis, Carteret, and Cook, Related by Dr. Hawresworth, Sidney Parkinson, Mr. Forster, and Captain Cook. Together with Those of M. de Bougainville. The Whole Compared with the Narratives of Former Celebrated Navigators, Viz. Mendoza, Quiros, Tasman, Le Maire, Schouten. Dampier, Roggewein, Anson, and Others. Part II Containing a Summary Account of Captain Cook's Attempts to Discover a Southern Continent in 1773, 1774, and 1775. Also Voyage of the Honourable Constantine John Phipps (Now Lord Mulgrave) towards the North-Pole, in 1773. With Maps and Prints*. London: Printed for J. Johnson, St. Paul's Church-Yard, 1778.

Nickollis John (M. de Dangeul). *Remarques Sur Les Avantages et Les Désavantages de La France et de La GR. Bretagne Par Rapport Au Commerce, & Aux Autres Sources de La Puissance Des Etats (Traduction de l'anglais)*. Leyden, 1754.

*Observations Sur l'Italie et Sur Les Italiens, Données En 1764, Sous Le Nom de Deux Gentilshommes Suédois. Par l'auteur Du Livre Intitulé Londres*. Amsterdam: Chez Costard, Fils & Compagnie, rue S. Jean de Beauvais, 1774.

*O Investigador Portuguez Em Inglaterra Ou Journal Litterario Politico*. London: H. Bryer, 1811.

Petty William. *An Essay Concerning the Multiplication of Mankind: Together with Another Essay in Political Arithmetick, Concerning the Growth of the City of London: With the Measures, Periods, Causes, and Consequences Thereof, 1682*. London: Robert Clavel and Henry Mortlok, 1698.

Poivre Pierre. *Reisen Eines Philosophen: Mit Betrachtungen Über Die Gebräuche, Sitten, Künste, Ackerbau Und Den Handel Verschiedner Völker in Asien Und Afrika: Aus Dem Englischen Übersetzt*. Daniel Ludwig Wedel, 1773.

———. *Oeuvres Complètes de P. Poivre, Intendant Des Isles de France et Bourbon, Correspondant de l'académie Des Sciences, Etc. Précédées de Sa Vie et Accompagnées Des Notes*. Paris: Chez Fuchs, libraire, rue de Mathurins, 1797.

———. *Travels of a Philosopher, or Observations on the Manners and Arts of Various Nations in Africa and Asia*. Augusta: Kennebec, 1797.

Quesnay François. *Le Droit Naturel*. Paris: s. n., 1765.

Ratton Jacome. *Recordações de Jacome Ratton Sobre Ocorrências Do Seu Tempo Em Portugal Durante o Lapso de Sessenta e Três Anos e Mais Alias de Maio 1747 a Setembro de 1810 Que Residiu Em Lisboa Acompanhadas de Algumas Subsequentes Reflexões Suas*. London: H. Bryer, 1813.

Rebelo Manuel Joaquim. *Economia Política Feita Em 1795 Por M. J. R.* Lisboa: Banco de Portugal, 1992.

Rivière M. de la. *L'ordre Naturel et Essentiel Des Sociétés Politiques*. 2 vols. London: Chez Jean Nourse, libraire and Chez Desaint, Libraire, 1768.

Robinson Henry. *Englands Safety in Trades Increase*. London: E. P. for Nicholas Bourne at the South Entrance of the Royal Exchange, 1641.

Savary Philemon-Louis. *Dictionnaire Universel de Commerce...Continué Sur Les Mémoires de l'auteur, et Donné Au Public Par M. Philemon-Louis Savary, Chanoine de l'Église Royale de S. Maur Des Fossez, Son Frère. Nouvelle Édition, Exactement Revue, Corrigée, & Enrichie de Beaucoup d'additions*. 3 vols. Genève: Héritiers Crammer & Frères Philibert, 1742.

Serionne Jacques Accarias de. *Le Commerce de La Hollande Ou Tableau Du Commerce Des Hollandais Dans Les Quatre Parties Du Monde*. Amsterdam: Changuion Libraire, 1768.

Silva António Delgado da, ed. *Colecção Da Legislação Portuguesa Desde a Última Compilação Das Ordenes, Redigida Pelo Desembargador António Delgado Da Silva. Legislação de 179–1801*. Lisboa: Typographia Maigrense, 1828.

Sismondi J. C. L. *De La Richesse Commerciale, Ou Principes d'économie Politique Appliqués à La Législation Du Commerce*. Genève: J. Paschoud, 1803.

Temple William. *Observations upon the United Provinces of the Netherlands by Sir William Temple*. London: A. Maxwell for Sa. Gellibrand, 1673.

Uztáriz Gerónimo de. *The Theory and Practice of Commerce and Maritime Affairs. Written Originally in Spanish, by Don Geronymo de Uztariz*. Translated from the Original by John Kippax. Dublin: George Faulkner, 1752.

———. *Theórica y Práctica de Comercio y de Marina: En Diferentes Discursos y Calificados Exemplares Que, Con Específicas Providencias, Se Procuran Adaptar a La Monarquía Española, Para Su Pronta Restauración, Beneficio Universal y Mayor Fortaleza Contra Los Émulos de La Real Corona, Mediante La Soberana Protección Del Rey Nuestro Señor Don Phelipe V.* Madrid: Imprenta Antonio Sanz, 1757.

Vasco Giambattista. *La Felicità Pubblica Considerata Nei Coltivatori Di Terre Proprie*. Brescia: Presso Giammaria Rizzardi, 1769.

Voltaire. *Le Siècle de Louis XIV. Nouvelle Édition Augmentée d'un Très Grande Nombre de Remarques Par Mr. de La B.* Francfort: Chez la veuve Knoch et J. G. Eslinger, 1753.

———. *Letters Concerning the English Nation*. The Second Edition, with Large Additions. London: Printed for C. Davis in Pater-Noster-Row, 1761.

———. *Fragments Sur l'Inde, Sur Le Général Lalli et Sur Le Comte de Morangiés*. s.l, s.n., 1773.

Worsley Benjamin. *Free Ports, and the Nature of Them Stated*. London: William Du-Gard, 1651.

# Index

Note: **Bold** page numbers refer to tables, *italic* page numbers refer to figures and page numbers followed by "n" denote end notes.


*ab introitu iudicum* 164–5, 204
agriculture 54–6, 115–16; Asian 46; chamber of 145–7; Chinese 30, 93; free ports 197; in India 60
Andes 84–9, 92

Bloch, Marc 65
Botanophiles 52
Boulainvilliers M. de. 65–6
Bourgeois dignity 14
Brazil 121–2, 193–4, 196, 199
Butel-Dumont, Georges Marie 13, 170–2

Cantillon, Philip 6, 49, 90
Cantillon, Richard 168–9
Cape of Good Hope 7, 55, 192, 196–8
Carli, Gianrinaldo 88–91
*Casa da Índia* 190
Charles-Emmanuel I 186
Charles, Loïc 56
Cheney, Paul 84
China 23, 25, 28–30, 42–3, 54–5, 59, 63, 73–4, 83–4, 88, 92–4, 99, 101, 125–6, 203
*Cinque Savii* 184
Cochin-China 27, 30, 43–4, 55
Colbert 127, 132–3, 138, 146, 160
Cunha, Luíz da 195

D'Alembert 21, 33, 45
Darnton, Robert 20–1, 32
*The Delights of Holland* (Mountague) 178
delocalisation 142–3
dependence 8, 102, 111, 115, 120, 122, 130–2, 137, 170, 172–3, 203
deurbanisation 131, 142–3
D'Holbach, Paul Henri Dietrich 32, 64, 68
Diderot 21, 33, 45, 76
diversity 3, 128, 156
*doux commerce* 2–5, 8, 129–30, 202
drawback system 10, 153, 169, 173, 179, 189–90
Dulac, Antonio Maximinio 198–9
Dunkirk 152, 156, 160, 197
Du Pont de Nemours, Pierre Samuel 23–8, 30, 41, 49, 57, 63, 74, 91, 107
Dutch 5, 9–10, 32, 43, 55–6, 104, 132–3, 157, 167–9, 171–2, 174, 176–9, 199
Dutot, Nicolas 108–11, 113, 125, 127, 139–40; *Political discourse* 110

economic maxim *see* maxims (Goudar)
economic theory 19, 22, 42, 45, 163, 203
economic thinking 2–4, 11–16, 18, 20, 42, 49, 63, 82, 91, 113, 202
*économistes* (Poivre) 73–6, 78–9, 81–4, 89, 94, 121
*Encyclopédie* 52, 56, 75–6, 78–9, 81, 94, 107, 159
England 4–5, 9, 11, 13–14, 16, 30, 32, 49, 64, 69, 102, 104, 114, 121–7, 131–3, 137, 140–3, 152–3, 168–78, 190, 203
*entrepôt* 9–11, 157, 159, 167–9, 173, 183, 195, 199
equality 14, 88–91, 93–4, 169
*Essai sur la nature du commerce* (Cantillon) 168

fairs 162–3; artificial marketplaces 164–5; Champagne 164; continuous 160; everlasting 160; fair-wardens 165;

free cleared 198; global 196–9; glocal 194–7; international 163; Lyon 163; markets and 161–2; perpetual 160; regional 163
feudal/feudalism 42, 60–9, **61,** 82, 93, 162
*The Feudal Society* (Bloch) 65
Forbonnais, François Véron de 13, 49, 57, 107–8, 139–40, 170–3, 175
Foucault, Michel 50, 114
*Fragment sur l'Inde* (Voltaire) 67
France 4, 12, 16, 25, 27, 30, 32, 42–4, 49, 63, 103–4, 116, 125, 132–3, 137–8, 141–3, 145, 152, 154, 159, 168–72, 175, 194–5, 203
free market 195, 198
free ports 151–7, *154,* 184, 204; Cantillons model of 168; Cape of Good Hope 196–8; in England 176; of Genoa 184–5; limited 179; in Lisbon 177–8, 188–95, 197–9; marketplaces 159–65; misuses 192–3; Navigation act and 174–5; old model 191; at Savona 186; in Spain 195

Galiani, Ferdinando 45, 49, 66, 112, 121, 127–8
Galles, Jean-Marie 73
Gee, Joshua 175–6
Genoa 152–3, 157, 178, 184–6, 188–9, 194, 199
Genovesi, Antonio 7, 29–30, 127–8, 151, 184, 191, 195
Gibraltar 152, 155, 175, 189, 194
Goudar, Ange 4, 21–3, 31–3, 45, 49, 99, 101–2, 106–9, 114–17, 120–33, 136–43, 145–7, 167–73, 202–3; agriculture 136–7, 139; *auteurs économiques* 107; *Les intérêts de la France* 102–3, 108, 110–12, 125, 136–7, 167, 170; *L'espion Chinois* 99; lifestyle 102–4; machines and 116–17; maxims 102, 111–17, 122–3, 132, 136–7, 140, 145–6, 172–3, 203; to Naples 120–1; *Naples ce qu'il faut faire* 108, 111, 127, 136–7; *Réflexions Historique* 113, 121, 125; *Réflexions politiques* 109–11; *Rélation Historique* 111; universal society 129
Gournay 12–13, 46, 49, 107, 128, 170, 172, 177
Gourtey, Abbé de 90
great enrichment (England) 14, 122–7, 142
Greif, Avner 17

Henry VIII 171
Herodotus 50
Hirschman, Albert Otto 4–5
*Histoire Naturelle* (Poivre) 52
history of commerce 4, 6, 11, 84
Holland 10–11, 114, 132–3, 141–3, 152, 167, 169, 172, 175–9, 186, 190, 194, 199, 204
Homer 50
Hubner, Martin 82–3
Huet, Pierre-Daniel 10, 178–9
Hume, David 4–7, 10–11, 82, 108, 110, 129–31

Incas 27, 42, 88–9, 92, 203
independence 189, 196, 199
Indian Ocean 41, 43, 54, 190
Indo-Portuguese trade 189, 192
Industrial Revolution 14, 126
inequality 88–93, 95n16
institutional diversity 173–6
institutional innovation 15–19, 160, 163, 202, 204
*ius stepulae* 165, 204

jealousy of trade 2–4, 6–8, 129–30, 202

L'Abbaye, Bearde de 91
*laissez-faire* approach 107, 159
*Le Despotisme de la Chine* (Quesnay) 30, 62, 74, 83–4
Lisbon: earthquake 103–4, 121–3; failure 188–9; free port 177–8, 188–95, 197–9
*Livornina* 156
Livorno 9, 66, 151–2, 156–7, 160, 163, 174–6, 183–6, 196, 199
Loureiro, Francisco Gomes 193
Lycurgus 89–90, 92

Malacca 60–3, 67
Malais 60–1, 63
Marco Polo 23, 30, 50
markets: domestic 170–1, 173, 176, 193, 198; emergence of 161–2; foreign 142–3, 169; imperial 193; and the marketplace 1–3, 8, 10, 153, 157, 159–65, 167, 177, 197, 202, 204;

Mediterranean 104, 132, 190; in Portugal 124; universal 155, 177
Marseilles 132, 152, 154, 159, 197
maxims (Goudar) 102, 111–17, 122–3, 132, 136–7, 140, 145–6, 172–3, 203
Mediterranean 9, 50, 103–4, 132, 151–3, 155, 159, 174–5, 177, 184, 188–90, 199, 204
Melon, Jean-Francois 6, 75, 108–10, 113–14, 116–17, 125, 136, 138–9; *Essai sur le commerce* 109–10, 139
Mirabeau, Honore-Gabriel Riqueti 32, 64, 68–9, 108, 136
*Mondain* (Voltaire) 139
Monteiro, José Caetano 192
Montesquieu 1, 4–7, 10, 45–6, 49, 60–5, 68, 103–4, 107–8, 111, 118n16, 130, 137–8, 140
Morellet 49, 66
Mornet, Daniel 20
Muratori, Lodovico Antonio 91–2

Naples 7, 32, 67, 102–3, 116, 120, 127–8, 132, 138, 141, 155, 184, 203
Navigation act 9, 18, 125, 152, 169–75, 184
Neapolitan 45, 66, 102, 106, 120–1, 127, 132, 151, 185
N-gram google 64, *65, 154,* 155
North-South Europe 23, 31–2, 102, 120–33, 163
*Nuova imposta* 183

Paiva, João Correa de 193
Perrot, Jean-Claude 3, 13, 20, 76
physiocrats 15–16, 22, 26–8, 41–2, 45, 47, 54, 57–8, 62, 66, 69, 76–7, 79, 81, 84, 101, 107, 112, 136
Piedmont 186, 189, 191
Plumard de Dangeul, Luis-Joseph 13, 108
Poivre, Pierre 4, 21, 23–5, 27–8, 30–1, 41–7, 49–52, 54–8, 60–4, 66–7, 69, 73–4, 76, 83–4, 92–4, 99, 101, 108, 202–3
*Political Essays* (Hume) 4
Polybius 51
Pombal, Marquês de 121–2
Ponthiamas 57, 60, 62–3
Portugal 32, 49, 102, 111, 113, 116, 121–5, 131, 137–8, 140, 142, 175, 186, 188–92, 195–6, 199, 203
*Principes et observations* (Forbonnais) 57
property 15, 16, 27, 42, 54, 56, 60, 62, 66, 69, 78, 82, 84–94, 101, 115, 175, 203
property rights 15–18, 27, 42, 57, 60–1, 63, 66, 68, 81–94, 126, 164
*Puertos libres* (free ports) 153

Quesnay, Francois 13, 15–16, 23, 27, 29–30, 41, 45–6, 56, 62, 74, 76–8, 82–5, 88, 107, 113, 136, 203

Ratton, Jacome 189
Rebelo, Joaquim 190–2
reindustrialisation 141–3
Reinert, Sophus 11
Robinson, Henry 177

Savary, Philemon-Louis 5, 155, 157, 159, 162
*Serenissima* (Venice) 183
Serionne, Jacques Accarias de 179
Shovlin, John 76–7
Shushtari, Abd al-Latif Khan 51
Siam 55–61, *58–9,* 63
Sismondi J. C. L. 153, 194–5, 198
Smith, Adam 7, 20, 23, 29–30, 41, 49, 69, 75, 153, 197
Souza Coutinho, Rodrigo de 189–90, 195
Spain 16, 32, 49, 130–2, 153, 155, 175, 189–91, 194–5
Sparta 16, 42, 84, 89–92, 203
*The Spirit of the Laws* (Montesquieu) 4, 6–7, 60, 62, 65, 111

*tableau de comparison* (Poivre) 56–62
*Tableau économique* (Charles) 77, 85
Tanger 152, 155–6
Tarde, Gabriel 19
taxation 30, 45, 62, 93–4
topoi 2, 11
*Trade and Navigation* (Gee) 175
travellers 4, 27–31, 41, 50–2, 54–5, 57, 60–1, 63–4, 66–7, 74, 93, 99, 178–9, 203
travelogues 23, 49–52, 109
Turgot 30, 41, 46, 73, 93, 159–62, 164

utopia 1–3, 8–11, 88, 131, 204
Uztáriz, Geronimo de 13, 171–2, 178

Vasco, Giambattista 91–2
Venice 178, 183–5
Verthamont 30, 94
Voltaire 21, 32, 45, 64–7, 91, 104, 108, 122, 138–9
voyage journals 50–1
*Voyages* (Poivre) 23, 26, 30, 41–2, 44–6, 49, 54–5, 64, 74, 92, 99, 203

Weber, M. 163
Weulersse, Georges 76–7, 84
Worsley, Benjamin 174, 176–7